The Rock File

To Elaine

The Rock File

Making it in the Music Business

Edited by
NORTON YORK

OXFORD UNIVERSITY PRESS
1991

Oxford University Press, Walton Street, Oxford OX2 6DP

Oxford New York Toronto
Delhi Bombay Calcutta Madras Karachi
Petaling Jaya Singapore Hong Kong Tokyo
Nairobi Dar es Salaam Cape Town
Melbourne Auckland
and associated companies in
Berlin Ibadan

Oxford is a trade mark of Oxford University Press

Published in the United States
by Oxford University Press, New York

British Library Cataloguing in Publication Data
The rock file: making it in the music business.
1. Pop music industries
I. York, Norton
781.63
ISBN 0–19–816193–X
ISBN 0–19–816248–0 (pbk)

Library of Congress Cataloging in Publication Data
The Rock file / edited by Norton York.
Includes index.
1. Music trade—Great Britain. 2. Music—Economic aspects.
3. Copyright—Music—Great Britain. 4. Popular music—Great
Britain—Writing and publishing. I. York, Norton.
ML3790.R62 1991 781.64'023'41—dc20 90–22670
ISBN 0–19–816193–X
ISBN 0–19–816248–0 (pbk.)

Set by Hope Services (Abingdon) Ltd
Printed in Great Britain at
The Bath Press, Avon

Foreword

The rule is there are no rules. I get dozens of letters every year from unknown writers and musicians asking me how they can force their way into the worlds of popular music and/or theatre. I try not to be discouraging, but it is hard to give practical advice, even to the talented, when most of those who have already broken into the charmed circle have got there by following a route unique to themselves, unplanned and unexpected, only with hindsight obviously a good one.

I never intended to become a lyricist but as a result of pestering a book publisher with an idea for a history of the charts I was introduced to Andrew Lloyd Webber who in turn persuaded me to write some words for a musical he had composed. I had written a few pop songs before meeting Andrew, one of which had actually been recorded by a group called the Nightshift. I had in truth only ventured into songwriting because I needed undemanding vehicles for my own voice—my ambition in 1965 was to be Mick Jagger rather than Alan Jay Lerner (and I still have a way to go to emulate either gentleman). This insane dream was quickly put to one side as I became aware of the dazzling Lloyd Webber talent, which in turn enabled me to discover abilities of my own.

Our first efforts at creating a West End show ended in tears and it was with some reluctance that we settled for what we thought was second best with our next project. Our brief, the best we could get, was to produce a twenty-minute oratorio for the young choir boys of Colet Court School. No money up front, no bright lights, no international acclaim. Or so we thought. But the piece we wrote was called *Joseph and the Amazing Technicolor Dreamcoat*, and from that humblest of beginnings, it and we never looked back.

It would be unhelpful for me to suggest to an ambitious young lyricist that he approaches a book publisher in the hope of meeting his Andrew Lloyd Webber, and that when he does they should go straight to the nearest prep school choirmaster. My advice has to be less exact and usually consists of three maxims—be different, be organized and keep at it. Copying anybody else too slavishly hardly ever works and cannot be satisfying if it does; the business end of it really matters from day one, and the longer you keep going the more chance you give yourself of the lucky break, which you probably won't recognize at the time.

I can now also suggest that the stars of tomorrow read *The Rock File*. Norton York himself acknowledges in his preface the enormity of the task he has set himself in presenting as comprehensive a guide to the contemporary music business as has ever been attempted. None the less he has succeeded admirably. From the inspiration to the deal, from the recording to the writ, the minefield is immaculately charted and entertainingly laid bare by many rugged survivors of the music business. Those within as well as those without will enjoy this work enormously, and find it invaluable as they pursue their individual unpredictable careers.

I am the man who recorded 'How Much Is That Doggy in The Window' *backwards*, convinced it would be the big Christmas hit of 1972. I am not sure that *The Rock File*, had it been available at the time, would have saved me from that particular folly but I would have made a better recording and got a better deal. May this fascinating book do that and much, much more for many of its readers, however strange their ventures.

Tim Rice

Great Milton, Oxfordshire
March 1990

Editor's Preface

In the early months of 1988 the teen pop band Bros shot to national stardom asking us 'When Will I Be Famous?' In one phrase they captured the dreams of many young musicians, all in their own way aching for the popularity which the Goss brothers had begun to achieve. Finding a manager, getting a record deal, or just breaking into session work has been a lottery for so long that the answer to Bros' question for most aspiring players is 'never'. The effect of this situation on young musicians is often confusion and disillusionment. This book can't change the way the music business works; but it does give young musicians some reasons for their frustrations by letting the music industry explain for itself how it works, what it wants from musicians, and what musicians can expect in return. All in the hope this understanding may help the stars of tomorrow avoid various well-worn pitfalls, and develop their talent into their business.

Creating pop music is quite different to producing a jazz, classical or any other type of musical performance. To have a hit record, pop musicians don't have to be able to play anyone else's music, nor do they have to perform on their instrument technically very well. They must, however, be popular. One of the results of this is that teaching someone to become a pop musician is almost a contradiction in terms. You can learn how to play the guitar, but who could honestly show you how to be Jimi Hendrix?

This situation poses several problems for music educators. We are asked by students to help them realize their ambitions to work in the pop music industry, and yet we know our advice and training is only a small and quite possibly irrelevant part of what it takes to make a professional career. As an attempt to resolve this, I have found it constructive to give young musicians access to the advice and experience of professional performers and music business personnel.

My first venture in this direction led to an annual summer school, 'Brighton Rock', sponsored by the British Musicians' Union and held at Sussex University. The second is *The Rock File*. Neither of these promotes any 'right' way of playing or of making a career, but both propose that it is worthwhile for young musicians to understand the workings of the music business from the inside, to be shown ways of learning to play their instruments, and also to encourage an interest in the capabilities of other musical instruments and technologies. None of this education or information will produce a hit record in itself, but it may give young players some guidance as to the structures influencing the art and industry within which they want to work. As a result, *The Rock File* does not attempt to be a comprehensive guide to all the workings of the pop industry. Instead, it is a collection of informed descriptions and opinions.

The articles in this book are in two sections. The first is by a selection of leading British musicians, all of whom have worked with major artists and have experience in educating young pop players. They haven't written manuals of how to play an instrument because their approach has been to give an impression of their professional lives. They describe issues such as how they deal with different types of work, how they have found employment, and the ways a promising bassist, keyboard player, singer or DJ might approach developing into a creative musician. This involves discussions of anything to do with the practicalities of professional pop music, from finding a rehearsal room, to using parametric equalization, or even making sure your amplifier doesn't blow up. There are several articles which aren't strictly about performing—'Keyboards and their Associated Technologies', 'Recording', 'Production', 'DJing and Remixing' and 'Songwriting'. These reflect the range of skills modern musicians may need to take their career from a gig at the local pub to world-wide recording and touring success. Each author has found an individual way of writing about making music and building a career, so some cross-reference between their work may prove useful. As a guide, each article starts with a short piece of editorial.

The music business section is written by top industry professionals. Their contributions can be divided into three types. The first are two articles which, to an extent, give a gameplan for action. Horace Trubridge sets out his advice for starting a band, and Dave Hill poses a number of questions which would help any publicity campaign. Another two articles deal with the legal and financial implications of every stage in a band's life, from rehearsing in your bedroom to going on tour to promote an album.

The largest group of business articles is a set of profiles. These are a combination of information about the structure of the music business, and detail about the individual organization in which the writer works. This ranges from Ed Bicknell on management and managing Dire Straits, to Brian Engel's explanation of copyright and the Performing Right Society, and Brian Southall's use of EMI as a model for his discussion of major recording and publishing companies. Through these profiles there emerges a picture of the business environment of current pop music, so that musicians can benefit from having the opportunity to read for themselves the opinions and experiences of some of the people who help to make or break a pop career.

I would like to thank a number of people whose support has been invaluable during the production of this book: all the contributors, for the time, effort and enthusiasm they gave during their hectic schedules; Brian Blain of the Musicians' Union; David Osmond-Smith of Sussex University; Bruce Phillips and all at Oxford University Press; and my family, friends and colleagues, for listening so patiently. However, my biggest thanks must go to Elaine, to whom this book is dedicated. It was her unfailing support, advice and encouragement that really made it all possible.

N.Y.

London
January 1990

Contents

Part 1 Music

1. **Vocals** *Ian Shaw*
2. **Guitar** *Deidre Cartwright*
3. **Bass Guitar** *Robert Burns*
4. **Drums** *Richard Marcangelo*
5. **Latin Percussion** *Bosco De Oliveira*
6. **Playing Keyboards** *Adrian York*
7. **Keyboards and Associated Technologies** *Blue Weaver & Adrian York*
8. **The Horn Section** *David Bitelli & Raul D'Oliveira*
9. **Songwriting** *Tot Taylor*
10. **Production** *Mick Parker*
11. **DJing and Mixing** *Paul Oakenfold*
12. **Recording** *Dave Foister*

1 Vocals

IAN SHAW has been one of the leading British session singers of the late 1980s, as well as working extensively on the jazz circuit. He has toured and recorded with a wide range of top jazz and pop artists throughout the world. He is currently developing his own band. In this article Ian discusses beginning a singing career, getting advice and training, doing a sound check, and starting to gig and record.

There is a picture of me with my mouth wide open in the junior school lunch-time choir. From my earnest yet somewhat pained expression, I was singing the descant part of 'All Things Bright And Beautiful'—loud and very wrong. The following year I was demoted to the altos as nature began to strangle my angelic tones. As this process continued, I fell even further down Mrs Harrison's ranks by being forced to accept the rather unglamorous post of 'music parts monitor'. This ain't rock 'n' roll.

We all go through the school choirs, orchestras and recorder ensembles, often being forced into extra-curricular activities to keep us from under our mothers' feet. I was a very reluctant, young piano pupil. Every Saturday morning I feigned as many ailments and symptoms as the family medical book would allow, but with hindsight these lessons were an invaluable grounding. A basic knowledge of the piano keyboard is an asset to any singer. I know my favourite keys, I can practice some tunes on my own, and being able to read music and understand chords is a huge help when I rehearse my own band and at other people's sessions.

At senior school, I joined a band. The line-up was two female singers, a drummer and me playing a Crumar Roadrunner electric piano. We worked out a set of songs ranging from Stevie Wonder to Kate Bush, rehearshing madly after school. Our 'A' level teacher's husband, Alan, acted as our manager. We found an agent in Liverpool and toured the working men's clubs of the North West, performing between the Bingo and the 'Star Turn'. At such a young age I was very lucky to have the fun of singing in a rock band and being on the road. As a result, I would encourage any new singer to 'get out and do it'. Find a group of like-minded musicians and play anywhere (schools, pubs, village halls, colleges) just to feel what it is like to stand in front of a crowd who are as eager for you to fail as you are to succeed. As soon as you have a band which is playing well, with tight, thoroughly rehearsed songs, it is such a thrill to see audiences nod their heads in time to your music, or even better, dance. From my early experiences, I learnt how to react when people are talking *and* how to talk when people are reacting. There is a lot more to presenting a song than 'and my next number is . . .'. I have been pelted with tomatoes, dodged beer-mats and had the power switched off because my band were playing too loud. At one very unsavoury venue a dog even attacked my saxophonist on stage. Even so, I wouldn't change my job for anything or anybody.

Choosing a Style

Like trends in clothes, styles of singing come and go, always returning in one form or another. For example, rock 'n' roll—as a style of dance music brought to England from America in the mid-Fifties—was relived in the Seventies with Sha Na Na, Showaddywaddy and Shakin' Stevens. Similarly, if somebody had predicted at the beginning of his career how David Bowie's vocal style was going to develop, Bowie probably would have never believed them. Some singers start in jazz and move into pop; other folk and country vocalists now work in rock bands; and even promising opera stars have turned to gothic punk. Your voice is as unique as your thumb-print and it may be fun to experiment with a variety of styles during your career. However, if you want to create a distinctive musical character, it is worth keeping an open mind to the styles of other, more established artists.

Don't be afraid of 'imitating'. This is an important part of your development as a singer and what seems at first like a poor copy of your idol will fuse itself with your own personal style. This process of imitation and influence has always been part of developing vocalists' styles. Al Jarreau must have been aware of Johnny Mathis's velvety baritone voice. By copying Mathis's vocal texture and combining it with 'scat singing' (a wordless 'shoo bee doo-ing' said to have been invented by Louis Armstrong), Jarreau has created his own style of singing. Paul Young cites Marvin Gaye and Otis Redding as his heroes and from his searching, reflective phrasing, their influence shines through. Despite that, the sound of Paul Young's voice is unmistakable.

David Bowie

Vocal Training

Like any other instrument, your voice needs care and respect. For pop music, you don't need a full operatic training. Although after years of training an operatic voice might have an astonishing range and durability, there are other ways to develop a natural, but trained voice. There are many successful singers whose voices wouldn't be regarded as technically good, but with the right material, arrangements and image, this potential flaw has been made into a vital feature. The classic example is Bob Dylan. His quirky, almost whining style of delivery is perfect for his ballads and narrative songs. Janis Joplin also breaks the accepted rules of singing, screaming above her range and breathing in all the wrong places. By doing that, she evokes the pain and anguish which her music requires. Siouxsie from the Banshees is another case. Her monotonal, almost out-of-tune singing suits her gothic image perfectly. Despite this, Siouxsie has taken some singing lessons more recently. Listen to 'Dear Prudence' where she sings with a stronger, less frantic voice. It's in tune too.

Finding a Teacher

Most singing teachers now regard rock and pop as a worthwhile area for vocal tuition. They offer suitable lessons because the basis of a singing voice is the same whatever your style of singing. A lot of good singing teachers operate by word of mouth, so keep your eyes and ears open. If you can't find a teacher from a personal recommendation, look in the 'Tuition' section of arts, music and rock magazines. Phone the teacher and discuss your requirements, such as your singing experience, the style you want to develop, and your budget (a lot of teachers require an advance payment of up to six lessons).

It is important to build a good relationship with your teacher. After a few lessons, you may decide that you are wrong for each other. You may need to confront the issue then and consider changing teacher. Lessons shouldn't be an ordeal, but you must realize that a fair amount of your tuition will depend on how much you can cope with the emotional aspect of singing. Singing isn't just about opening your mouth to produce a sound. There is a tremendous emotional charge involved as well. Listen to gospel singing and hear how the voice can be a vehicle for the extremes of emotion. To get the most from your lessons, you need to feel uninhibited with your teacher and willing to do a little 'soul-searching'.

What to expect from Voice Lessons

Whichever type of singing you want to develop, most good teachers will have a general vocal workout plan for you. As most lessons only last for an hour, this warm-up can often be developed best in a group

David Bowie

workshop (see next section). Learning how to breathe and use your diaphragm (as a top-up for your breathing to create a strong support for your singing) is one of the first tools of the singer's trade. It is remarkable how this initial discovery (that the chief strength of your voice lies low down in your stomach and that you can use your breathing apparatus in a new way) improves your voice's sound and tone. I recommend other physical recreations to enhance this new-found strength, like yoga and swimming.

Once you are using your lungs and diaphragm in your singing, your confidence and stage presence soars. Listen to some of the legendary jazz singers like Sarah Vaughan, Ella Fitzgerald and Mel Tormé to hear how breath control can be quite stunning. Sarah Vaughan bases her long drawn-out phrases on her ability to use her diaphragm to reach for quick breaths. Also, breathing can be a decorative and effective musical punctuation. Working with the jazz guitarist Joe Pass, Ella Fitzgerald's little gasps and snatches of breath are a beautiful compliment to Pass's fretboard finger squeaks.

Voice Workshops

The workshop is one of the most positive results of the performance-based approaches to music education developed in the Seventies. The music workshop has become an exciting method of group teaching which is vital to performing arts education. Vocal workshops are an ideal situation for exercising the human voice. When you team up with other singers in a workshop, you realize just how diverse and flexible the voice can be.

Every singer has specific problems which can be aired and solved with the help of the workshop leader. The format of a good vocal workshop will usually run something like this. First of all, there is a general discussion to find out people's names, why they have come and their preferred singing style. Next there is a warm-up. Most good teachers will do a physical warm-up, limbering up the neck and shoulder muscles for example, and loosening the jaw and activating the lungs. Then the breathing process will be explored, maybe lying on the floor to discover the importance of the rib-cage. Workshop teachers have different techniques and approaches to these rather more technical aspects of singing, but they amout to the same thing. The rest of the workshop will be devoted to producing vocal sounds—by using group improvisation, looking at shapes and rhythms, calling and responding, and maybe even attempting a large group 'a capella' piece. It is extraordinary how a collection of people who have never sung in public can produce a group sound which would enhance any concert, all in about one hour.

Bob Dylan

It is important to realize the value and social attraction of music-making in groups. Unlike a one-to-one lesson, voice workshops not only broaden your outlook on singing, but they can liven up your social life as well. After attending a few workshops why not use some of the methods with which you have worked and form some workshops of your own? It is amazing how this group feeling can soften the heart of even the most cynical thrash guitarist.

If you live in a city there will be a variety of ways to find workshops. Some are sponsored by local councils while others are run privately. In London there are various organizations aimed at providing workshops and outlets for music-making at all levels. Of these, Community Music and Musicworks are the two best known. Also it is worth looking at short residential courses. Wavenden, established by John Dankworth and Cleo Laine, and the Guildhall both run very prestigious jazz courses offering an intense all-round and jazz vocal training. For pop vocalists, the Musicians' Union and the University of Sussex run the Brighton Rock summer school. Most arts magazines, such as London's *Time Out* and *City Limits*, have details of workshops and vocal courses for the whole country. You may even form a band at one.

How to begin Work as a Singer

Once you have put a band together, or if you can accompany yourself on keyboards or guitar, there is a wealth of gigs waiting for you in wine bars, pubs, restaurants, theatre foyers and the increasingly popular cabaret circuit (although for this, your style and material would need a particular focus, with a socially or politically satirical edge).

After finding out who is responsible for booking music in each venue, try to organize an audition over the phone, although some bookers insist on hearing a demo tape. Think carefully about where you target. If you want gigs in pubs or wine bars, the booker isn't necessarily going to respond positively to a demo tape of original songs, unless it is lively and immediate. Choose about six songs for your audition and demo tape. This is more than for a record company demo, because bookers sometimes want to be sure that you have sufficient, suitable repertoire for the gig. Don't be tempted to sing slow ballads as they often bore the booker. If you are making a demo as a soloist, there is no need to clutter your songs with additional keyboards and backing vocals. Again, that is suited to the record company demo. For gigs, all that is wanted is a good clear presentation of how you sound when you perform live.

Gigging

Your first gig will be an important milestone. It may also be a disaster. If it is in a pub or wine bar, no one may listen, but you will quickly learn the reasons why. You may not be on a stage, so you aren't seen by the audience. Perhaps you are performing too loud or too soft, too much or too little, or maybe you lost your confidence. Whatever the reason, try to learn from the experience and don't get down-hearted. If you are a solo singer, using piano, keyboards or guitar as an accompaniment, make sure your arrangements aren't too complicated, because your voice is your best means of communication. As an example, listen to solo artists accompanying themselves, like Roberta Flack singing 'The First Time Ever I Saw Your Face'. Immediately, she evokes a power and atmosphere with simple chords and a quiet, almost trance-like vocal. She demonstrates that loud singing doesn't always attract an audience's attention. I always include a quiet song in my set to re-establish my presence. If nothing else, it can embarrass a persistent talker into silence. If you are sitting at a keyboard, try to be seen by the whole room. Your face is almost as important as your voice in this situation, so arrange the mike stand at a comfortable and visible position (a twisted head can promote a lost voice due to singing from the throat).

Fronting a Band

To be a lead singer in a band is every vocalist's dream. Although there are no rules about fronting a band, it is worth pointing out some methods. To help you find your own way of doing this, explore the vast collection of rock videos in the high street and at your local libraries. Check out the Cure, with their idiosyncratic front man, Robert Smith. He uses twitchy face movements, barely opening his eyes and hardly moving away from centre stage, to create the Cure's popular and characteristic style and personality. By contrast, the athletic Bruce Springsteen throws himself on to speakers, leaps off monitors, establishes an eyeball-to-eyeball contact with his audience and, like many rock performers, he uses the microphone stand as a dramatic prop. By contrast, Kate Bush uses all aspects of theatre and dance in her rare live performances. To incorporate these visual elements into her shows, she uses a radio chest mike to be free from leads and microphone stands. However, the volume on this type of microphone is very difficult to control, so it is only recommended if it is absolutely necessary.

The Soundcheck: How to Use a Microphone

Most rock gigs involve a sound check. When electronic instruments are used, this is a necessity. The vocals usually sound check last. At the sound check, make sure the microphone lead is free of its stand if you want to move around when you perform. Also, ask for a monitor (or 'wedge') directly in front of you so that you can hear yourself and everyone else. The vocal mikes should be as loud as possible without producing feedback (that painful whistling sound). This is when mike control becomes important. If you are singing loudly, move away from the bowl of the mike. If you sing softly, move back in. Most good live mikes are uni-directional, which makes you sing into them rather than across them. However, you can produce a very special, soft tone quality by 'eating' the mike. Also, remember your plosive mouth sounds, 'P's and 'B's when using any microphone. Try to soften them in ballads. If you think 'M', you will stop words like 'please' and 'baby' exploding out of the speakers.

I always insist that backing vocalists are at the same volume as the lead singer. Backing vocals (or 'beevees') are often much harder than the leader. They take power, precision and concentration, so they need to be *heard*. Top backing vocalists use microphone control with consummate confidence and accuracy to support the total sound of the band.

At the end of the sound check, the band should run through a couple of songs. This isn't only to hear if the sound is good out front, but to check whether everyone in the band can hear the whole sound through their monitors on stage. At bigger gigs, there is a sound on stage person to help with this. A simple gesture to him or her during the gig will change the volume in your monitor.

The Gig

At the gig, your performance should be direct and confident, reflecting the style of your band. Project your songs out to your audience. Open your eyes. Only close them for effect. Use the space you have on stage, though be careful how close you go to the monitors as you could cause serious feedback! Announce each song clearly—there may be A&R staff in the audience. Acknowledge your band members. Some bands use repeated choruses to introduce each person by name. Finally, make sure you have a good encore. That just might be your first hit single.

Sessions

Session singing can be musically rewarding and financially lucrative. Each session can lead to another, more interesting, and better paid project. Some singers commit their entire working lives to doing sessions, working on every album and television advert imaginable. As a result, they are constantly in demand because they can sing whatever an artist or producer needs.

For advertising work, a sessions singer has to be technically good, be pitch perfect and have good breathing and tone control. Also, the session singer needs the ability to modify his or her voice to the requirements of the product. For example, on a recent chewing-gum advert, I performed a very rocky, Bruce Springsteen type vocal, which had to match the pictures of sportsmen, urban skylines and rather overtanned young people cavorting on beaches and high streets. Top pop performers are sometimes imitated as an effective way of making TV viewers associate a product with a familiar sound. This is an increasingly popular advertising method. Turn on the television and you can hear session musicians' versions of Queen, Joe Cocker, Nina Simone, Ella Fitzgerald, Bryan Ferry and a host of other stars, all singing the delights of a particular chocolate, carpet cleaner or crisp. I have sung Scottish accents, cockney slang, ridiculous opera, rasping blues and country 'n' western, all to accompany a visual advert. In many ways, session singing for advertising is similar to acting—the more flexible you are, the better. Of course, some singers are valued and used for their individuality, such as Joe Fagin, whose gravelly tenor voice can be heard on many adverts.

Getting into Sessions

Like being a backing singer, sessions singing is a very demanding and specialist field, requiring technique and confidence. Most studios or agencies will require a 'showreel'. This is a tape of anything and everything you have recorded, from a simple four track with just keyboards or guitar, to your first session. Unlike in record companies, agencies don't let your tapes sit on producers' shelves gathering dust. Every jingle writer and producer is constantly on the look out for new and different voices, so yours might be just the one they want for an international fizzy drink advert. But vocal sessions don't only concern advertising. There is a wide variety of recording opportunities for singers: theatre music, independent films, video promotional 'shorts', industrial films, educational videos and records.

To be asked to sing on a band's album or single is a real thrill and often a good way into the record industry for your own material. This is a vague area, even though there are agencies which specialize in singers (like the famous General Bookings agency). Although record companies have a list of singers they trust, a lot of new bands ask people they have heard singing at gigs or who they met at the pub to record with them. The way to get into this area is to advertise yourself as a singer and get your face known. It is remarkable how your guts in saying, 'I'm a singer, here's my card', can result in a session with a new band. Have business cards printed, with your name, telephone number and 'Singer' on them. I often have phone calls from people who have kept my cards for years, asking me if I still do sessions.

Like everything else, there is a legal side to singing sessions. For doing jingles and anything to do with broadcasting, most agencies will insist on membership of British Equity. Don't panic! It is much easier to join Equity as a singer than as an actor. This can be achieved by doing gigs, any gigs, and asking the bookers to write a contract stating for how long you have performed and for how much. The amount of contracts you need changes from month to month, but getting an Equity card isn't impossible. At least as a singer, you don't have to compete with aspiring actors for jobs as strippers or as performing sidekicks for killer snakes. Also, being a member of the Musicians' Union is a prerequisite for anything connected with the music industry.

In the Studio

After a few months gigging or touring, either with your band or as a solo artist, you may be ready to produce a demo for record companies. The demo has to be a good reflection of you as an artist, while the vocal needs to be clear, strong and true to your live performance, because if an A&R person likes your tape, the next step is for him or her to see you live.

When you are choosing a studio, check out the vocal sound to make sure that you are happy with it. Ask the engineer to play you some work that has been recorded there recently. Once you are in the studio, the backing track will be 'laid down' with a 'guide vocal'. This is your chance to get the feel of the vocal 'booth' and to get used to working with headphones or 'cans'. Experiment with one 'can' on your ear, and the other off. Often, this helps your tuning. Be careful not to be carried away by all the special effects available for vocals, like reverb (an artificial acoustic which places the voice in a large space lending it an echoey sound) or delay (a repeat effect which can sound very attractive, but an unnecessary gimmick when overused). These effects can be experimented with in the final mix. All you need in your cans is a good, toppy sound, reasonably dry, with a good volume in proportion to the backing track. Try and take the rough mix home and listen to it carefully, noting sections which you can patch the next day. Most engineers are happy to drop in and repair sections of the vocals.

I love to do my own backing vocals in the studio. Singing with yourself produces a very special effect. Listen To Chaka Khan—she is the best exponent of layering her own beevees. As a contrast, sometimes it is a luxury to have another vocal texture above or below your own. But be careful not to clutter the lead vocal with layer upon layer of stunning beevees.

Three songs is a good introduction to your talents for a record company, accompanied by a photograph of your band and a letter of introduction. Who knows, this bold gesture may change the rest of your life.

Listening Guide

I have compiled a list of a wide cross-section of singers. Try to hear these artist' recordings. Your local record library may help with the more obscure ones. Then you can open your heart, mind and ears to the array of styles which other vocalists have developed, and use that knowledge to forge your own.

Early Crooners and Torch Singers

Nat King Cole
Frank Sinatra, *Songs for Swinging lovers*
Ella Fitzgerald, the *Songbooks* (Porter, Gershwin, Rodgers and Hart)
The Platters
Judy Garland, *Live at Carnegie*
Frankie Laine
Connie Francis

Rock 'n' Roll

Elvis Presley
Little Richard
Brenda Lee
Chuck Berry
Bill Haley and the Comets

Jazz and Blues (early)

Bessie Smith, *The Bessie Smith Story*, vols. 1 and 2
Ella Fitzgerald, *Ella Sings with Louis*
Billy Holiday, *Lady in Satin*, *The Billie Holiday Story*
Joe Williams
Louis Armstrong
Sarah Vaughan, *Sarah Vaughan Sings*, *Tenderly*
Dinah Washington

Jazz and Blues (late)

Sarah Vaughan, *An Evening of Gershwin with Sarah Vaughan and the Los Angeles Philharmonic*
Ella Fitzgerald, *Ella with Joe Pass*, *Sunshine of your Love*
Al Jarrreau, *Live in London*
George Benson, *Tenderly*
Diana Reeves
Dee Dee Bridgewater, *Live in Paris*
Mel Tormé
Nancy Wilson, *This Mother's Daughter*, *Lush Life*
Bobby McFerrin
Joni Mitchell, *Mingus*
Aretha Franklin, *The Early Sessions* (on Atlantic)
Sheila Jordan
Mark Murphy
Take Six

Rhythm 'n' Blues and Soul

Percy Sledge
Bill Withers
Tina Turner
Aretha Franklin, *Live at Filmore West*
Ray Charles
King Pleasure
Carol Grimes, *Eyes Wide Open*

Rhythm 'n' Blues and Soul (cont.)

Earth Wind and Fire, *I Am*
Ann Peebles
Betty Wright
Millie Jackson, *Still Caught Up*
Diana Ross
Martha Reeves
Marvin Gaye, *What's Going on?*
Phoebe Snow, *Something Real,
Looks like Snow*

Gospel

Mahalia Jackson
Sweet Honey in the Rock
Aretha Franklin, *One Lord, One
Faith, One Baptism*
Mighty Clouds of Joy

Rock

Kokomo
Todd Rundgren, *Healing, Nearly
Human*
Bon Jovi
Foreigner
Toni Childs, *Union*
Heart
Guns and Roses
The Who
David Bowie, *Aladdin Sane, Let's
Dance*
The Rolling Stones, *Let it Bleed*
Spandau Ballet

Women Singers

Laura Nyro, *New York Tendaberry,
Nested*
Joni Mitchell, *Court 'n Spark, The
Hissing of Summer Lawns*

Joan Armatrading, *Me, Myself, I*
Sandie Shaw
Lulu
Judie Tzuke, *Sports Car*
Tracy Chapman
Joan Baez
Carole King, *Tapestry*
Janis Joplin, *Pearl*
Elkie Brooks
Shirley Bassey
Barbara Streisand
Carly Simon, *Hotcakes*
Cher
Kate Bush, *The Kick Inside, Hounds
of Love, The Sensual World*

Punk, Gothic, New Wave, Eighties Pop

Siouxsie and the Banshees,
Kaleidoscope
The Sex Pistols
Blondie, *Parallel Lines*
The Undertones
Culture Club, *Colour by Numbers*
Duran Duran
All About Eve
The Cult
The Alarm.

Folk, World Music, Ethnic

Miriam Makeba
Salif Keita
Le Mystère des voix bulgares
Trio Bulgarka
Bob Dylan
Joni Mitchell, *Ladies of the Canyon*
The Chieftains
Edith Piaf

Further Reading

There are many books on singing techniques, but the skills of rock and pop vocals can't be readily acquired from reading. Most publications present an introduction to the basics of singing technique, for example, the physiology of the torso, and the head/chest/mouth/diaphragm relationship.

F. Husler and Y. Rodd-Marling, *Singing: The Physical Nature of the Vocal Organ* (Hutchinson).
Cleo Laine, 'Singing', in George Martin (Ed.), *Making Music* (Barrie & Jenkins).
M. McCalliom, *The Voice Book* (Faber & Faber).

Siouxsie Sioux

2 Guitar

. . . .

DEIRDRE CARTWRIGHT is a guitarist, composer, arranger, author and teacher. She has toured and recorded with various rock, pop and jazz bands including the critically acclaimed Guest Stars. She was one of the presenters in both series of BBC TV's 'Rockschool' programme which was shown world-wide. This led to her co-writing the two 'Rockschool' books, *The Rockschool Sessions* and her own guitar tutor. Currently, Deirdre is writing for her own jazz fusion group, runs a jazz club in London, 'Blow the Fuse', and gigs and records constantly. She cites her main musical influences as Jimi Hendrix, John Schofield, John Coltrane and the people she works with. Here, Deirdre discusses the practicalities of playing and recording rock guitar, and includes a safety guide for using electric instruments which is essential for all musicians.

This article is full of information and ideas for anyone who wants to be a rock or pop guitarist. It also mentions some of the pitfalls just waiting for new-comers to the business. In fact, I wish that somebody had written something like this when I began playing! This is all based on my experiences of professional guitar playing—from miming in front of the mirror to being called up to play on sessions and tour with a band. I hope that this personal view helps you in becoming a successful musician.

First Stages: Joining a Band

I am going to assume that you own an electric guitar and an amplifier (see the equipment section in this article for hints on buying these) and that you are learning to play some songs. It would be even better if you had a guitar book and a teacher, and if you practised every day on different skills such as scales, fingerings, technique exercises, chords and learning new songs from your favourite albums. The next step is exciting, challenging and very rewarding: you form or join a band. You may be lucky and a bunch of your friends also want to play music, so you can form a group. You exchange ideas and records, hold rehearsals, try writing some songs and who knows, someone may even offer you a gig! But if you start off on your own, how do you get into a group? It is never easy to find people you want to play with (and who want to play with you!). A practical approach is finding and answering adverts—in music shops, rehearsal rooms or the back pages of *Melody Maker* or *Loot*. Also, try to make personal contacts by asking around at school, at youth projects, in music shops, or guitar and music teachers. Which style of music do you want to play? Which groups do you listen to? Have you written any songs? All of this will help you assess what you have in common (or not!) with other musicians. You could even try advertising yourself, for example:

'Guitarist playing six months into HM seeks bass and drums'

or:

'Guitarist into folk and blues wants to meet other musicians to rehearse and jam'

Write out a card and put it in a local music shop or studio and see if you get any response.

Rehearsals

If you are in a group, then you'll need to think about rehearsal rooms because you'll face problems of volume and space at home (you probably won't get the drum kit and the rest of the group into your bedroom). A good rehearsal room is very important because it will let you set up and play in conditions similar to performing on stage. It is often useful to have a few smaller and quieter rehearsals at each other's homes to write songs and settle on a general band style. However, for your band to progress you will need regular full group rehearsals. To find a cheap rehearsal space, you could try schools, youth clubs, church halls, factories, garages or shops in the evening. Yes, it has all been done. If you can afford it, go to a professional rehearsal studio. This has several advantages including a PA system, the cheap hire of amps and drum kits, and storage space for your gear (especially useful if you do not have access to a car or van). Unfortunately, some poor rehearsal studios also include the dubious delights of stroppy staff, no heating or ventilation, not enough soundproofing from the band next door, toilets that never work and ten years of graffiti on the walls. You have been warned! Don't just book over the phone. If you haven't got any personal recommendations, compare a few studios by looking them over. Then you can make the right decision for your band.

Performing: On Stage/ On Tour

When it comes to playing your first gig, you have to deal with several factors which are different to the rehearsal situation. If you always rehearse in the same place, you will be used to your band's sound and set-up in that room. The sound on a stage can be very different. Try to position your equipment on stage so that you can hear each other clearly. Also, you may find that some of your gear isn't adequate for gigging. For instance, if you have a short guitar lead, you are going to find yourself stuck at the back of the stage next to the amp.

At most gigs, you will have to rely on PA monitors to hear the vocals, and the bigger the stage, the more reliant the whole band becomes on the PA to hear each other. Consider which parts of your band's sound are the most important for you to hear. For example, you may want some bass and drums through your monitor. This is why sound checks are so important. If you sing with the lead vocalist on one number, you may find that as you move forward and away from your guitar amp, you can hardly hear your own playing. Also, the lead singer may not have asked for any of your vocal to be put through his or her monitor so you can't hear your own singing, which is very unnerving. As you do more gigs, you will become used to coping with different stage sounds and how to identify the instruments which you need to hear on stage. Then you will be able to use the sound check to anticipate and solve some potential problems. Of course, you may be playing gigs with three or four other groups on the bill, sharing equipment and performing on a small stage with hardly any time to set up or sound check.

The guitar 'cuts through' a band's sound more than other instruments such as the bass. This allows guitarists to use a small amp and still be heard clearly. Often, bands set up at a gig and the guitarist thinks she or he sounds great, with just the right volume. Then a friend or a sound engineer comments that the guitar is far too loud out front. If you need to turn down your amp for a better overall group sound, but your guitar still seems too quiet to you, try putting your amp on a chair or beer crate just behind you. Bringing the amp closer to you still gives you the impression of a powerful sound, although the guitar's volume can still be reduced out front in order to stop it dominating the group's sound.

At bigger gigs where most instruments are miked up, try experimenting with your amp facing sideways across the stage, or even towards you like a monitor speaker. This gives the PA engineer more control over the guitar's volume as part of the band's sound and lets you play at an ideal volume. In a mid-sized venue (approximate capacity 500) a 100W Marshall amp and cabinet should amplify the guitar quite satisfactorily. However, the quality of the guitar sound is

Chuck Berry

usually better if it is reinforced by a large PA system because the sound can be evenly distributed by large stacks of speakers on both sides of the stage.

Image

When you are performing, you have to be aware of how you look. Everyone projects an 'image' on stage, even if it is in no way outrageous, such as wearing jeans and a T-shirt. Classic rock showmen have included Jimi Hendrix, Angus Young (AC/DC) and Pete Townshend, but guitarists like Eric Clapton and Mark Knopfler also portray a strong if quieter image. Obviously, image isn't just about clothes and make-up. It concerns your ability to be comfortable playing on stage and in front of an audience as well. If you can, ask someone to video your group playing at a gig and have a close look at yourself.

Recording and Session Work

The recording process makes its own demands on you as a guitarist. In the studio, the emphasis is on the band's sound and not your image. When you are recording you need to lay down parts quickly and accurately but still manage to perform with a good feel. There are many different ways of recording songs which depend on the type and size of the studio, on the style of the music, and on the engineer's and producer's work methods.

Let's consider some areas where recording really differs from live work. If you were the guitarist of a rock group, you could be recording a song in which you play a rhythm part as well as taking a short solo. Even though the basic track could be recorded with all the group playing together, the engineer may use screens, with a separate drum or vocal booth. This means that you will have to use headphones to hear everyone else. You need to find out whether you can hear your own headphone mix or if everyone in the band hears the same balance of instruments. This is quite similar to using a monitor system on stage except that you are sometimes more reliant on a studio headphone mix. You need to be comfortable with what you can hear in your headphones. If you have a good balance of bass drum, snare, hi-hat, bass guitar and the rest of the backing track, it makes all the difference to your playing. Is it loud enough? Think about what you can't hear. Sometimes, guitarists record their parts by themselves, without the band. If you are recording alone, consider whether you mind the rest of your group standing around in the control room while you play. If you prefer to record with just the engineer and producer in the control room, say so.

When you are doing a solo, there may be several tracks available for you to try two or three versions and to listen for the best one. If you

Eric Clapton

take advantage of these, the producer may make up a composite solo from the best parts of each version. Some guitarists work better with the safety net of keeping several tracks free. Others like to feel the pressure of 'one go', almost like being on stage.

If you aren't used to recording in a studio, these different ways of working, the usually drier sound and the pressure of getting it right without the buzz of an audience, can all badly affect your performance. Experience really does help, but try to become familiar with these studio techniques so you can start to relax and enjoy yourself.

Equipment for Recording Sessions

It is obviously best for you if you can record with your familiar gigging set-up, but the limitations in the studio of space, volume and tracks may require a compromise. Generally the guitar is recorded by positioning a microphone just in front of a speaker and other microphones are placed further away to pick up the sound of the guitar in different parts of the room. This 'ambient' sound is what you usually hear. Various effects pedals add extra noise and hum to your sound in the studio, despite being excellent units for stage work. To cope with this, try to avoid recording with your full stage set-up of effects. Instead, limit yourself to the effects which feature in each particular song.

Another way of recording the guitar is to 'direct inject' (DI) into the desk. Usually this makes the sound cleaner and quieter, although the sound can lose sustain and warmth. Another method involves 'DIing' the guitar from a 'Rockman' or similar purpose-built mini amp/ effects unit. This boosts the guitar's volume, and if it contains built-in effects these will help give your guitar sound more substance and character. If you are working with no separate recording room, like in most home studios, you will probably have no choice but to DI the guitar. In this case some kind of 'in line' effect like the Rockman is essential if you want a rocky sound. Sustain, overdrive and wah wah type effects should be recorded with the guitar. Reverb and delay effects, including chorusing and phasing, can easily be added afterwards. The engineer may suggest doing this so that you can hear the sound of the guitar in the overall mix. Then you can judge much better the amount of delay or reverb which needs to be added. All this also has to be weighed against the possibility that your performance in the studio may suffer because the 'dry' studio makes the guitar sound very different to normal.

Try to work creatively with the engineer. Listen to a playback of the guitar sound and ask him or her to change things if necessary. When you do this, it is worth being as specific as possible. Telling someone 'it doesn't sound like me' isn't very helpful. 'Could you add more treble or bass?', or 'can you make it cleaner or warmer?' are far more descriptive and practical suggestions.

Doing Sessions

Earning money from playing sessions is something to which many guitarists aspire and only a tiny percentage manage. Generally, people like using session players who are well known and experienced. Also, they will be expected to read music, chord charts and be quick, accurate performers. Usually, session players have equipment which can deal with most recording situations and styles of music. For instance, they might have two electric guitars, an acoustic guitar with steel or nylon strings, a small versatile amp and several effects. Sometimes players are asked to do sessions because they are known for a certain style of sound, such as Eddie Van Halen on Michael Jackson's 'Beat It', but that is unusual. Most session work requires extreme flexibility. Players need a good working knowledge of several different styles and musically it can actually be quite boring although it is well paid.

If you want to work as a session player, your attitude is very important. You should be punctual, pleasant and patient so that you can interpret what are sometimes very vague or abstract musical ideas. 'A bit more oomph' or 'the sound of a squeaky spring' is the sort of guidance you might get. Even if you aren't sure what you are being asked to do, still convey confidence and keep trying until the producer suddenly says 'That's it!' Don't make the people who are employing you feel musically inferior or stupid, or say that their music is awful, even if you think it is. Your job is to perform. Unless you are asked, you aren't there to give your artistic opinions.

It is very hard and competitive to break into session work, but if you are serious, have some cards printed with your name, telephone number and skills. Get an answerphone and leave your card around at studios. Ask people to help you get in with a session fixer and make as many contacts as possible so that people know that you are interested in this type of work.

Guitarists for Guitarists

Listening is essential to becoming a good musician. By paying close attention to the sound and style of rock's great guitarists, you can hear how these performers have developed and established certain styles of guitar playing which have become the standards of rock technique. All these great players learnt from each other. By observing and listening, copying and practising, they all found a distinctive sound and style. To help structure your listening, I have made a list of guitarists (which is by no means comprehensive) who have been major influences on whole generations of guitarists. Some of them completely changed the sound of the electric guitar, while others have been imitated so often that their playing no longer sounds quite as revolutionary as when they were first heard. (Artists marked with * are essential listening.)

The 1950s

*Chuck Berry Wrote and played rock 'n' roll classics like 'Johnny B. Goode', 'Roll Over Beethoven', 'Sweet Little Sixteen'. With his clean, sharp sound, he was known for his driving rhythm playing and memorable introductions and solos.

Carl Perkins A composer and guitarist, his playing has influenced generations of rockabilly players. He wrote 'Blue Suede Shoes' and 'Honey Don't'.

Scotty Moore The guitarist with Elvis Presley for his first recordings with Sun Records, he also worked with Gene Vincent. Scotty had a clean sound, using lots of reverb, which complimented his succinct and melodic jazz-influenced solos.

B. B. King As the blues guitarist who was known for making his guitar 'sing' in his solos, he influenced the next generation of British rock players as well as other guitarists of the 1950s like Chuck Berry. However, his best album recordings were released in the 1960s, like *Live at the Regal*, *Alive and Well* and *Completely Well*.

The 1960s

A period of incredible change, starting with the sound of Hank Marvin and ending with Jimi Hendrix. Young British guitarists, like Jeff Beck, Eric Clapton and Peter Green, redefined the blues and exported it back to a young American audience. This was an era when music's technology developed fast. Louder amp stacks from Marshall and new effects like the fuzz box, the echo unit, and the wah wah pedal changed the whole sound of the electric guitar.

*Jimi Hendrix From a background in blues and R 'n' B, Hendrix created a distorted, howling, monster guitar sound that set the instrument free into the realm of sustain and feedback. He wrote 'Purple Haze', 'Voodoo Chile' and 'Little Wing'.

*Eric Clapton A blues-influenced guitarist whose great playing graced John Mayall's Blues Breakers, he was lead guitarist with Cream. With them his playing was still bluesy, but with more effects such as wah wah. Hear him on Cream tracks like 'Tales of Brave Ulysses', 'Crossroads' and 'White Room'.

Other great lead players included *Jeff Beck* (hear the *Truth* and *Blow by Blow* albums), *Jimmy Page* of Led Zeppelin (whose great tracks combining folk and rock influences include 'Whole Lotta Love', 'Black Dog', 'Rock 'n' Roll' and 'Stairway to Heaven'), *Ritchie Blackmore* of Deep Purple (known for his fast bluesy, rock playing—hear him on 'Smoke on the Water'), and *Peter Green* (who graced early Fleetwood Mac tracks like 'Albatross').

For rhythm playing:

Pete Townshend (The Who) He used a powerful, open chord sound on songs like 'Substitute' and 'My Generation'.

Roger McGuinn (The Byrds) With The Byrds, he created a classic 'jingly jangly' rhythm guitar sound using 12-string guitars. Hear it on 'Tambourine Man'. This is often simulated today by using a chorus pedal.

The 1970s

This was the era of glam rock, pub rock, pomp rock, country rock, the supergroup, punk and the growing popularity of ska and reggae. One musical fashion followed another and a host of good guitarists emerged to develop the guitar sound of the 1960s. As a result, the 1970s consolidated more than revolutionized the techniques of playing rock guitar.

Carlos Santana He blended Latin and rock to become popular in the early 1970s with his smooth, sustained sound. Listen to his album, *Abraxas*.

Brian May (Queen) A smooth, exciting and fast player who began experimenting successfully with tape delay devices like the Wem Copycat on live gigs. Hear him on tracks like 'Dead on Time' and 'Brighton Rock'.

Andy Summers (The Police) A particularly inventive rhythm player who combined melodic lines with strong rhythm, as on 'Can't Stand Losin' You' and 'Every Breath You Take'. He often used delay and chorus effects.

The 1980s

Despite the massive growth of synthesizers in the 1980s, the sound of electric guitar continued to be more popular and diverse than ever, especially with the growth of world music.

*Eddie Van Halen Van Halen revolutionized the sound of heavy metal guitar. He is famed for his speed, fast picking, two-handed finger-board tapping, high harmonics and the whammy bar (actually the tremolo arm, but when you use it to raise and lower the guitar

strings like Van Halen, what else can you call it?). Listen to 'Spanish Fly', which was actually played on acoustic guitar, and 'Eruption' from his first album, *Van Halen*.

Johnny Marr (The Smiths) Continuing the legacy of The Byrds, his jangly rhythm style proved an ideal accompaniment to Morrisey's songs.

The Edge (U2) He has a beautiful use of harmonics and delay effects, while he plays sparse but soulful, rhythmic solos.

Joe Satriani He became known as an excellent teacher to professional players and has released several albums which showcase his fantastic technique and control.

Dozens of good heavy rock players—Michael Schenker, Gary Moore, Randy Rhodes, Jake E. Lee; 'hi-tech' performers (fast and flashy)—Vinnie Vincent, Tony Macalpine, Yngwie Malmsteen, Steve Vai; jazz fusion stylists—Scott Henderson, Frank Gambale.

The Equipment You Need

1. A Guitar. There are literally hundreds of guitars around. Many are based on the designs of the Fender Stratocaster or the Gibson Les Paul, though a few new shapes have become popular recently. If you are buying a guitar for the first time, take someone more experienced to a good music shop. There you can try out and compare different makes, pick up free advice from the assistants and see what a more expensive guitar feels and sounds like. Having done all of that, go for something within your budget with which you feel happy. Sometimes shops have secondhand guitars which are less expensive and often better value for money. Above all, take your time.

Although buying secondhand guitars privately should be cheaper than in the shops, you need to know how much to pay for the different models of a guitar. Otherwise, you may get ripped off. So, until you are experienced, a shop is probably a better bet. At least you can test out the range of guitars in their display and be sure that you will really get what you pay for.

2. An Amplifier. Something quite small and portable would be a good start, perhaps with some built-in effects like reverb and distortion. Or you could plug in to a home hi-fi unit, if it is fitted with a microphone socket. However, be careful not to take the volume up too high, as you might blow your speakers.

3. Guitar Lead. Buy a 15–20 foot good quality, straight lead. They are the most useful. Poor quality leads tend to become noisy and crackly and they break down much faster. Even a top class lead will stop working some time, so it is worth keeping a spare close at hand.

4. Guitar Strings. These come in different gauges. The most common sets are either 009–042 or 010–046. Buy a spare set—you never know when you might break a string.

5. Effects Pedals. The most popular effects are distortion, chorus and digital delay. Listen to how the guitarists I have mentioned use them.

Eddie Van Halen

6. Sundries. Plectrum and spares; a guitar tuner is useful if you can afford one (share it with the bass player); a small electrical screwdriver, which is useful for adjusting your guitar or looking inside mains plugs.

Always carry spares with you. If you start doing gigs, you will soon need them! Your kit of spares should include spare strings, batteries (for effects), plectrums, guitar leads, as well as mains and amp fuses. Also, the band should carry a plug board. Lots of venues don't have enough power points.

Safety Note

If you are using a hired or borrowed amp, check that the plug is wired properly and that there is no sign of strain where the mains lead is connected to the amp. If you plug into an amp and you hear a buzz which disappears when you touch the strings, then the equipment isn't properly earthed. Check the mains plug first (familiarize yourself with how a plug should look when it is wired up correctly). This is a very basic safety procedure, but a number of guitarists have been killed using faulty equipment. If you are unsure of the plug's wiring or you receive a small shock when you touch a microphone, STOP. Get someone to check out the problem. I know this has happened in rehearsals, at sound checks and in a television studio. The problem then has always been somebody's else's faulty equipment, plugboard or mains supply, although there might just as easily be something wrong with your gear. There are devices available which cut out the electrical current before you receive a shock and which protect you from this hazard. Another good safety check is a 'Martindale mains tester'. Plugging this into a power socket or plugboard will display whether the mains wiring is correct and properly earthed. I have found this a worthwhile tool.

Guitar Synths

There isn't space here to detail exactly how guitar synths work. Unlike keyboards, the guitar has been a difficult instrument to use as a trigger for synthesized sound. If you try one out, you will quickly understand some of the problems. Currently you have to adapt your playing technique in order to get the best out of these instruments. Some guitar synths only use synthesized sound while others are basically guitars with a special pick-up which lets you mix the guitar's sound with the synthesiser's. That can be really effective.

The big advantage of these instruments is that if you are interested in synthesized sounds, MIDI and sequencing, you can use this technology without learning any keyboard technique. Guitar synths are constantly being updated and improved. Pioneering names were the Synthaxe, Stepp guitar and various Roland products. More recent models have been made by Yamaha and Casio. Look in magazines and go to music fairs to keep up with this young and exciting technology.

Further Reading

Deirdre Cartwright and others, *Rockschool I* (BBC Publications).
Julian Colbeck, *Rockschool II* (Music Maker).
Ralph Denyer, *Guitar Handbook* (Pan).
Rockschool Sessions (Boosey & Hawkes).
Rockschool Guitar Tutor (Boosey & Hawkes).
What Guitar (Making Music Books) available through *Making Music* magazine.
Guitar Player
Guitarist
Loot (for second-hand equipment)
Making Music (good for reviews, equipment comparisons, prices, general info)
Melody Maker

3 Bass Guitar

....

ROBERT BURNS is a studio bassist and producer. Having studied at the Guildhall School of Music and Drama, he spent much of his early career touring before becoming involved in film music composition and production. His playing credits range from Pete Townshend and David Gilmour to countless television sessions and jingles. Robert is also head of bass guitar studies at the Bass Tech school in London. In addition to discussing the bass, this article includes an informative description of how many players break into professional playing, and of the attitudes and working methods they adopt to make a successful career.

Starting Out as a 'Pro'

Since turning 'pro' in the mid-1970s, I have witnessed huge changes in how bass guitarists regard themselves, and how they are perceived by other musicians. As a young player, I found myself in a country where it was unheard of to study the bass guitar at music college. In addition, I was no different from many young musicians whose parents disapprove of music as a career, regarding music merely as a pleasant hobby to accompany school work. However, my parents' plans for my medical career bit the dust the moment I was accepted to study trumpet at the Guildhall School of Music and Drama in London.

In fact, I left the Guildhall without finishing my course. I went on tour instead with some of my teenage heroes, Edwin Starr and Sam and Dave. How I got this job is typical of the way musicians break into professional work. Before I studied at the Guildhall, my musical aspirations were higher than just playing in two local bands. To begin my career, I decided to look at the 'Musicians Wanted' adverts in *Melody Maker*. After lots of phone calls, I made the train journey from Hemel Hempstead to London very regularly in search of fame and fortune. Usually, my destination was a back street garage where I would play with a band who 'wanted commitment', 'NO hardened pros', 'own gear', and offered 'management interest' along with an unpaid gig at the Marquee in a year's time! Eventually I auditioned for a band wanting a bassist who read music for some gigs and BBC recordings (I only read treble clef at the time). I got the job but the band quickly split up. However, the band's guitarist remembered me when he was offered a job with Edwin Starr, and he got me in as well. Suddenly, I was a working, professional bass player.

Persistence is essential to success in auditions. For every worthwhile audition, there will be at least ten which have wasted your time. But if you play well, people will notice, take your phone number and maybe book you one day for a gig, tour or recording session.

Working Professionally

My first professional job was quite a shock. Before then, bass playing had been a hobby. Touring with an American soul band gave me my first lessons in professional discipline. I was working for an American musical director who knew what he wanted, and how to get it (in my case, quite brutally!). I lasted the tour and was offered the subsequent ones. These first professional experiences taught me several invaluable lessons which I still appreciate. When I do bass clinics with young players, I always stress these points as they apply to any style of music, and to both freelance and band playing. These aren't in order of importance. They are simply a guide to what would be expected of you as a professional bass guitarist.

1. Broaden Your Musical Listening

Listen to all the music you can. I used to avoid country music until I had to perform on a country album. It may not be the most exciting music to play on the bass, but it isn't all two notes to the bar and it requires a great deal of discipline. If country music is one of your favourites, try something else with which you are unfamiliar, like fusion or Latin. One day, your interest will pay off. Your versatility means you can work with a wide variety of musicians. If you are having a bad week and get a call from a Latin band, it would be heart-breaking to turn it down just because you can't play salsa!

2. Develop Your Musical Skills

Study subjects from harmony to slapping and cross-handed tapping. You will need every facet of modern bass playing at your fingertips to make a career. For instance, some players regard plectrum playing as old-fashioned, but many recording engineers still prefer it. If you have never played with a plectrum, get used to it. In the past, I believed that reading music wasn't too important for young players. Now I recommend it. If you want to be a professional player, it is worth learning how to sight-read music. Then you can wait for your band to get the 'big deal' while getting out and working with other musicians. You can begin to establish yourself as a 'dep' (deputy) for various players, and even do a few sessions. This doesn't imply a lack of commitment to your band. It is simply the most reliable way of starting a career which has some chance of success. Otherwise, if your band fails, so will you.

3. Learn How to Work under Someone Else's Direction

Try to be open-minded about new ideas. If you are rehearsing with your band, let the songwriters experiment with different ideas for the bass part without making them feel uncomfortable. As a freelance session player, you can't afford to look down your nose at the music which you are being asked to perform. Be prepared to be told what to play, and do it as well as you can. You may be asked to work with a conductor on a session or on a gig, so take note of his or her musical direction.

4. Work on Your Timing

Most modern music uses a time code in recording. Your band might sequence parts of its music, or you may play for a film, television or jingle session when the music has to be perfectly synchronized with the pictures. For all these, it isn't just the drummer's job to keep time, the bass has an important role as well. Try to practise as if you are playing along with a computer so you can build up an inner 'body clock' which keeps you in time. To develop this, practise bass parts or scales with a drum machine or a metronome. If you can't afford one of these, make some tapes of beats from other people's drum machines, all at different speeds, so you can get used to playing in time to any music, however fast or slow. But be careful not to play robotically. If you do, the music's groove will be lost. The groove is essential, because it attracts people to dancing and liking your band's music. The trick is always to be aware of timing, groove and dynamics as you listen and react to your fellow musicians' playing.

5. Be Prepared!

You and your equipment should always be ready for work, twenty-four hours a day. This means that your bass must be set up, with clean strings and correct tuning. Many sessions start at 8.30 a.m.— contrary to popular belief, music isn't always made at night. Sometimes I get up at 6 a.m. to practise for an early session so that I am warmed up and alert when I arrive at the studio.

6. Practice

Practice is essential to your musical development. Apparently, Jaco Pastorius walked with a bass around his neck for all his waking hours at home, and many players practise up to six or eight hours a day. Such intensive work can backfire, so never force yourself to do more than is comfortable. Music practice is like running. Find your limits and push them just a little further, every time you work out. If you want to practise for several hours a day, try breaking up your time into hour-long sections to keep your mind fresh. If you can only practise for a short while each day, regularity is the key to progress. In this case, divide your time into the areas you need to develop. For example:

10 minutes—Hand exercises, with or without the bass, to strengthen your hands and make them more flexible. Piano books sometimes include these.
15 minutes—Scale practice. Consult any bass guitar tutor book.
15 minutes—Reading music.
20 minutes—Individual improvisation, perhaps to develop slapping, or listening to records and working out how to play interesting bass lines.

7. Keep up with the Times

Every professional bass player is aware of how music recording changed in the early 1980s. Suddenly, work for bass guitarists and drummers dried up as synthesizers and drum machines became fashionable. I was lucky to be on tour almost permanently from 1983 to 1986. When I was at home, I noticed that sessions were becoming more scarce. A friend advised me to become 'MIDI literate'. Until the 1980s, many bass players had assumed that their techniques, bass guitar and amplifier would see them through their careers. Now top bass players have to be mini rhythm sections. They can programme bass *and* drums, like David Franks, who works with Michael Jackson, Steve Winwood and many others. But what if you aren't a good keyboard player? MIDI bass guitar is still in its infancy. Several companies have tried to make a bass guitar which would accurately trigger a synthesizer or sequencer. They have enjoyed mixed success because of problems with getting the bass's notes to sound in time with the rest of the music. As a result, bass players haven't been able to use MIDI guitars to sequence conventional pop music bass parts. MIDI basses have been used for soloing and chordal sounds.

All this MIDI equipment is quite expensive, but there is no need to buy everything all at once. Read the 'Keyboards and Associated Technologies' article in this book and the relevant keyboard and MIDI magazines to familiarize yourself further with MIDI's capabilities. If you learn how to use MIDI equipment, it may make the difference between you or the other guy getting the gig of your dreams.

The 1960s

This was a pioneering decade for the bass guitar. Although it was featured on several hit singles, the bass remained very low in the studio mix of records until players like Paul McCartney, John Entwistle, Muff Winwood and Chris Squire brought the instrument to the foreground of pop's sound. These players began to write 'melodic' bass lines which were very different to the more usual 'rhythmic' ones of earlier pop music. The standard, rhythmic role of the pop bass guitarist was simply to underpin the chord sequence of a tune and to keep the groove with the drummer. In early James Brown you can hear how the bass pumps the rhythm along. It was very exciting and new when McCartney, Entwistle and Squire started to play bass lines which contributed to the melody of a song as well as providing a solid, rhythmic feel.

Paul McCartney wrote his bass lines as integral parts of his songs' melodic lines. He started his career with the Beatles playing a Hofner violin bass, but by the *Sergeant Pepper* album, he used a Rickenbacker. With that, he produced a warmer sound, particularly when he played high notes. On 'Come Together' and 'Hello, Goodbye' McCartney's style is clear.

John Entwistle was the first player to use round wound strings which he developed with Rotosound Strings. He did this out of frustration at not being heard above Pete Townshend's guitar. By boosting the treble (as it was known then!) on his amplifier and using these new strings, his sound cut through to become his trademark. One of the best known examples of this is Entwistle's playing on *Quadrophenia*'s opening track, 'The Real Me', and on the single 'My Generation'. He is also famous for his collection of bass guitars, which currently stands at around 150!

Muff Winwood inspired me to try bass playing with his performance on the Spencer Davis Group's hit, 'Keep on Running'. He used a Framus bass, with a slightly distorted sound. He went on to become a major record company executive.

Chris Squire played bass in such a melodic way that he sounded like a cello! As well, he always maintained the job of underpinning the rhythm of his band, Yes. Like McCartney, he used a Rickenbacker bass, but his was a much brighter, almost brittle sound which he produced on 'Roundabout' from the *Fragile* LP, and on *The Yes Album.*

Paul McCartney

The 1960s Americans

In America, the Stax, Atlantic and Tamla Motown record companies promoted the idea of keeping the bass high in the mix, using players like James Jamerson, Bob Babbitt and Carole Kaye. These were the great session players of the 1960s and the 1970s who performed with a slightly more rhythmic approach than the bassists in Britain.

James Jamerson was a jazz player who was tempted to become Tamla Motown's house bass guitarist. He played for a pittance on most of the company's early hits, all on the promise of a Tamla Motown jazz record label which never materialized. His style remains unsurpassed in soul and R 'n' B.

Carole Kaye was a freelance session player and American housewife. She became Quincy Jones's first-call player, using a plectrum on her Fender Precision which always looked too big for her. Along with her many albums for Quincy Jones, the Beach Boys' 'Good Vibrations' (Brian Wilson played the second, simpler bass part) and her performances with The Supremes and Joe Cocker are essential listening.

Bob Babbitt was James Jamerson's stand-in at Motown, although he was an established player in his own right. He worked with Elton John, Jeff Beck, Jimi Hendrix and Bette Midler. His characteristic style can be heard on 'Tears of a Clown' recorded on Motown by Smokey Robinson and the Miracles.

Slapping

By the 1970s, the bass guitar had come of age and was established at the forefront of pop music's live and recorded sound. In Philadelphia, a young double bass player, Stanley Clarke, saw a British bass guitarist, Colin Hodgkinson, performing at a gig. Hodgkinson had worked with Alexis Korner and Jan Hammer, helping to pioneer slap technique. Stanley Clarke took this up while working with Chick Corea, and soon he had influenced a whole generation of bass guitarists. You can hear his bright, characteristic sound on *Stanley Clarke*, *School Days*, and with Chick Corea on *Light as a Feather*, (playing double bass), *Romantic Warrior*, 'No Mystery' and 'Where Have I Known You Before'.

The slap technique dates from the 1930s. This was when double bass players started pulling their instrument's strings so far away from the fingerboard that the resulting slap could be heard over the drums and the rest of the band. This style was used in particular by American Rockabilly players. Listen to Bill Black backing Elvis. Later on Larry Graham developed the slap technique on the bass guitar when he played for gospel meetings as an accompaniment to his mother on the piano. There was no drummer, so the sound of Graham's slapping and pulling provided their music with some percussion. His individual style is featured with Sly and the Family Stone on 'Higher' and 'Dance to the Music', but the Graham Central Station albums feature his slap style most prominently.

Fretless Basses

In 1965, the Fender and Ampeg companies both tried making a bass guitar without frets, aiming to produce a sound similar to a double bass. But it wasn't until the early 1970s, when Jaco Pastorius stripped the frets from his Fender jazz bass, filled the resulting holes with wood filler, and covered the fingerboard with boat varnish, that the possibilities of a fretless bass guitar began to be explored more fully. Suddenly, the bass guitar had a new dimension. Without its frets, it could be used to emulate the lyricism of a cello or double bass, and the vibrato technique could be developed into a natural chorus effect. You can hear the remarkable groove and lyricism which characterized Pastorius's playing on the following recordings: 'Teentown' (fast be-bop), 'A Remark You Made' on *Heavy Weather* (lyrical), 'Black Market' on *Black Market* (rhythm playing), 'Night Passage' by Weather Report (his soloing), 'Portrait of Tracy' on *Jaco Pastorius* (use of harmonics), and 'Bach's Chromatic Fantasy in C minor' on *Word of Mouth* (stunning!).

Writing a Bass Line

There are many ways of inventing a bass line for a song. Sometimes the bass is the inspiration for the whole song. In another situation, it is the last thing to be composed. Here are the two most common situations in which bass parts are created.

1. In a band, new songs are often jammed around until the melodic content and rhythmic groove feel right. This process of trial and error has created great pop music, particularly soul and R 'n' B. Alternatively, the band's songwriter (if that isn't you) may produce a chord chart, with the song's basic chords written in letters and bar format (e.g. C/C/F/C etc.). This still leaves you to construct a bass line, but the song's structure is already laid out. You may even be presented with notated music, but I have found this is only common in fusion, jazz or 'art' rock. I have rarely come across a notated bass part in mainstream pop sessions and tours. In America, chords are sometimes written numerically. For example, C, F and G chords would be written as 1, 4 and 5. Using this method, the C major scale becomes C-1, D-2, E-3, F-4, G-5, A-6, B-7. Minor chords are written as Em and 3m, or E− and 3−. This system makes changing key very simple, as the tonic chord is always number 1, the dominant chord is number 5, and so on.

2. As a session player, you are expected to read music, to improvise and to know when to put in an idea. Sometimes you also need to realize when to

Jaco Pastorius

keep quiet and just do what you are asked. This requires a lot of self-discipline, but it can be rewarding to help someone else's ideas become reality. Session players are often considered mercenary. However, most session players are usually happy and keen either to work under someone else's direction or to contribute their ideas when they are invited.

Your Equipment

I believe in buying the best instrument within your budget. You may have to beg, borrow (or steal!), but there is nothing worse than having your enthusiasm dampened by an instrument which doesn't feel good to play. If you buy an unsuitable instrument, you will almost certainly replace it as soon as possible, or give up. But if you have a good instrument, even if it costs more than you intended to spend, your progress will be astonishing and exciting because you won't want to put your new bass down.

Most Japanese basses are good beginner's instruments. Try Yamaha, Ibanez or Aria. Some professional players use these guitars as main instruments or spares, and they achieve startling results. You don't need a specialist bass for your preferred type of music. Most modern basses can cope with the whole range of musical styles.

Check the width of the guitar's neck. If you have big fingers, it is generally better to avoid narrow-necked basses, while if you have small fingers, a broad neck will make you work much harder than necessary. Take an experienced bass player with you when you buy your instrument. He or she can check the basses for neck warpage and wear of the frets which, as a beginner, you may not be able to judge. Another option is to buy a bass which feels comfortable to hold but doesn't sound good. You can enhance its sound by replacing its pick-ups and bridge. Try Reflex, Bartolini or Seymour Duncan pick-ups, with a Badass bridge, to improve an average guitar's performance.

Like guitars, amplifiers improve as their price increases. If you are on a limited budget, the simpler answer is to buy a good, inexpensive bass and spend a little extra on a fair amplifier. Session or Carlsbro amps are worth trying at the cheaper end of the market, whereas Trace Elliot, Gallien Krueger and SWR are all more expensive. Bear in mind that a poor amp will almost certainly spoil the sound of an expensive bass. The answer is to strike a balance between the cost and quality of your guitar and amp.

Strings are a matter of personal taste. Wire wound (round wound) strings are the most versatile because they can sound bright and mellow. Tape and flat wound strings always sound mellow and they are suited to jazz and big band playing. Half wound strings are neither one thing nor the other, so they are probably best left until you are more experienced. String quality is also related to price. I use Scalar. They cost slightly more than most strings because they last longer and, I believe, sound better. For recording, heavier strings often get good results, while lighter ones suit slapping and soloing. You need to experiment with different gauges and weights to find the right strings for you.

The effects pedals which you buy must reflect your musical interests. A good combination is a chorus pedal, for slapping, soloing and broadening your bass sound, with an octave pedal, which gives the effect of two basses playing one octave apart.

Learning

There are many ways of learning the techniques and skills I have described. The cheapest is to ask a friend who is a bass guitarist to show you how to start. If you are serious, the best way to progress is to have a teacher and a tutor book as a guide to the basics. Here are some recommended books for further study and reading.

Further Reading

Laurence Canty, *How to Play the Bass Guitar* (IMP).
—— and Tony Bacon, *What Bass* (Making Music Publications).
John De Witt, *Rhythmic Figures for Bassists*, i and ii (Charles Hansen Publications).
Dotzauer Cello Studies (Augener).
Adam Novak, *Bass Harmonics* (AMSCO).
Tony Oppenheim, *Slap It!* (Theodor Presser Company).
Chuck Sher, *Improviser's Bass Method* (Sher Music).
Standing in the Shadows of Motown: The Life and Music of Legendary Bassist James Jamerson (Dr Licks and Hal Leonard Music Publishing). This comes complete with tapes.

4 Drums

RICHARD MARCANGELO is a drummer and programmer/producer. With his wide experience of studio and touring work for name acts, Richard now concentrates on his own production projects and the freelance session business. Here he discusses the history and role of drums in pop music as well as clearly setting out one way of dividing a music career into 'art' and 'business'.

Drummers have a crucial role in modern rock and pop music. They supply the 'backbeat', the heart of any band's sound. The backbeat is usually played on the snare drum, on beats two and four, while the bass drum strikes the 'down beat' on beat one, and then on or around beat three. This pattern is the basic rhythm of all rock, pop and soul. There are two other essential elements in a drummer's performance—POWER and GROOVE. Some of the greatest drummers just 'sit on the groove', happy to play the backbeat and to use only a few cymbal crashes and drum fills. Before dealing with anything else, let's consider some of the drumming 'greats' who have helped to develop what we know as modern rock drumming.

The Related Styles and History of Modern Drumming

Bands like the Who, the Jimi Hendrix Experience, and Led Zeppelin, were the homes of the first rock star drummers. Listen to the Who's 'Substitute', or watch footage of them playing live. You will see and hear one of rock's greatest performers on drums—KeithMoon. Not only did he play with a new creativity and power, he was also an arch-comedian, one of rock's first wind-up artists! Mitch Mitchell, Hendrix's drummer, was an early innovator in jazz-rock drumming. On 'Hey Joe' (an early hit single) or on 'Is This Love or Confusion' (off Hendrix's first album *Are You Experienced*), you can hear Mitchell's loose, flowing but powerful style, with his characteristic jazz phrasing. Ginger Baker, Cream's drummer, used

The Who

African influences. Check out 'Sunshine of Your Love' and feel Baker using his tom-toms to lay down the backbeat and the groove. In Led Zeppelin, John Bonham moulded the rock/metal style of drumming which is still the standard. He is essential listening for any drummer. Try 'Whole Lotta Love' on the Zep's second album.

Along with Led Zeppelin, other great British bands like Deep Purple and Black Sabbath took British rock into the 1970s. In America, a host of other stars did the same, but generally rock had become smoother and safer. The real explosion was brewing in a new musical fusion of jazz and rock. Miles Davis, the legendary jazz trumpet player, influenced bands like Weather Report and the Mahavishnu Orchestra, who also drew rhythmic influences from soul acts like Sly and the Family Stone and James Brown. Their music was a new earthy brand of soul, with jazz melodies and rock rhythms. This was funk. Suddenly a shattering rhythmic sound was happening. Billy Cobham, Mahavishnu's drummer, stunned everbody. His innovative style combined an incredible technique with a power reminiscent of John Bonham. Cobham used two bass drums, a battery of tom-toms and brought the drums further forward in the music than ever before. To hear him at his best, listen to *Inner Mounting Flame* and *Birds of Fire*, the first two Mahavishnu albums, as well as his first solo album, *Spectrum*.

While Cobham and others were refining their new approach, glam rock exploded into the music business. The Tubes, Styx and Kiss headed a host of bands who dressed up in sci-fi style clothes, put on extraordinary make-up and who turned the rock gig into a wild extravaganza. Then came punk. Suddenly, the Clash and the Sex Pistols were playing fast, loose anarchic music. For drummers, the term 'thrash' was born. Topper Headon of the Clash and Rat Scabies of the Damned led this style of playing, which was not far from Keith Moon's earliest antics. Alongside punk, the emergence of reggae prompted Stewart Copeland to fuse these two opposite styles. He formed the Police using a new rhythmic idea, reggae/rock. Listen to 'Walking on the Moon' on the *Regatta de Blanc* album to hear how he harmonized rock with reggae's rhythms.

As punk developed into New Wave, another rhythm emerged—disco. The Bee Gees, on *Saturday Night Fever*, and Chic, with 'Le Freak', made records based on mesmerizingly repetitive grooves. Often they used four bass drum beats to the bar as they aimed for the discos and the dance club audience. Ever since, this audience has held a tremendous influence over all pop music.

Around 1980, Roger Linn designed and produced the first drum computer. A then unknown and young producer, Steve Levine immediately got hold of one. With it, he produced Culture Club. The age of the New Romantics had begun, with Duran Duran, the Human League, Spandau Ballet and Depeche Mode dominating the scene. The drum machine's metronomic beats and clear sound (which were sampled drum sounds, effectively) seduced the ears and wallets of record companies, radio programmers and eventually the public. This was a difficult time for drummers. Suddenly, their instrument was out of fashion. Their skills were almost redundant. Drum programming was the new art and many professional drummers were out of work. The ones who survived found out about the new technology and learnt how to use it creatively. As a result of their work, drum machines have developed and improved the standard and importance of modern drumming. Now drums are much more important on records. This is due to a fashion which emerged during the 1980s for using a 'gate' type of reverb on the snare drum to create an explosive sound within a powerful 'heavy' groove. To hear this, listen to Tony Thompson's work on the Power Station's *Powerstation* album, Robert Palmer's single 'Addicted to Love', or on Prince's *1999*.

In the 1980s, soul/dance music took over the charts. Relying on drum machines and samples, music like rap, hip-hop, house, acid, and rare groove drove the music business into a club frenzy. If music didn't work in the clubs, no one would record it. But pop music includes a wide variety of styles, from straightforward rock and heavy metal, to folk and country. In the 1990s, drummers need to play great, programme great and look great. It all sounds so easy. Let's do it!

Technique

You need to play and practise with a solid, well-formed technique. The longer you play badly, the harder it will be to improve. Go to a recommended drum teacher. At your lessons, you can check how well you grip the sticks, the way you sit at the drum kit, and how you strike the snare drum. That is just the beginning. You have also got to consider how balanced you are when you play and the quality of your snare-drum rolls.

The first thing to get right is holding the sticks. Without a proper grip, some things will always feel difficult. For rock/power playing, the matched grip has taken over from the orthodox one. That old-fashioned grip was designed for marching-band snare drum players who had to cope with their drum bouncing up and down on their leg as they walked. But don't discount the military grip, as you might need it one day in your band's video! Apart from lessons, books and practice, the best way to develop your skill is to go and watch as many top drummers as possible. Or watch them on video. There are a number of master class videos available as well as concert performances. Seeing is believing. Don't get despondent when you see a great drummer. Get excited. Learn from being blasted by someone else's power, phrasing, technique and confidence. Those are the qualities you need to develop to get your picture on the front cover of magazines like *Modern Drummer*. If you still need convincing, watch a video of Omar Hakim (with Sting or Bowie). Just look at where he starts those big backbeats when he is playing on the groove. You will never develop that class of powerful accuracy without starting off with a big dose of technique and a steady practice routine. Playing an instrument like the drums is similar to sport. You practice and train to reach the highest level of technique, style and skill. Then you join up with the rest of the band and play like a team.

Practice Routine

To make any progress in the art of drumming you will have to start a rigorous practice routine. You can vary your schedule to suit your particular needs, but your rudiments and time keeping are essential. A simple example of a routine would be this:

Rudiments. Do all of them at varying speeds. Also, lead with your weaker hand to strengthen it.

Time keeping. Play along with records, a metronome or a drum machine to develop a solid groove.

Experimenting. This could be anything from learning a salsa cowbell rhythm off a record or trying out a new technique from a book.

It is up to you how much you practice, but you can be sure that the drum heroes of today spent a great chunk of their youth developing their technique and style. If you do that, then you might find that your dream of being a big-time drummer becomes a reality.

Buying Equipment

If you are just starting to play, and have a limited budget, try to buy the essential parts of a kit: snare drum and stand, bass drum and pedal, hi-hat stand and cymbals, ride and splash cymbals and stands, and a stool. The next additions would be a mounted and floor tom-toms. There are always drum kits and accessories for sale in the classified sections of *Melody Maker*, *Loot* and other magazines.

If you can, take an experienced drummer to check any second-hand kits you might buy. There are good, old kits around, particularly Gretsch, Ludwig and Camco, which improve with age and can be bargains, but their metal fittings can need updating.

Be sure to get a kit which suits your music. For instance, if you play heavy rock, an 18″ bass drum would probably be a handicap.

Technology

The technical advances of the last few years offer drummers the use of a wide and possibly confusing range of electronic equipment. Drum machines have more recently been superseded by samplers linked to computers or dedicated sequencers.

A sampler like the Akai S-1000 allows a drummer to record drum sounds from his or her own kit or from sounds cheekily (and illegally) taken off records. Once these sounds are arranged in the sampler, the drummer can trigger them using a pad system like the Roland Octopad. Separate MIDI information can be assigned to each of these eight pads. This MIDI data can be logged and edited in a sequencer or a computer like the Atari 1040 ST (running the C-Lab Creator software).

Beginning

To improve your playing and start your career it is crucial to find other musicians to work with. This could be just to jam and play covers, but it might lead to forming a band and playing original material. It is not easy finding other musicians, especially in smaller towns. You will have to seek them out by asking around in music shops or advertising in the local paper. Growing up in the country and wanting to be a rock star is very difficult. There are not the same opportunities to play and to meet musicians that you find in London or other major cities. Wherever you live, you will quickly find that the old saying 'if you don't ask you don't get' is the motto of every level in the music business.

As soon as you start playing in bands, you will realize that your fellow musicians are all very different. Some will want to give the orders and others want to be told what to do. It is up to you to fit in. If you can't, you are probably in the wrong band. Songwriters and singers often hold the balance of power because they create the music or are the focus of the band's image. There are no rules about how a band works or communicates, but as a drummer you can make your life easier. Try to learn arrangements fast and get a good sound and feel as quickly as possible. That means interpreting the songs by listening and reacting to what the rest of the band is playing. Don't be afraid to offer ideas about the music. They are its life-blood. However, try to be clear in what you say, otherwise your band's musicians will lose interest. There is always a time and a place for new ideas. It may be worth keeping quiet to let a heated situation cool down before expounding your theory about why you hate a song's intro and why it should start with an instrumental chorus! Also, try to turn up on time. This is essential to professional work and others expect it of you. As drummers usually have a lot of equipment to set up, try to arrive at gigs, rehearsals or recording sessions a bit early. Then you can set up, warm up and feel relaxed when you perform. Finally, don't irritate the rest of the band by playing your kit while they are trying to discuss or rehearse the music.

Playing for a Living

To earn a living from playing the drums, you are almost certainly going to play music at gigs and sessions which you would prefer to avoid. This sort of experience is invaluable to build an understanding of the practicalities of being a professional musician. Having accepted this, we can divide your career into two types of work: the creative and the business. The business gigs are those you do to pay the bills and to make new contacts with other musicians and music business professionals. This work can vary from gigging with a guitar and drum duo in a pub to filling the drum chair in David Lee Roth's band at Madison Square Gardens. Your creative work is where you develop as part of a band or as a writer and individual performer. To show how these co-exist in most musicians' lives, I have put down a gameplan for each. This isn't a set of rules, it just describes the varied musical situations in which you will be involved as you chase your drumming dreams.

Business

Gigs

For freelace gigging in pubs and clubs, you will be expected to play whatever the band wants (which can be a great way of learning different styles and classic pop material). You will get paid a fee, the value of which depends on the grade and size of the venue. Usually you get booked for these gigs by word of mouth. Pass your telephone number around as many musicians as possible.

Recording Sessions

The fee depends on the type of session you are doing and the number of hours you work. The rates are set by the Musicians' Union. The different types of sessions are: live radio/TV session; pre-recorded radio/TV session; jingle sessions; recording company sessions for commercial release; demo sessions, which are usually lower paid than 'master' sessions.

If you are hired as a session musician you are very unlikely to get royalties from music which you have performed, but if either the band or the producer (preferably both) like you and your work, you may find they offer you regular employment. The band may give you the chance to sign their recording deal or they may keep you on a salary to go on tour, do rehearsals and TV shows. The producer may ask you to work on another project. Suddenly, you are on the way to becoming a hot session drummer. To keep your career on the boil, make sure you keep up with the changing rhythms of musical fashion. Also, a lot of session work entails reading music. To be a top session player, you will need all the expertise and confidence which is now exuded by your drumming idols.

Until recently, most of this work had been arranged by word of mouth, but now a lot of it is controlled by 'fixing agencies'. You get on to their books by personal recommendation and building a good reputation. Once you are there, these agencies call you for jobs for which they think you are suited. Often, this means doing an audition. Auditions (or just going for a blow with David Bowie) probably get a little easier with experience. Try and get used to playing on an unfamiliar drum kit. At the first meeting David Bowie, or whoever it is, just wants to know if you can play in the groove and whether he or she likes you. Try to relax and play as well as possible.

There are many ways of handling rock stars at close quarters. Usually, they enjoy a laugh. They certainly like it when you give them the beat which makes their popular music groove. They have to please an audience of millions, so give them what they want. Serious moaning on your part will definitely endanger your job. If you have a positive attitude, you can at least make the best of every situation.

Touring

The chance to go on tour is very exciting, but too much touring can be tiring and very destructive to your personal life. Your fee depends on the success of your employers. A major act will pay much more than a young band on their first British tour. The advantage of working for a support act is that you get the invaluable experience of playing to a large audience of thousands. You can discover how to project your sound and style the best way—by doing it in a huge arena. As the tour progresses, your confidence should grow so that you develop into a powerful, live drummer like your idols. When you have done that, you may find yourself playing with a major artist and beginning to realize ambitions which you still haven't dreamt of.

Creative

The first thing to realize is that playing original material in a band isn't going to earn you much money, if any. After you have rehearsed your music, you need to get on to the local pub and club gigging circuit. Most cities and large town have one. These venues are a market place for new bands, especially in London. A&R staff from record companies check out any bands who are creating a buzz.

If anyone shows interest in your band, they will want to hear a demo tape. This is your chance to shine in the studio. The first few times your band goes into the studio are very important. They may make the business aware of your music, or not. Try to make the music groove like it has at your best gigs.

As a drummer, your first recording sessions may be a real eye-opener because the tape recorder never lies. Little errors of timing and accuracy can slip past in the excitement of a gig. In the studio, every mistake is there on tape. So, solid time keeping, groove and consistency are vital if you are going to lay down a great drum track.

If the rest of your band match your stunning performance in the studio, you should have a demo tape which will interest record companies. On the strength of your gigs and your tape, 'BIG' Records Inc. offer you a deal to make an album, and to do a prestigious tour support. You make the record using all your confidence and technique. The record company likes it, the radio stations play it and it sells. Suddenly, you have a hit record. Your record company is relieved because they have invested thousands of pounds in your talent. And you are a rock 'n' roll star. In fact, you are a star drummer. As long as your record deal was fair, you should start getting some royalties in the year after your record's release.

This sequence of events is unlikely to happen all in one go. With some bands, it takes years to start a successful run. What you must do is to keep analysing your playing, while trying to be creative. Above all, have fun. It will show in your playing.

Further Reading

There are a lot of drum books around, so these are just two classic examples:

Louis Bellson, *The Musical Drummer* (Warner Brothers Publication).
Buddy Rich, *Buddy Rich's Snare Drum Rudiments* (Embassy Music Corporation).

5 Latin Percussion

· ·

BOSCO DE OLIVEIRA left his native Brazil in 1974 and performed in Africa, Spain and Portugal before moving to London in 1979. In the UK he has worked with a wide variety of musicians from Working Week, Sade and Phil Manzanera to Loose Tubes, Charlie Palmieri and Airto Moreira, and has recorded on soundtrack albums such as John Boorman's *The Emerald Forest* and the Comic Strip's *Supergrass*. Bosco was a founder member and first musical director of the London School of Samba, and has written numerous articles on percussion and on Brazilian music and folklore for *Rhythm* magazine. This article is an introduction to Latin percussion as well as a guide for percussionists to professional work.

Percussion in Western Pop

With the development of the modern communications industry, there has been a wider acceptance of different music from all over the world. As a result, percussion has left behind its ethnic surroundings and moved into the market of pop and rock music. By realizing the value of other people's music, the 'West' (Western Europe and the USA) has begun to develop a new, hybrid musical culture. For example, the tablas have been an essential element of Indian music for centuries. They became known to the general Western public only during the 1960s when the hippie movement looked to Indian music as a spiritual experience. Ravi Shankar, the sitar player, and Alah Rakha, the percussionist, became gurus to many Western musicians. Since then, tablas have been used by many groups in pop recordings and live performances.

Having been born and brought up in Brazil, I started playing percussion at a very early age. My musical background was Brazilian popular music, but I have been lucky enough to hear many different kinds of music. As a professional percussionist, I have spent a year working and travelling in Southern Africa, including Mozambique and Angola. Later on, I lived in Spain where I came into contact with Flamenco and other non-Brazilian Latin American music. All of this, as well as my ten years in London, has given me an insight into a variety of musical cultures. This has influenced my interpretations of other people's music and how I play my own. Percussionists need to hear as many kinds of music as possible so they can develop a flexible and informed approach to playing. The best way for young players to learn their trade is to use the traditional rhythms of percussion which are the basis of modern playing.

In this article, I am not going to lay down any infallible rules. I will simply pass on my professional experience of music. If you find this helpful, I shall be happy.

The Function of Percussion

Many people in the West regard percussion as the icing on the musical cake. I disagree. A conga or a timbale pattern, a cowbell or a shaker, is an integral part of any rhythm track. It is not an embellishment. Although percussionists sometimes use their instruments for obvious sound effects, these are the only percussion parts which can be treated separately to the rhythm of the drums. After all, a drummer is only one musician doing the work of several percussionists.

Many artists, producers and sound engineers understandably feel concerned about the percussion cluttering the sound of a track, but if you listen to music in which the percussion is mixed quite high, you will hear that it has a special place in the track which doesn't interfere with the other instruments. That doesn't just happen in Latin and other ethnic music, but also in American funk, soul and dance music. When the percussion is mixed too low, it can clutter a track because the pattern which is being played is only faintly audible. One of my most frustrating experiences is making a studio or live concert recording and being told afterwards that 'The percussion could not be heard'.

Percussion can change a track dramatically. A cowbell on a chorus can lift a song which seems sluggish and dreary, or the bass line, drums and keyboard patterns can seem bitty and disjointed until a shaker blends the whole thing together. So, a percussionist has to take account of more than just the drum parts when working out his or her pattern. The rhythms of the bass, guitar, keyboards, vocals and brass all need to be considered. Percussion is rhythm and colour. Use your imagination and listen carefully to what is going on around you.

The Importance of Traditional Drumming

To know about traditional drumming, whether it comes from India, Brazil, Nigeria or Cuba, doesn't mean you have to specialize in ethnic music. Traditional rhythms help you understand how to blend instruments when arranging a percussion section. The technique of each percussion instrument is linked to one or a number of cultures. If you want to play tablas, you would need to learn through Indian classical music. If you want to play talking drum, you would have to study the music of a West African country such as Nigeria, Ghana or Senegal.

Percussion is particularly difficult for a European as it isn't a strong tradition in Europe's music. To play congas, you couldn't use the German or English techniques. They simply don't exist. You would have to master the African, Brazilian or Cuban style of playing. As percussion becomes more popular in the West, it may develop into an integral part of Western popular music. Perhaps, after a century or more, European percussion may have its own technique.

To develop a solid style of playing, you need to learn the basics of one or more of the established techniques of percussion. To make progress, work with the traditional rhythms which are the foundation of all percussion playing. Then you can pass them on to the next generation of players who can use them in their own way. Study how Brazilian music has developed. You will notice that it took 400 years to blend Indian, Portuguese and African musics into several different rhythms. These rhythms differ from one another depending on the strength of these three ethnic influences (and according to where in Africa that continent's influence originated). For example, in Rio de Janeiro, the slaves were predominantly of Bantu extraction and their music developed into the samba.

Even these divisions aren't as clear as they seem because slaves weren't housed in their ethnic groups. Often, families were split up and slaves' languages, beliefs and music mixed into one black culture. Within this, various ethnic groups became dominant in various parts of Brazil. Brazilian black culture was influenced by white and Indian cultures. Where the black population was large, it dominated, but where blacks lived in small isolated groups, on remote farms and plantations, their culture was subjugated. Cross-fertilization created the hybrid society which is now Brazil. Although the rhythms of Brazil are the result of this mixture of African, Portuguese and Indian influences, Brazilian music has an identifiable character, personality and set of techniques.

Adapting Traditional Rhythms to Modern Music

To adapt and use traditional rhythms, a percussionist must understand them. Otherwise, how would you choose a percussion pattern for a song? What criteria would you use to decide which rhythms would fit the music? Some musicians write a song and tell the drummer and the percussionist 'to play a samba'. In fact their music usually has nothing or little to do with samba because it was written either without any consideration of the samba's rhythm or with the wrong percussion pattern in mind.

To write a song using a traditional rhythm you need to know how that rhythm is put together. Unless you understand all the rhythm's components, its main accents and groove, you can't write a melody within the spirit of that rhythm. In Brazilian, Cuban, African and other ethnic music there is always one pattern running through a song. It doesn't have to be played all the time, sometimes it is just implied, and that is the pattern which must be understood to get the feel of the rhythm. As an illustration, look at the main pattern for samba:

If the melody and the accompaniment don't follow the feel of this pattern, the music will be disjointed and pedestrian. However, modifications can be made without losing the soul of the rhythm. For example, the main samba pattern spawned another rhythm called samba partido alto, which is as follows:

In modern Western music there is a very similar pattern:

snare drum

bass drum

To adapt a traditional pattern to a modern rhythm, you need to match up the feel of your melody with the pattern of your rhythm. In Cuban music the clave can act as this link. Simultaneously, it is an instrument (two sticks played one against the other), the rhythm played by that instrument and a concept of musical creation and performance. The composer chooses a clave pattern as the basis of his or her song, and uses it throughout the composition so that the melody, brass lines, keyboards and percussion patterns are all played within the same clave.

The two main claves are the '3/2' (nothing to do with time signature):

and the '2/3' (an inversion of the 3/2):

As a simple example of the clave's use, consider the well-known tune 'The Peanut Vendor'. Here are the first few bars of the melody and the rhythm of the piano and the brass parts.

melody

piano and brass accompaniment

If you sing either the melody or the accompaniment, and clap the clave at the same time, you will discover which clave the composer used for this tune. Clap the 3/2 first, and then the 2/3. Which sounds better? I definitely think the 2/3 is best!

The clave is an important part of Afro-Cuban and the Puerto-Rican music, but the idea of the clave can be used in any type of music. The Cubans and Puerto-Ricans who emigrated to New York brought lots of different rhythms with them, like the rumba, mambo, son, guaracha, bomba, plena, guaguanco, cha-cha-cha and many others. During the 1950s and 1960s, their mambos and guarachas were very popular. People would gather to play, sing and dance in the parks and street corners. When the rhythm peaked they would shout SALSA! SALSA! (which means hot sauce, or 'put some pepper in your rhythm'). Salsa incorporates all the rhythms I have listed. The main salsa rhythms came from the pattern for son, mambo, guaracha and cha-cha-cha. They are all basically the same rhythm played at different speeds and with a variety of feels. I have set out in Fig. 1 how it goes on the conga drums.

Fig. 1

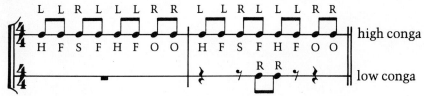

L – left hand   R – right hand
H – hitting as close as possible to the centre of the drum with the heel of the hand
F – tip of all fingers open or closed hitting the drum simultaneously
S – slap: with the left hand resting on the drum, hit with the right hand, with the tip of the fingers closed, as if trying to grasp the drum head with the fingers, and leave on the drum head after the strike
O – open tones: hit drum with the hand quite straight; lift the hand from the head immediately to get a ringing tone

Most of the strokes in this pattern, like the heel of the hand and the fingers, are fairly muted. They contribute to the feel of the rhythm while the main accents come from the right hands:

If we simplify the accents we arrive at one of the most common conga patterns in pop and dance music:

I have given these few patterns only as examples for you to understand how traditional rhythms can be adapted to modern music, but don't limit yourself to just these. If you learn about the thousands of traditional rhythms from all over the world, you can use them to enhance your music.

Techniques

Of all musicians, percussionists probably need the widest range of instrumental techniques. As a result, percussionists are rarely masters of all instruments. Most players specialize in one and have a reasonable command of others. This is the case in every music where percussion plays a fundamental role. In Brazil, percussionists may specialize on instruments like the surdo, cuíca or pandeiro. These musicians wouldn't necessarily play congas very well, or even other

Brazilian instruments, but they would be in complete control of their chosen tool.

In the West, percussionists are expected to play most available instruments, so practising stick technique for timbales, cowbells and electronic pads is just as important as 'hand' technique for congas, bongos and other instruments. For basic technique, follow any drum method. For timbales, there are two ways of learning. The first of these is the more traditional Cuban style. In this, the notes are sparse and completely inside the clave. The best example of this drumming is Manny Oquedo (Conjunto Libre, Grupo Folklorico y Experimental de New York). The other approach leans more towards jazz drumming. This is busier, more outside the clave and with a wide use of double strokes. For this, listen to Tito Puente, Orestes Vilato (Ray Barreto, Santana), Ralf Irizarry (Ruben Blades) and Marc Quinones (Carabali).

For basic conga technique, you can choose between Afro-Brazilian or Afro-Cuban technique. Although both came from Africa, their conga techniques are very different. The Afro-Brazilian is closer to the traditional African technique, being quite loose. The Afro-Cuban is lighter, with the hands working very close to the drum. The Afro-Cuban slap is crisper as well. It is played as if the fingers were trying to hold the skin of the drum. By contrast, the Afro-Brazilian slap is more muffled and needs the whole hand. Also, the Afro-Cuban technique uses the heel of the hand.

As examples of Afro-Brazilian conga players, listen to Paulino Da Costa (Sergio Mendes) and Landir De Oliveira (also Sergio Mendes, Chicago). For Afro-Cuban playing, try Los Papines, Patato Valdes and Totico. For salsa, check out players like Ray Barreto, Milton Cardona, Bobby Allende and Giovanni Hidalgo.

A third option for congas is the American technique. This came out of Afro-Cuban and salsa music. The American style developed its individuality by incorporating drum kit technique. As most percussionists in Ameria also play drum kit, they make use of the double strike technique. This style is 'off the wall' playing which reacts constantly to whatever is happening in the music, rather than holding a steady pattern. The important players of American conga technique are Don Alias, Ralf MacDonald, Bobby Thomas and Bill Summers (Herbie Hancock, Anita Baker).

Most other instruments have one basic technique and the variations are down to personal styles.

Tito Puente

Reading and Remembering

Reading music is not as difficult as people think. To do it well requires dedication, study and practice. If you can read music, you can do any gig with the minimum of rehearsal. It is worth using your memory as well. Reading is fine for a gig at short notice, rehearsing a new show, playing a very long complicated tune or for doing a recording session. But after you have learnt your band's set, try and play without reading. This improves your concentration and your adaptability to cope with any unpredictable changes which might occur in a song.

Rehearsing and Creating

When rehearsing a new song or set always find out whether the composer, arranger or band leader has any ideas of what he or she wants from the percussion. Often they don't and they just leave it up to percussionists. But if they do, use their ideas as a starting-point. As you get to know the songs, you can make suggestions and try your own ideas. If there are no written parts for you to play, make a few notes to help you follow the tunes' structures until you know them by heart.

Inside a Studio

When you are asked to do a recording session, find out what sort of music is being recorded and which instruments are required. You don't want to carry instruments to the studio which you won't need. However, always take a few extra things from your set-up which might be useful. Arrive at least half an hour before the session, to set up and look through any parts which you may have to play. If you arrive late, you are wasting people's time and money, and you may not be called again. It is useful to note the position and types of microphones at the session. You never know when you will need that knowledge. If you can work fast, and efficiently, if you are creative and helpful, you will do many, many sessions.

Basic Set-Up

Percussionists' set-ups vary a great deal. Some like to play the congas sitting down; others stand up. Some put their instruments in a rack; others have them on a table. This is a very personal aspect of playing. Your set-up depends on your physique and the type of music you play. (If you have short arms, for instance, it is often better to use a rack rather than reaching across a table.)

I prefer to play congas sitting down, with the leading drum between my legs. If I play with a band who require me to move quickly from congas to timbales or to shakers in one song, it is better for me to have the congas on a stand because there is no time to sit down and adjust them. If you are playing the congas sitting down, resting them on the ground, remember to put a plank of wood under your instruments. It helps them to resonate. If the congas are laid directly on the floor, they lose their characteristic sound. Finally, if you sit down to play the congas, make sure that the lugs are wiped clean of excess oil. Otherwise you will soon ruin all of your trousers!

However you choose to set up, there is a minumum number of instruments which a Latin percussionist needs.

at least one pair of congas
one pair of bongos
one pair of timbales and stand
two or three different types of shaker (one with a light and crisp sound, another with a heavier sound)
two or three cowbells (with different timbres)
two choices of tambourines
one cabassa
one reco-reco or one guiro (scrapers)
two or three triangles
one set of sleigh bells or one set of chimes
one cymbal (16" or 18")

Optional: agogo bell, cuíca (friction drum), caxixis, wood blocks.

Try not to restrict yourself just to conventional instruments. I often use odd things like old casseroles or saucepans as cowbells. Shakers can be made out of a variety of containers, from beer cans and cat food tins to washing-up liquid bottles. Take the tops off two cans, fill half a can with rice, beans or split peas. Stick the two cans together. Experiment with different 'filler' ingredients. Each one makes it own special sound. Even an envelope with some sugar inside can be useful in a recording situation. Although it is very quiet, it is very effective with close miking. Instead of a set of chimes (or bell tree), you could improvise with a lot of old yale type keys. Hang them so they will hit each other when they are moved and avoid bunching them up too much. Then they can ring freely.

Use your imagination and create your own sounds. As a percussionist it is important to develop your own style of playing, and the sounds you use are part of that.

Care of Your Instrument

Whichever instruments you play, you must look after them. Here are some tips:

Keep all lugs lubricated, especially those which are under high tension, like the ones on bongos and congas. For timbales and snare drums don't use too much lubricating liquid. It makes the lugs slip and the drum detunes by itself.

All drums with natural heads, like congas, bongos and cuícas, must be detuned before being stored away. After you play, slacken off all the lugs until the head sounds a low note without being completely loose. This increases the life of your drum heads. If you leave heads tuned, they lose their tension by themselves, due to humidity. As a result, you will have to stretch the skins further and further every time you play to get them back in tune. After a while, your heads become overstretched and lifeless. With bongos, stretched heads can become overheated by the sun, lights or heating, and then they just split.

To tune and detune a drum, work around the head with one turn per lug so the tension is even all around the drum.

Wipe clean any excess lubricating liquid from around lugs, especially on congas and bongos.

Bongo heads come from a variety of sources, like calf, goat and deer skins. The high bongo head should be thinner than the lower one. The high head usually needs changing most often because it is subjected to a tremendous amount of tension. I prefer goat skin for a high bongo and deer skin for the low one. You can buy heads already lapped, or you can get the skin and lap it yourself. But lapping is a difficult process. If you have never done it before, get some help from an experienced player.

Conga heads are also from deer, goat and cow hides. The thickness of the skin is a matter of personal taste. Whichever sort you choose, make sure it isn't a split skin. Split skins don't have a shiny surface. They have two rough sides because some manufacturers try to economize by making two or three heads out of one very thick buffalo skin. It is fine if you buy the top one of these split skins, but the others have no life and therefore no true sound.

If you have a new conga head and the skin is quite hard, the best softener is fat and sweat from your hands which takes years to penetrate the skin. You can help the softening process by rubbing bacon or pork belly fat on the skin. If your hands are dry when you play be careful not to let your skin crack, it will be very painful and difficult to play without moistened hands. To cope with dry hands, rub some oil or cream on your palms and fingers. The oil will also penetrate the drum head. The best oil is clear palm oil.

For storage and transport of instruments, use your common sense. Put all the fragile shakers and caxixis together. All the stands and metal should go in another box, while all the wood should be in a further compartment.

Working with a Drummer

Every percussionist has his or her favourite drummer. The understanding between the drummer and percussionist is crucial for a successful rhythm track. A percussionist should know exactly what the drummer is doing. Where is the bass drum being placed? Is there a back beat on the snare? Is the right hand playing the hi-hat or the ride cymbal?

Playing instruments which give a contrasting sound to the drum kit is one useful approach to percussion. You could play a shaker when the drummer is riding a cymbal, or a cowbell against a hi-hat. Also, ensemble drums and percussion phrases can be effective, particularly if you aren't afraid of changing roles. The drums might play a straight pattern while the percussion is free. Next, the percussion may keep it straight as the drums do all the fills. It is very exciting to hear a drummer and percussionist who really understand each other's playing.

Percussion and Electronics

When dealing with electronics there are normally two attitudes. There are musicians who totally oppose electronics and regard it as a threat to their livelihood, while others believe that without electronics a musician is old-fashioned. I believe in a healthy balance between the two.

The use of electronics as a substitute for live performance impairs rather than enhances the musical possibilities of percussion. It is possible to use samples of all percussion sounds with electronic pads as triggers, but this is quite impractical if you want to use a lot of percussion sounds. A live percussionist can get seven or more sounds out of one conga drum. Imagine the number of pads and triggers you would need to replace all the sounds of a professional percussionist's recording set-up!

To me, it is more interesting to combine a range of acoustic sounds with the electronic sounds not made by acoustic instruments. An inspiring approach to electronics and percussion has been the work of Joe Zawinul, the keyboard player. After classical piano training in his native Austria, he emigrated to the USA. There he played with jazz giants like Cannonball Adderley, and he produced the mid-1960s hit, 'Mercy, Mercy'. Next, Zawinul founded the fusion group Weather Report. Although Zawinul moved from playing acoustic piano to electric piano and the latest synthesizers, he always used an acoustic drummer and percussionist. That combination of the most modern synthesizer sounds and the primitivism of acoustic percussion was very effective. On his 1986 solo album, *Dialects*, he programmed all the drums and percussion on computers, but since then he has returned to using a combination of acoustic and electronic percussion sounds. Why not follow Zawinul's lead and be creative with your use of acoustic and electronic percussion sounds?

Discography

The following records are recommended as examples of various artists' music. It would be useful to listen to other music by these artists. These records don't always have a percussionist as the band leader, but they all make extensive use of percussion.

Artists	Record	Type of Music
Martinho Davila	*Batuqueiro*	Brazilian Popular
Alma Brasileira	*Alma Brasileira*	Brazilian Percussion
Djalma Correa	*Musica Popular Brasileira Contemporanea*	Brazilian Instrumental
Nana Vasconcelos and Egberto Gismonti	*Duas Vozes*	Brazilian Instrumental
Sergio Mendes	*Alegria*	Brazilian Popular
Airto Moreira	*Identity*	Brazilian Fusion
Uakti	*Uakti*	Brazilian Classical/ Ethnic
Miton Nascimento	*Missa Dos Quilombos*	Brazilian Popular
Les Étoiles de Dakar	*Les Étoiles de Dakar*	African
Totico	*Totico y Sus Rumberos*	Cuban Popular
Grupo Folclorico y Experimental de New York	*Grupo Folclorico y Experimental de New York*	Cuban/Puerto Rican Folkloric and Popular
Conjunto Libre	*Conjunto Libre*	Salsa
Ruben Blades	*Buscando America*	Salsa
Los Papines	*Para mis colegas*	Cuban Popular
Weather Report	*Heavy Weather*	Jazz Fusion
Ralph MacDonald	*The Path*	Fusion
The Zawinul Syndicate	*The Immigrants*	Fusion
Ravi Shankar	*Portrait of a Genius*	Indian

Here are just a few books you might find useful. If you are a beginner try to combine learning from a book with help from a teacher.

Further Reading

Airto Moreira, *Master Classes: The Spirit of Percussion* (21st Century Music Prod. Inc.). Brazilian percussion in the very personalized style of the great percussionist Airto Moreira.

Edgar Nunes Roca 'Bituca', *Ritmos Brasileiros e seus instrumentos de percussao* (Escola Brasileira de Musica, Rio de Janeiro, 1986). It might not be available in the UK but it is well worth trying to import.

Birger Sulsbruck, *Latin American Percussion* (Wilhelm Hansen, Copenhagen). Good Afro-Cuban and Salsa section; ignore the Brazilian section.

6 Playing Keyboards

ADRIAN YORK is a freelance keyboards player, pianist, programmer and producer. After studying music at Sussex University, he became a member of the chart band, Roman Holliday. Since leaving them, he has toured and recorded with numerous top pop, rock and jazz artists and bands. In this article Adrian has given a comprehensive guide to professional piano and keyboards work, as well as assessing the capabilities and functions of keyboards in commercial music.

In today's musical world, the keyboard player has to be a complete musician. He or she is expected to provide harmony, rhythmic impetus, melodic lines, differing timbres and sound effects, as well as having arranging skills and the ability to create or get access to almost every type of sound. Keyboard players come from a variety of musical backgrounds. Some read music and have studied classical piano or the organ, while others play totally by ear or learn by being shown styles and licks by more experienced musicians. Also, there is a new breed of keyboard player who uses the keyboard as a means of inputting note information to a computer-based music composition package (probably either a computer, a dedicated sequencer or a workstation). Obviously, the number of musical skills learnt by any keyboard player influences the range of work which he or she can be involved with.

Education

There are a variety of places around for aspiring players to get tuition, advice or, just as importantly, playing experience. Many people have bad memories of classical piano lessons, with teachers who rap their pupils' knuckles for every wrong note, but thankfully those days are over. Many modern piano teachers have grown up with pop or jazz, and often have some experience with electronic keyboards. Don't be afraid to approach a classical piano teacher and tell them what your needs are (perhaps a sound playing technique and a wider knowledge of harmony and music theory). Also, don't succumb to the 'necessity' of taking piano exams. I have never heard of a pub landlord or nightclub owner who has been impressed with a Grade 8 pass certificate. For pop playing, exams aren't essential, because it is your feel and creativity that counts. There are teachers, music schools and short courses which deal exclusively with pop and jazz playing. However, many of these don't concentrate on playing technique, and that can be the main use of a classical teacher.

For students following the classical route, a lot of music colleges, universities and teacher training colleges now offer options in jazz, improvisation, synthesis, sequencing and sampling. When you apply for a higher education course, it is worth investigating what is on offer and the quality of the teachers. Many of the older generation of teachers have found difficulty with coming to terms with new technology, both morally and practically, whereas a younger and less traditionally qualified 'MIDI wizard' might be of more use. For sixth-form college and school students, investigate whether your school runs a pop group or big band. If there isn't one, pressurize your teachers! They should be able to provide equipment, tuition and any supervision you need. Many local education authorities are starting up big bands and pop music courses, as pop and jazz education is developing into a growth industry. This isn't surprising as popular music education is often more relevant to an aspiring performing musician than a purely classical background.

Starting Out

If you are just beginning your playing life, maybe in a pop group, playing in hotels or in a West End show may seem a long way from your basic aim of being a professional pop musician, but you can be sure that all the piano-playing pop and rock stars, such as Elton John, Billy Joel and Barry Manilow, as well as most top sessions musicians, learnt their craft doing some of this less glamorous work. As a keyboard player you have to earn a reasonable living to be able to buy the equipment you need to keep up with the constant stream of new keyboard technologies. It is unfashionable at the moment to discuss musicians having to 'pay their dues', but this process of working in a variety of situations and styles improves your knowledge of music, your awareness of song structure (particularly useful if you want to be a writer) and if you play in a 'covers' band, it keeps you in touch with the current hit sounds.

Most pop pianists own at least one electronic keyboard. There are too few venues with good quality acoustic pianos, so it is a necessity to have an electronic back-up. However, there is a considerable difference between a pianist who uses a synthesizer and a keyboard

Elton John

player. Keyboards require a specific set of skills which even a first-rate player may not possess. Many musicians cover both areas, but to play keyboards well you need to develop a good knowledge of keyboard styles, an understanding of synthesis, MIDI and sampling, as well as the ability and interest in creating a whole range of sounds on request. You also need a strong back. Moving equipment around has always been a problem for keyboard players, and although a D-70 is much lighter than a Hammond organ, a keyboard player with a large rig still has enough gear to keep even a professional roadie busy for quite a while.

Professional and semi-pro keyboard playing can be divided into four main categories, and many people work in more than one, if not all four of these.

1. Session Work as a Keyboard Player

There are several ways of working as a session keyboard player. A band may put you on a retainer, which is a weekly wage. This means that your first professional priority is the band or artist who is paying you. On top of the retainer, you may be paid for recording, rehearsing and gigging. If you aren't on a retainer, you should charge a weekly or daily amount for your work, for which you must get a written agreement in advance. There are Musicians' Union rates for recording, but many session players tend to have daily charges well in excess of the union's minimum payments. You are worth whatever you can get from a particular client, but you have to be careful not to price yourself out of the market. There is a danger in working for just one band over a long period. If you are sacked, decide to leave or if the band splits up, you could be left with a lot of expensive gear and no work. Some session players hop from band to band but this can also be a trap which only leads to an endless cycle of touring.

Some employers and session booking agencies are beginning to understand that keyboard players should be more highly paid than other musicians because of the level of investment which they have needed to make in their equipment. This commitment to buying new technology is also reflected in the difficulty keyboard players find in getting sponsorship deals with manufacturers. Drummers, for instance, may not find it too hard to persuade percussion manufacturers to give them some free gear once they are doing a fair amount of television and touring work. Keyboard players don't have this option because they change their equipment so frequently—the investment from the manufacturer isn't worth the small amount of exposure. So the equipment you use will be whatever you buy.

If you are particularly good-looking or striking, there is session work appearing in videos or miming on TV shows. With this, it is important to realize that the band or artist who is employing you is a product; and that product has to look right. Your job will include looking the part. It may be worthwhile not to have too radical a haircut so your appearance can be easily modelled to the image of the artist you are backing. You should also acquire a basic rock 'n' roll wardrobe of a credible leather jacket and jeans.

2. Programming Work

The programmer/keyboard player may do the type of live work where a lot of the music is sequenced, or he or she may do the programming for a keyboard player going on tour. However, the real home of the programmer is in the recording or pre-production studio. The first programmers weren't always musicians, they were technicians employed to get great sounds out of synthesizers. This type of work still exists, and these technicians often work for instrument manufacturers creating new sounds for their keyboards. Working with drum machines and sequencers was the next area to open up for programmers, and with the advent of digital sampling and sequencing, as well as the development of the Synclavier and Fairlight systems, the programmer really took on a vital role in modern music recording. The programmer could put together complete tracks in a pre-production studio without any live musicians apart from the vocals and maybe a sax solo.

Many musicians were made redundant by the success of programmers. On some tracks in the early 1980s almost all of the music was run off sequencers. More recently, artists only use programmed music when they need it. If they want a live drum feel, it makes sense to employ a drummer to play in the studio. Good programmers are expensive to hire, but they are cost-effective as they avoid the need for a rhythm section and extra brass, string or percussion players. As a result, the programmer needs to know how to arrange for all the instruments that he or she is replacing.

3. Pianists

Background music Many pianists with a classical or jazz background earn or supplement their living by playing in hotels, restaurants, wine bars, theatre foyers, nightclubs, pubs or on cruise liners. The common ingredient with all these gigs is that unless the pianist is backing a cabaret act, or accompanying his or her own singing, the usual requirement is for 'wallpaper music'. The pianist doesn't have to work alone on these dates. He or she may perform with a bass, sax or voice, or in a trio with a drum kit as well. Whatever the musical combination, if you don't react to the restaurant or wine bar manager's criticisms of your playing (it may be too loud or intrusive), you will soon have lost your job. However, the sack and your sanity may prove a more beneficial long-term reward than the restaurant's wages. It can be soul destroying to play music to people who aren't listening, just to create the right atmosphere for a hotel foyer.

The type of music you play at these gigs can vary from the classical repertoire (nothing too avant-garde, but impressionist and 'pretty' music goes down well) to jazz and popular standards from musicals. If you don't have an extensive knowledge of jazz and popular tunes, it is worthwhile building up a library of music to play at these gigs. There are many collections available. It is useful to know at least a handful of songs from memory such as these commonly requested standards: 'Misty', 'Smoke Gets in Your Eyes', 'As Time Goes By', 'Evergreen', 'My Way' and 'Girl from Ipanema'. People who request songs often get the titles wrong, or else sing the melody with a technique from the school of indeterminate pitch. However, your patience and co-operation can sometimes elicit a substantial tip!

If you are a jazz player, these gigs aren't the setting for you to delve very deeply into your knowledge of advanced harmony or rhythmic displacement. If you do, you'll soon be displaced at the keyboard by a less adventurous performer. A trip through the melody followed by a few choruses of light variations (trills and arpeggios are the done thing) are all that is required. No Thelonious Monk. Certain elements from George Shearing's 1950s style, much to his annoyance, have been absorbed into the 'cocktail' piano sound, so he is definitely worth hearing for a role model as well as for his musical genius. Payment at these gigs can vary wildly, from hundreds of pounds to just a few, but it is general practice to be provided with a meal and at least some soft drinks. In London there are several agencies who control most of the big hotels' work, and who can be approached for an audition. A lounge suit or a tuxedo is certainly the required dress for any of these gigs.

Pubs For pub work (apart from jazz gigs) you will be required either to sing, to back a singer, or to lead a singsong. There is a specific repertoire for this work. The required 'old-time' songs or 'party favourites' can include anything from 'The Birdy Song' and 'We'll Meet Again' to many of the numbers made famous by Frank Sinatra. If you are going to lead a singalong, or sing by yourself, you need to learn material such as 'My Old Man's a Dustman' and 'Underneath the Arches'. The pub may have booked a singer for you to back, who may or may not have brought along any music. If they have no music for you at all, you'll have to be able to busk through tunes you don't know, or tunes you know which you are having to play in an unfamiliar key. There is no time for a quick rehearsal when the singer on stage calls out 'Lady is a Tramp in Ab, . . . 1 2, 1 2 3 4'!

Quite often pub regulars get up and sing songs you have never heard of, probably without any regard for pitch, rhythm or key. If this happens, keep smiling, close your eyes and hope that the end is near. In these situations, people are either very warm-hearted or quite hostile, so be prepared. Organists also face these situations in pubs as well as in working men's clubs where the antagonism from the audience is almost legendary. Money for pub work is quite variable, but gigs like this in holiday camps and on boats are subject to fixed Musicians' Union wages.

Dance classes Classically trained pianists can earn a more genteel living either by teaching or by playing for ballet or other dance classes. For most classical ballet classes, the music is fairly standard and it is often provided by the ballet school. For some modern dance groups, however, the pianist is expected to improvise around a specific feel or rhythm.

Jazz work For the jazz pianist, there is the possibility of wine bar work in most towns and cities. Also, you can look for jazz supper clubs or try convincing a pub landlord or restauranteur that a Sunday lunchtime jazz session will bring in extra punters. There may be local jazz clubs based in pubs, theatres or at colleges. Any of this work is usually hard to get, irregular and it is often not well paid. The most lucrative jazz gigs are generally those with some outside funding such as from a local council, an arts council, a business sponsorship deal, the Musicians' Union or the Performing Right Society. The country is divided into 'jazz regions' and touring subsidies are available to cover specific geographic areas, such as Jazz South.

4. Piano/Keyboard Work

Function bands Many session musicians supplement their income playing for private functions. Work exists for everyone from the solo performer to 18-piece bands. The repertoire will cover most styles of popular music from the 1920s to the present day, and this can be a good way of learning different styles, improving your sight-reading skills (as charts are nearly always used) and of keeping in touch with the current hits and sounds which you may be asked to imitate.

Night-clubs Night-club work is often taken by underemployed jazz pianists. You are sometimes expected to back cabaret artists and so you need to be able to read music. This work means regular money, but it can be very tiring with five or more sets per night which may run well into the early hours of the morning. Working conditions are frequently poor with a shabby dressing-room if there is one at all. These gigs often require keyboards as well as or instead of a piano.

Theatre and cabaret shows You may be asked to beome a musical director (MD) for a cabaret artist or a theatre company. To do this, you need to write arrangements, book musicians, and liaise between the artist, musicians and a venue's management. West End work is quite well paid both as an MD or as a keyboard/piano player, but as with all repetitive work it can become tedious. Some musicians stay with the same show for years as it is a very satisfactory way of paying the mortgage, but for more creative musicians this work can be very dispiriting. One of the best ways of getting into doing West End shows is working as a 'dep' (deputy) for another musician you have got to know and who wants a night off. One of the big musicals may employ up to five or six keyboard/piano players.

TV sessions These are very well paid but can be boring. You need to be able to sight-read to a high standard and be willing to back a lot of middle of the road artists. You often find some of the best musicians playing some of the least interesting music in these situations, so it is extremely hard to break in to this area of the business.

Jingles Recording advertising jingles is how many session musicians earn their bread and butter wages. This frequently involves copying various playing or programming styles and getting access to a wide range of sounds with which to fulfil the client's requirements. Sometimes the client can want a near copy of a hit song, so if that is what is requested, that is what you have to produce. As a result, this type of work involves providing more of a musical service than a high degree of creative input. There are specialist jingle companies which control much of this work and employ musicians directly.

Equipment

Which equipment to buy, and when, has always been a problem for keyboard players. For the professional, it is important to use up-to-date instruments with the most modern sounds, but prices can be prohibitive. You must also remember to budget for flightcases, leads, accessories and insurance for all your keyboards. One approach to the equipment dilemma is to try and buy at the lowest possible price new gear which has been judged to be an 'industry standard', such as the Yamaha DX7 in its time. This may seem obvious, but a lot of people have been happy to pay the recommended retail price when it isn't necessary. Try to find out the trade price +VAT, add a few pounds on to it and wave some cash at the sales person; and play off dealers against each other—competition in the music instrument retail trade is very fierce. It is best to buy from an accredited dealer if you want good after sales service (like servicing and repairs), despite the temptation of taking a good 'off the back of a lorry' offer. Second-hand equipment can be very good value if bought privately. Look in the classified section of magazines like *Melody Maker* and *Loot*.

Industry Standards

There is generally one piece of equipment in each area which is judged to be the best of its kind. For instance, the Roland MC500 II was thought of as the 'industry standard' dedicated sequencer in the late 1980s. It is always possible to buy equipment which isn't quite as expensive as the industry standards, but usually cheaper models can't do as much as their more flexible cousins. That doesn't mean there aren't good quality pieces of equipment at the lower end of the market. One such example is the Midiverb series of effects units. However, if something has become the mythological industry standard, you can be sure it is reliable, good value, effective and it will have a good second-hand resale value. If you want to upgrade your equipment, try to sell your old gear for the best possible price just before a new industry standard comes on to the market. For instance, the second-hand DX7 price dropped when the Roland D-50 was released, as did the Akai S-900 on the appearance of the S-950 and S-1000. If you read magazines such as *Keyboard*, you can keep in touch with the products the manufacturers are about to release.

Different Set-Ups

Exact recommendations for which equipment to buy are almost impossible to make as everything depends on your budget and specific musical needs. However, a classic set-up may include this equipment (the instruments in brackets are only examples and not necessarily recommendations): an analogue synth (Roland JX10, JX8P or an Oberheim), a digital FM synth (a DX7 I or II), an LA synth (D-50) or Korg M1), a hybrid synth (Yamaha SY77, with FM and sampled sounds, or Roland D-70, with LA and sampled sounds), a digital piano, an organ (Korg CX3 or BX3) and a sampler or sample player (Akai S-1000 or Roland U-220). However, many keyboards players aren't interested in having a multi-keyboard set-up any more, preferring to use a complex MIDI rig with one controller or master keyboard such as the Roland A-80 and everything else racked up in module form and accessed through a MIDI patch/routing system. This type of set-up is particularly useful if you are working with a lot of sequenced parts on live gigs.

Jerry Lee Lewis

Piano players may want either a digital piano or a master keyboard controller. Most of these have a weighted piano-type action and a good MIDI specification, which is vital in any set-up. There is nothing more frustrating than trying to play sensitive piano parts on a springy synthesizer keyboard. Also, you should look for a master keyboard with touch sensitivity and after touch. The former gives you a wide dynamic range for each note, while the latter allows you to use UFO effects such as vibrato, open filter and amplitude envelopes as you hold a note down, the amount of the effect depending on the pressure of each particular finger on any one key.

If you are buying your first synthesizer, a 'workstation' may be a good investment (such as the Korg T1 or M1, Yamaha SY77, or the Roland W-30). They have a broad range of good quality sounds, digital effects and equalization, as well as an on-board sequencer. For professionals, their need will always be for a wide variety of sounds with the best affordable sampling and sequencing hardware. This means that dedicated units are usually mose useful so that only one piece of equipment needs to be changed when a new desirable product comes on to the market.

Accessories

For a gigging and recording keyboard player, the expense doesn't end with the keyboards. There are lots of accessories, mixing and amplification equipment to buy as well. Leads can be very costly if they aren't properly maintained (to do this, learn how to coil them without kinks or twists and always pull them out by the jack rather than the lead), and you will need a good supply of jack-to-jack as well as MIDI leads for any professional work. Good quality leads are very expensive in shops, so try and find a local electronics expert to make leads up for you. It can save you almost half the retail price. Always make sure you have plenty of spare leads of every type (including mains extensions) and that your leads are long enough. For instance, most MIDI leads supplied with equipment are far too short for realistic gigging use. Check that your mains leads are fitted with rubber plugs because plastic ones are easily broken.

When you buy a synthesizer stand think ahead and plan for your future needs. Is it sturdy? Will it hold more than one synth? Most players start with a simple X stand which can take on extensions to support other keyboards. These stands are fine for up to two keyboards, but in my experience with three keyboards, X stands can be unstable and the threads on the base section can wear out. Tubular A-frames are a more expensive option which take up more room and are very stable. There is a new generation of stands being developed (similar to the Roland KS-9) which hopefully will be strong, lightweight, stable and easily dismantled. Depending on your set-up, you may require a number of stands to give you the flexibility and mobility you need.

MIDI Equipment

For any multi-keyboard or MIDI sound source set-up, a MIDI 'thru' box or a MIDI patch bay is vital. If you need to patch together several sound sources, you can avoid the time-consuming work of going from the MIDI 'out' of the keyboard controller into the 'in' of another keyboard or a module (and then out of the 'thru' of this second sound source and into the 'in' of the third one in a 'chain' connection!). Instead, you can set up a 'star' connection using a MIDI 'thru' box or patch bay. This has the MIDI 'out' of the controller keyboard connected with the 'in' of the 'thru' box, and then the several 'thru' channels of the patch bay send the master keyboard's MIDI data to the 'ins' of the various other connected sound sources.

A simple 'thru' box such as the Roland MM-4 has one MIDI 'in' and four MIDI 'thrus'. You can set each sound source to receive different MIDI information on an individual MIDI channel, and the master keyboard can then be used to control each sound source by tuning the keyboard into the appropriate MIDI channel. You can set all your sound sources to receive the same MIDI information as well. Using a MIDI patch bay reduces the time delay which often happens when MIDI information has to travel down a 'chain' connection from the master keyboard through eight or nine keyboards in a chain. A more sophisticated unit is the Akai ME30 PII which has four MIDI 'ins' and eight MIDI 'thrus'. This is obviously useful with a multi-keyboard set-up which involves using a sequencer as a controller as well as several keyboards. The Akai has thirty-two midipatch memories which remember the different MIDI configurations so you don't have to re-patch MIDI leads in the middle of a gig. At the top end of the market, though still not too expensive, are units such as the Digital Music Corporation's MX-8 MIDI patchbay/processor and the 'Function Junction'. The MX-8 features six MIDI 'ins' and eight MIDI 'outs', and it incorporates MIDI 'merge'. This means that information from any two inputs can be merged and sent to any of the outputs. This is useful if you want to have a sequencer and a keyboard able to control a sound source at the same time.

The processing functions on devices such as the MX-8 (also available on keyboard controllers such as Roland's A80) represent a new level of MIDI control. This increased flexbility makes a gigging keyboard player's equipment more sophisticated in its set-up and simpler in its operation, giving greater and easier access to more sounds at any one time. These functions are as follows.

MIDI delay is similar to digital delay. *MIDI filtering* takes unnecessary MIDI information from the data stream to avoid unwanted time delays. *Map function* allows you to split your control keyboard into as many as four key zones, each sending on a different MIDI channel and allowing you different sounds in each of those areas. *Transpose function* transposes up or down 64 semitones on any MIDI channel, enabling you to use a key zone of low MIDI note numbers to trigger high MIDI note numbers, or vice versa. *Compander function* lets you increase or decrease the range of MIDI note velocity and hence dynamic ranges. *Velocity cross switch* means you can change MIDI channels when you play a note at a specified velocity, so you can switch between sounds by playing harder or softer. *Channel shift* enables you to move all the information from one MIDI channel to any other MIDI channel. This is useful if you have several modules. You can always be sending MIDI data on one specific MIDI channel from your controller, but for each MIDI patching setting (i.e. for each song) your information can be routed to different sound sources, each receiving different MIDI channels. If you had just one keyboard controller on a gig, and were sending your MIDI data consistently on channel 1 for every song, you could programme the MX-8 to route that information to different MIDI channels and therefore to different sound sources during each song in your set. *Patch chain facility*: the MX-8 can send up to eight programme change commands on each patch setting. This means that it can change the actual sounds you use as well as your MIDI configurations on each song.

Multi-timbral Sound Modules

With the growing use of sequencers and MIDI, rack-mounted multi-timbral sound modules, such as the Roland D-110 (synthesized sounds) and U-220 (sampled sounds) and the EMu Systems' Proteus (sampled sounds), give you great flexibility. For example, the D-110 offers up to eight different sounds simultaneously (eight part multi-timbral) as well as a full percussion specification and on-board digital effects. When combined with a dedicated sequencer multi-timbral modules are very powerful compositional tools. Manufacturers often offer multi-timbral modules which are essentially their workstations without the sequencer or keyboard. For instance, Yamaha's TG77 contains the sounds of the SY77 workstation. If you already own a sequencer and a master keyboard it can save you money and space if you buy a module version of a keyboard package.

Amplification

Amplification is vitally important. If your amp and speakers don't perform well, all your time and effort preparing sounds and sequences may be wasted. Also, what sounds good on headphones or in the studio may need some adjustment for live work. You will probably start off with a keyboard 'combo' or a speaker and amp. However, keyboard sounds cover a very wide frequency band, so your amplification set-up needs to be able to handle these extreme highs and lows. A 15″ speaker with a horn gives a good balance, and a combo such as the Roland JC120 gives excellent all-round results. If you have more keyboards and sound sources than inputs on your amp, you may need a mixer. A simple 6-into-2 mixer would give you six inputs going to a stereo output with some basic equalization (tone control) and panning (positioning the signal between the left and right speakers). An 8-into-4 mixer may provide better quality equalization and also the ability to use outboard effects such as reverb, delay and chorus. Also, you could split the four outputs into two stereo pairs, one for monitoring and one for the out-front sound. (For more detail on mixing desks, see the 'Recording' article.) If you use this type of set-up, you will also need a large rack for your mixer, outboard effects and sound modules. If you are working with a large PA system you may not use a backline, and just be put through the monitors.

Practical Ways of Improving Keyboard Technique

1. Harmony

Learn the shapes of all major and minor triads, dominant sevenths, major sevenths, diminished sevenths and augmented triads in both hands and in all keys (see scales and chords at the end of this article). This will give you a wide palette of chords to use.

Try building up chord sequences out of these chords, and work out the sequences of your favourite tunes. You could transpose these sequences into every key. You will find some chord sequences regularly occur in many hit tunes. Change around the order of notes in your chords to create different voicings. If you have a sequencer or a workstation, write in some bass and drum lines to accompany your chord sequences. Try as many different voicings as possible over these bass and drum patterns. Also, transpose the bass parts and see if you can play the same chord sequence in the new key. Or programme a bass line which vamps on one note, and experiment with different chords and voicings against the bass. You'll be surprised by some of the chords which can work in certain circumstances.

2. Rhythm and Timing

Always practice everything with a metronome or drum machine. This is by far the best way of learning how to play in time. Practice playing scales, arpeggios, chords and octaves with both hands and each hand separately using the following rhythms:

(a) crotchets

(b) quavers

(c) triplet quavers

(d) semiquavers

Do this all at a variety of speeds.

Learn to play different rhythms in each hand. For instance, try working out a rhythmic pattern for the left hand, such as

♪ ⁊ ⁊ ♪ ⁊ ⁊ ♪ and another for the right hand,

⁊ ♪ ♪ ⁊ ♪ ♪ ⁊ ♪. Then, play both hands together. Try this

with different chords and by swapping the left-hand part with the right hand. This type of exercise develops good co-ordination. Work out your own exercises too.

3. Feel

The best way to improve this is to play along to recordings of keyboard players you admire. Analyse their use of harmony and rhythm, as well as the licks they use, and try to copy their rhythmic feel. When you have picked out the distinctive characteristics of a player's style, learn any tricks you have worked out in every possible key, get together with a bass player, drummer and maybe a guitarist, and recreate the sound and feel of the artist you want to emulate. You could also programme some bass and drum parts in to your workstation or sequencer to play along with.

4. Soloing

Transcribe or learn by ear any of your favourite solos. Analyse the scales, patterns and effects which the soloist uses, in particular pitch bends and vibrato. Common scales used in solos are the blues scale and the major and minor pentatonic scales. Learn to play these scales in every key and create your own patterns with them. There are many other scales to use but these are a good foundation. Programme bass and drum sequences into your sequencer either vamping in one key or going around a sequence of your choice, so you can practice soloing over them.

5. Sound Programming

Always bear in mind the context in which you are using a sound. Get to know your equipment thoroughly and consider each sound in relation to all the other sounds in any one song. Your favourite sound may be overwhelming and totally unsuitable in certain circumstances. Remember the characteristics of individual synthesizers. For instance, for a warm sound with a bright attack, you may use a plucked digital sound in combination with a warm analogue sound. Make sure your bass sounds have enough bottom end, your bright sounds cut through, and your pads (three- or four-note sustained chords which follow the harmony of a piece) are warm.

Before any gigs, recording or rehearsals, try to do as much pre-production as possible. Try to work out your parts and sounds before you arrive at rehearsals so the rehearsal time can be used for making the band work as a unit rather than for arranging. When you are choosing sounds for particular parts, try to think logically. If you want to put a synthesizer pad in a moody rock ballad, or underneath a chugging guitar to give rhythmic impetus, you will probably need a mellow sound, with the filters quite closed. If you opened up the filters, you would get a brighter sound which would be more suitable for a more dominant or rhythmic part. Listen to the rest of the music and decide whether you should be in the background or in the foreground. Digital synthesizers are generally better for brighter sounds, while analogue ones are often used for fatter, warmer ones.

Developing your Style

If you want to be a good keyboard player never neglect your technique. Study Hanon and Czerny (published by Schirmer), and practise your scales and arpeggios, all in consultation with a teacher so you don't injure yourself by playing with a faulty technique. Familiarize yourself with all twelve keys. Study and try to emulate the great players, and don't be afraid of programming and sampling your own sounds. All this will help give your playing an identity. You can do more with keyboards than any other instrument, so enjoy your playing and the freedom you have.

Listening Guide

Rock 'n' Roll Piano: Jerry Lee Lewis, Little Richard.
Blues piano: Otis Spann.
Soul, R 'n'B, funk piano/organ/keyboards: Ray Charles, Fats Domino, Booker T., Georgie Fame, Alan Price, Bill Payne, Richard Tee, Billy Preston, Stevie Wonder, Herbie Hancock, Simon Law (Soul II Soul).

Pop Piano: Elton John, Billy Joel, Neil Sedaka, Carole King, Kate Bush.
Jazz piano: Herbie Hancock, Kenny Kirkland, Keith Jarrett, McCoy Tyner.
Country piano: Floyd Cramer, Charlie Rich.
Latin piano: Eddie Palmieri.
Jazz organ: Jimmy Smith, Jack McDuff, Jimmy McGriff.
Jazz, rock, fusion electric piano and synths: Jan Hammer, George Duke, Joe
Zawinul, Herbie Hancock, Don Grolnick.
Rock piano and organ: Jon Lord, Keith Emerson, Bruce Hornsby, Steve
Nieve, Bill Payne, Ray Manzarek, Stevie Winwood.
Progressive rock keyboards: Rick Wakeman, Tony Banks, Tangerine Dream,
Roger Waters, Keith Emerson, Vangelis.
Programmers/keyboard players: Wally Badarou (Level 42), J. J. Jeczalik and
Anne Dudley (Art of Noise), Robbie Kilgore (Hall/Oates), Greg Phillinganes
(Michael Jackson/Eric Clapton), Vince Clarke (Erasure), Howard Jones,
Adamski.

Practical Ways of Improving: Chords and Scales Chart

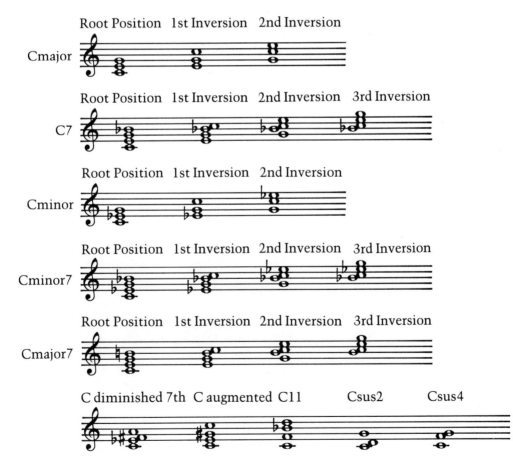

C blues scale   C major pentatonic scale   C minor pentatonic scale

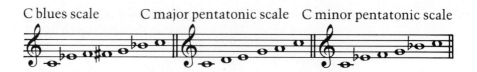

A typical keyboards pattern (minor pentatonic)

etc

7 Keyboards and Associated Technologies

BLUE WEAVER is a freelance programmer/producer who has his own 24-track recording studio and was a founder member of the Fairlight Users Group. Since leaving the Bee Gees several years ago Blue has worked with many major chart acts. Blue wrote this article with **ADRIAN YORK** who is a freelance keyboard player, programmer, and tutor on the Guildhall School of Music and Drama's postgraduate Jazz and Studio Techniques course. Blue and Adrian explain the workings and role of technology in pop, and some ways of beginning to use technology whether you are a keyboard player, guitarist or drummer.

In the last twenty years the keyboard player has been at the forefront of the developments in music technology. For drummers, bass players and guitarists, their basic equipment has remained constant up until the last few years, but the keyboard player has seen very rapid advances in technology, and has had to keep on top of it all. The old image of the organist with the Hammond and Leslie in the back of the car, or the pianist hoping to find a decent piano at a gig, is surely dead and buried now that synthesizers and samplers have become the standard. At last, keyboard players can turn up for work with instruments that are reliable, controllable and, very importantly, not too heavy.

Since the 1960s (when the first production synthesizers were developed by Robert Moog), keyboard players have grasped the chance to expand their range of sounds and capabilities. Now any sound can be synthesized (created by manipulating various waveforms). Analogue synthesis uses oscillators as a sound source. Digital synthesis uses FM (frequency modulation) tone generators, as in the Yamaha DX range. Linear Arithmetical synthesis uses high-level computational techniques of linear arithmetic to synthesize sound digitally, as in the Roland D-50. Combinations of digital, analogue and sampled sounds can be very effective, as in the Roland D-70 where a combination of LA synthesis, sampled sounds and an 'analogue feel' function is found. Another modern technology has enabled musicians to sample any sound; that means the sound is stored as digital information in a sampler such as the Fairlight or Akai S-1000, so it can be recalled, edited and played back at any time.

Despite modern technology, the techniques of playing the piano, organ or electric piano are still relevant to the contemporary keyboard player. The study of past styles, for instance, and a knowledge of music from other cultures is a definite advantage to the professional keyboard player because differing styles are used in various contexts. What happens now is that the sounds and styles of the past are still used, but are often reproduced by modern technology and are sometimes combined with more contemporary noises (for example, Jimmy Smith, the great jazz organist, was featured on the Michael Jackson/Quincy Jones *Bad* album; and the use and adaptation of Latin piano styles has recently been apparent in house and pop hits). The ability to MIDI (Musical Instrument Digital Interface: the standardized form of communication between electronic devices such as synthesizers, drum machines, studio effects (FX) units, sequencers, computers, samplers and so on) traditional instruments such as organ and piano has created other new avenues to explore.

Synthesis has always been associated with keyboard players, from the earliest analogue monophonic instruments (Mini Moog, Arp 2500/2600/Odyssey, and the EMS VCS3) to the most recent digital developments. In the same way that the organ player was able to control the timbre of his instrument, so the contemporary synthesist has an even more varied array of options available, from the warmth of analogue oscillators and filters to the clarity of digital, or combinations of both. Also, MIDI can now be retrofitted to most older electronic instruments, making them controllable from other keyboards and sequencers.

The developments of sequencing and sampling have opened up totally new areas for keyboard players. It is now taken for granted that a keyboard player is capable of arranging, playing, sequencing and creating the parts and sounds of many other instruments (such as brass, strings or drums), and the presence of on-board signal processing on much of the latest equipment, and the ability to MIDI with most modern studio outboard equipment has meant that a knowledge of production and studio techniques is also required.

Learning

In the past many children had piano lessons. Nowadays they are just as likely to have their first creative musical experience with a computer. This means that many of today's players haven't developed traditional keyboard skills, and many of the older players have adapted to modern technology. Many young musicians with an interest in keyboards and/or computers wonder whether it is necessary to have a training in piano technique, and also whether they should have the ability to read music. There is no definitive answer to this question as modern music incorporates people from both backgrounds; each musician has to decide. Sometimes without consciously realizing, a modern musician may have learnt traditional skills. For instance, working with the C-Lab Notator (a MIDI-based software sequencing programme for the Atari-ST computer) involves understanding the notes on a stave, so you can learn to read music while you are programming.

Technique is another area with no set approach. For some keyboard players and programmers a lack of technique might be regarded as a positive advantage as they haven't been sidetracked into a conventional approach. Many of the great keyboard players had very little training in conventional technique and have developed their own very identifiable style with a lot of feel, despite lacking a high degree of classical training. Stevie Wonder, Jerry Lee Lewis and Booker T. all created much imitated styles, feels and sounds not because of any formal training but due to their musical roots and creativity. This doesn't mean that any form of classical technique is futile, quite the opposite. Herbie Hancock and Kenny Kirkland both had quite advanced classical and jazz training and have managed to cross over very successfully between both pop and jazz, breaking new ground in each.

Dealing with Technology

Today's musicians are constantly having to update their knowledge as new technological advances are made and the areas in which they need expertise expand. There is no substitute for 'hands on' experience with a new piece of equipment and because many manuals are less than satisfactory, trial and error can often be the only way to learn. Communication with other users through user groups such as the 'DX Owners Club', 'Juno-6 Appreciation Society' (and, if only it existed, the 'Wish I'd Waited for the S-1100 . . . S-1000 Owners Club') can be very useful for exchanging sounds and information; and manufacturers are beginning to run courses on the use of their products, as well as usually having a help line. There are courses at colleges throughout the country and also privately run centres where tuition and help is on offer. Ask your local music store

or local education authority for details. Magazines such as *Keyboard*, *Home and Studio Recording* and *Studio Sound* print useful advice and information on a wide variety of topics and there are books available on specific subjects such as MIDI, recording, FM programming, synthesis and sampling (see further reading section at the end of this article).

The rest of this article will present some hints and tips on using modern music's technology. The areas you need to study if you want to use this equipment are: MIDI, sequencing, sampling, sound programming, signal processing, and synchronization.

MIDI

In January 1981 Dave Smith developed a system of communication for synthesizers called USI (Universal Synthesiser Interface), which was the precursor of MIDI. In December the following year Dave Smith worked with Chet Wood to improve USI, incorporating ideas from several Japanese technologists, and created MIDI. The need for some sort of communication between electronic musical instruments was obvious and MIDI has become the international standard adopted by all the major electronic musical instrument manufacturers.

MIDI devices communicate information by means of digital signals. This information can be stored and edited on a microcomputer or dedicated sequencer. To make communication possible between MIDI devices, the MIDI 'out' socket of the sending unit should be connected to the MIDI 'in' of the receiver via a MIDI lead. There are sixteen MIDI channels in all, and the receiver's MIDI 'in' channel has to be set to the same channel as the sender's MIDI 'out'. If you are linking more than two devices you can use the MIDI 'thru' socket which is on most MIDI devices. This socket can be used on a second device in a chain to send on to a third device all the information which the second device is receiving from the first device. If you find the last sentence a bit confusing, let that be a warning! You can get very confused if you chain MIDI devices. If you need to connect more than two MIDI devices it is particularly worth buying a MIDI patch bay. These let you connect and usually store MIDI configurations (what is connected to what). The more recent of these can store and recall complete set-ups including patch settings, levels and MIDI channels, and allow you to have several controllers in use at once (for example, a sequencer, two keyboards and a MIDI guitar). For more details on this, see the 'Equipment' section in the 'Playing Keyboards' article.

A simple and cheap way of achieving more than one MIDI 'out' without linking up a chain connection (by means of MIDI 'thru') is by

Stevie Wonder

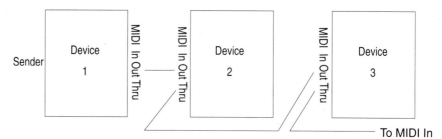

Fig. 1 A MIDI 'chain' connection

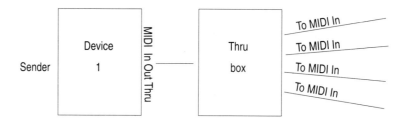

Fig. 2 A MIDI 'star' connection

using a MIDI 'thru' box such as the Roland MM-4, which gives four MIDI 'outs' from one 'in'. It is better to start off this way if you can afford it because when you link many devices using MIDI 'thru', you can begin to experience timing delays. Also, some manufacturers' MIDI implementation is slower to respond than others.

Information related to an event on a keyboard or MIDI device (i.e. a note on/off or pitch bend etc.) is converted by the MIDI electronics into digital information. This digital data is transmitted in bytes, strings of eight 1s or 0s (known as 'bits'). There are sixteen channels through which this information can be transmitted down MIDI cables at a speed of 30,125 bytes per second. These cables have 5-pin DIN plugs and are connected to MIDI 'in', 'out' and 'thru' ports on MIDI devices. Each MIDI event is labelled, and there are two main areas for this, channel messages and system messages.

Channel Messages

There are two types of channel message: **Voice** and **Mode**.

Channel Voice Messages Channel voice messages are as follows: note off, note on, poly key pressure/after touch, control change, programme change, channel pressure/after touch, and pitch bend mode messages.

MIDI Note On event messages send information about which key is pressed on the keyboard (as a MIDI note number such as C3 = 60 = Middle C), about the MIDI channel the note is being sent on, and about the velocity (loudness) at which the note is struck (on a range from 0 to 127). **Midi Note Off** information is the same except its velocity is the velocity of when the note is released, and not when it is pressed.

Poly Key Pressure/After Touch and **Channel Pressure/After Touch** these messages send information about after touch (the presure applied to a note after its initial note on information has been sent). After touch is used to bring in effects such as vibrato or other low frequency oscillator (LFO) controlled effects. Polyphonic key pressure allows just one note in a chord to have a vibrato, while channel pressure affects all notes on the keyboard. **Programme Change**—when you change a patch setting on your controller, this information will also change the patch setting on your receiver, so be careful!

Control Change when you change any of the controls on your master MIDI device, that information can be transmitted to your receiver. This type of data includes sustain pedal, tremolo, and modulation wheel information.

Pitch Bend Mode pitch bend information can be transmitted from your sender to your receiver, but make sure that the increment and range of the pitch bend wheel controls are set to the same amounts on your linked sound sources, otherwise your pitches won't bend at the same rate!

Channel Mode Messages The MIDI standard consists of four keyboard modes. The mode to which the MIDI device is set determines how data is interpreted when it is received.

Omni/Poly or **Omni Mode** means the device receives and interprets messages on all sixteen channels.

Omni On/Mono Mode means the device receives messages on any of the sixteen channels, but only plays one note at a time.

Omni Off/Poly Mode means the device interprets messages only on the same MIDI channel as the channel selected on the sending device.

Omni Off/Mono Mode allows you to send up to sixteen channels of mono information. This is a very useful mode as it means each channel could control a separate instrument or voice. For example, MIDI channel 1 = piano, channel 2 = drum, channel 3 = strings and so on.

System Messages

System messages have no channel numbers attached to them so they can be read by all MIDI devices at any give time. There are three types of system messages: **Common/Real Time** and **Exclusive.**

System Common Messages include the following:

Song Select chooses which song is played by a sequencer from the several in its memory; **Song Position Pointer** chooses where in that song the sequencer starts playing; **tune request** sends messages to all devices to tune themselves up.

System Real Time Messages allow you to link, for instance, a drum machine, synthesizer and a sequencer. If the sequencer were the master device, it would send MIDI clock information (this tells you where you are in the song) and start/stop messages to the other devices to make sure they all start/stop and stay in time together.

System Exclusive Messages are only implemented by the specific device for which they are intended. This means that if you wanted to change a programme on one device without affecting the others you could do it by sending a system exclusive message. You can also bulk dump banks of information via system exclusive. This is useful for saving banks of sound on your computer. Each manufacturer has their own system exclusive number and within that there is a sub-number for each of the MIDI devices a manufacturer makes. Here is a list of manufacturers' system exclusive ID numbers (0–127 are available for manufacturers, but these are the ones currently in use):

1 Sequential	19 Digidesign	41 PPG
2 IDP	20 Palm Tree	42 JEN
3 Octave-Plateau	21 JL Cooper	43 SSL
4 Moog	22 Lowrey	44 Strueven
5 Passport	23 Adams-Smith	45 Neve
6 Lexicon	24 EMU Systems	47 Elka
7 Kurzweil	25 Harmony	48 Dynacord
8 Fender	26 ART	64 Kawai
9 Gulbransen	27 Baldwin	65 Roland
10 AKG	28 Eventide	66 Korg
11 Voyce Music	31 Clarity	67 Yamaha
12 Waveframe	33 Siel	68 Casio
13 ADA	34 Synthaxe	70 Kamiya
14 Garfield	36 Hohner	71 Akai
15 Ensoniq	37 Twister	72 Japan Victor
16 Oberheim	38 Solton	73 Mesosha
17 Apple	39 Jellinghaus	
18 Grey Matter	40 Southworth	

A good tip when working with MIDI, especially with MIDI sequencers, is to keep any parts where timing is critical on the lower MIDI channels. This is because MIDI information is transmitted as serial data and this means that the channels are sent down the line in a strict order of 1 to 16. Information on any channel higher than 1 (i.e. 2–16) obviously arrives after data which is sent on channel 1. If there were more than one MIDI port out of your sequencer/computer, you could have two sets of MIDI channels 1–16, running simultaneously and without interfering with each other, thus allowing you to have more information on lower MIDI channels so that the timing delays inherent in a serial information system can be reduced. The hierarchy of the MIDI ports is also important for timing, so refer to your manual for details of this.

MIDI was at first used to link two or more synthesizers together to create more interesting sounds. When recording, creating a multi-layered sound was quite time-consuming and also only as accurate as the performer; without MIDI a performer would have to repeat his or her performance many times so it could be recorded on several tracks of the tape which then would be mixed down on to one or two tracks to make a new sound. With MIDI you can play many instruments at one time with all the sounds controlled simultaneously by one keyboard, called the Master or Mother keyboard. These have now been developed into dedicated keyboards which produce no sound, they just send MIDI information, such as the Yamaha KX88, Roland A80 and the Akai MX76. MIDI is now being used on a vast array of effects from guitar pedals to reverb units. If an effect is still used in modern music-making, it will almost certainly have MIDI or be able to be retrofitted.

It is important not to think of MIDI as being only keyboard-oriented. MIDI controllers now come in all shapes and sizes, such as guitar, wind, vibes, percussion, microphone and voice controllers. There are devices now being sold which allow you to programme their sliders, switches or knobs to send out any MIDI data. These also include a number of factory presets which allow for a change of level for instance on a Lexicon PCM-70 reverb or Oberheim Matrix 1000. MIDI is also being used to control the muting on mixing consoles and is now available on lower budget models. This works by switching off the mixer channels when they are not needed, and can reduce recording noise considerably.

Keeping track of MIDI paths (what is connected to what) is a must or you could end up in a MIDI jungle. If you don't have a programme or device which remembers your total set-up, write it down as you may well need it again some day.

Manufacturers are now working on devices that allow MIDI connections over long distances via fibre optic cables (up to 2.5 km with Lone Wolf's FiberLink). Also, manufacturers are developing MIDI networking devices which provide MIDI routing, merging and modification for multiple devices. For example, with Lone Wolf's MIDITap you can control any number of MIDI devices from one controller, or have many controllers merging into just one device. Used with the FiberLink, this networking can be done over large distances. This means, for instance, that a keyboard player in one studio can control the MIDI sound sources in another studio by connecting the MIDITap in the first studio to that in the second. In essence, this makes both studios into a Local Area Network (LAN) of MIDI devices. Each LAN is connected to its own MIDITap which provides for a free flow of data from the one LAN to the other. Manufacturers are also currently hatching 'MIDI 2', a more advanced form of MIDI.

Sequencing

Sequencing, in its most basic form, is a method of storing note information which can be recalled, edited and replayed. A sequencer has no internal sounds, it has to trigger an external sound source such as a synthesizer or sampler to create a sound. The first sequencers did this by patching together the gate and trigger connections on early synthesizers with the corresponding connections on an analogue sequencer. (A Gate is an on/off signal used to define how long a note sounds. A Trigger is an electrical impulse used as a timing signal.) This process has become less haphazard and more versatile with the use of MIDI.

A MIDI sequencer can be thought of as a musical word-processor (that doesn't usually mean it plays you a song as you type, though some can do that as well), and it accepts information sent to it via any MIDI device. The types of information it stores are: note on/off (duration), pitch, velocity (volume), song-pointer position, after touch, pitch bend, modulation wheel, pedals, programme changes, and all other MIDI data. It even saves your synthesizer patches. In practice this enables you to play or write in to your sequencer musical parts (stored as MIDI data) which can be played back on any MIDI sound source.

Sequencers come in two basic forms. Dedicated sequencers are computer based pieces of equipment (hardware) which are made specifically for sequencing. Each dedicated sequencer has its own way of displaying information, usually on a small liquid crystal display (LCD) screen, and they have a keypad for inputting and editing information. Some synthesizers/samplers also incorporate dedicated sequencers in packages now commonly known as 'workstations' such as the Korg-M1, Roland W-30 and the Yamaha V50. A lot of people regard the reduced immediate visual access to data as the main disadvantage of these systems. On the plus side, though, is the proven reliability of units such as the Roland MC500 II and Yamaha QX1.

Software-based sequencers have to be used in conjunction with a computer, the most popular computers being the Atari ST, Apple

Macintosh and IBM (usually clones such as Compaq because of their portability). There are quite a number of music software packages for these computers. Here is a brief list:

Atari ST range C-Lab 'Notator/Creator'; Steinberg 'Pro-24/Cubase'; Dr. T 'KCS'; Composer's Desktop Project 'Midigrid'; Hybrid Arts 'EZI TRAK PLUS'; Passport 'Mastertracks'; Hollis Research 'Trackman/Midiman'.
Apple Macintosh Mark of the Unicorn's 'Performer'; Hybrid Arts' 'Master Trak'; 'EZ Vision/Vision/Studiovision'; Steinberg 'Cubase'.
IBM: Voyetra Sequencer Plus; Passport 'Mastertracks'.

MIDI sequencing is probably the most important development in modern music composition and recording during the last twenty years. It has given a control and flexibility which hadn't been thought possible. For instance, you can record a performance by a fellow musician, let him or her go home, and then edit and control all aspects of the performance as you wish. Many musicians have been put out of work by MIDI technology, since you may not need a drummer or a brass section if you have those sounds sampled already. You can just sequence the brass, string or drum parts yourself, and a knowledge of how these instruments would sound and be arranged makes your sequencing sound more realistic. Using this technology has also created new styles which many musicians, especially drummers, now have to copy to survive.

A lot of sequencers use the track system to record data, in a similar way to recording on different tracks on a multitrack tape recorder. Some sequencers are limited to just a few tracks, and others have sixty-four or an unlimited number. What is more important is the sequencer's note capacity, as it isn't much use having unlimited tracks if you can only store up to 1,000 notes. Note capacity on sequencers is generally based on the amount of memory (RAM) that your computer or dedicated sequencer has.

One track in a MIDI sequencer can contain data for up to sixteen MIDI channels. This data could also be inputted to different tracks, and it would be played back exactly the same either way. For the sake of visual clarity you benefit from separating MIDI channels and parts as you would if you were scoring music. Having all MIDI parts on one track would be like looking at a music score with all the instruments' parts written on one stave.

You can input data into a sequencer in two ways: Step Time and Real Time. Real Time sequencing means that the sequencer records the MIDI information as you play it on a keyboard, guitar synthesizer or drum pad. It records all aspects of the performance which it receives via MIDI, such as note events, pitch bend, modulation wheel and so on. It is possible with most sequencers to filter MIDI information

coming in so that the sequencer only records what you want. This can be useful to filter out, for example, after touch information if you don't need it, as it clogs the MIDI data stream unnecessarily. It is quite easy to record parts which may be difficult to play at the required tempo simply by decreasing the BPM (beats per minute) time of the sequencer, performing the part at a slower tempo, and then increasing its BPM once the sequencer has recorded it.

Step time sequencing involves manually inputting data either from a QWERTY keyboard (such as a computer keyboard) or any other MIDI keyboard/controller, one event at a time, although some sequencers allow chord input. For a musical part, this process is the equivalent of writing the music on to the stave. You begin by stating the pitch of the note (each note has a MIDI note number, e.g. Middle C = 60), its duration (also determined by a number), its loudness and each note's other musical parameters.

Quantisation is a function found on most sequencers which pulls notes into a defined time position, such as 16ths (semiquavers), 8ths (quavers), quarter notes (crotchets) and so on. The maximum quantisation value of a sequencer, commonly 96, 384, 768, 1536, is dependent on the resolution of each sequencer. There is no such thing as 'real' real time in a sequencer as every event has to occur on a fixed time position. If your sequencer has a resolution of 24 beats (positions) pqn (per quarter note) this means one 4/4 bar of music can contain 96 events (notes, etc.). The higher the resolution/quantise value, the closer to your original performance your music will be recorded and replayed. The ideal would be like a tape recording which doesn't need to assign events in any fixed position. Many sequencers now give you several quantisation options. You may be able to choose whether your performance is quantised as you play or afterwards. You aren't generally restricted to quantising all of your performance, as certain bars, individual notes or sections can be chosen. This can improve the timing of your performance without affecting your feel.

Non-dedicated sequencers seem to have more quantisation options than dedicated ones. Some have various forms of so-called 'musical quantise' which correct the note on and off events without altering the notes' lengths, helping to keep the music's original feel.

Sampling

Sampling is the storing of sound as digital information which can then be replayed by a MIDI controller. To sample a sound, the sampler works by looking at the input signal (the sound to be sampled) at a rate usually selected by the user (this is known as

Herbie Hancock

the sampling rate). One of the industry standard rates is 44.1, which means the sampler analyses the input signal 44,100 times per second.

Analogue audio signals, either from a microphone, instruments such as a synthesizer, electric guitar or a record/cassette/CD, are turned into a series of numbers, 0s and 1s, by the sampler. This is the analogue to digital stage commonly called A to D. These numbers are initially stored in the sampler's RAM (Random Access Memory). Most samplers can save this data either to a floppy or a hard disk. This process is reversed to play the sample as the numbers are converted back to analogue (the D to A process). These sounds can be played back at virtually any pitch, reversed or mixed together, or they can be looped to produce a longer sound (this is achieved by a section of any size being infinitely replayed).

Samplers have become the tools by which many sounds on recordings are produced. The Fairlight Orchestra hit (Orch 5 . . . possibly from Stravinsky's *Firebird Suite*) was one of the most heard samples of the 1980s. There is no limit to the use of a sampler in a recording. Drums, bass, guitars, keyboards, brass, and voices are all being sampled and used in modern music; nothing is sacred, so if it makes a noise, sample it and more importantly use it!

Mixing samples together or using the front of one sample and the back of another, such as the attack of a piano note and the sustain of a trumpet, can be very rewarding and innovative. You could mix several preset sounds on your synthesizer into one big sound or get some friends to bring their keyboards, guitars or drums to play them together and create a new sample.

Samplers can really save you time and money once you've made the initial investment. In the studio, for instance, vocalists only need to sing one chorus if you sample it and put it into the rest of a song. A lot of pop records use this form of sampling, and its other uses are the fast triggering of short samples, mainly words such as Paul Hardcastle's single 'N-N-N-N-Nineteen'. House records actually sample whole sections of other people's records and use them to create their own tracks; but these artists do sometimes get sued for doing this. The moral of this is not to leave a kick (bass) drum or snare being heard on its own in one of your recordings because if it is good or unusual it will soon be appearing on other people's hits. Optical disk and hard disk recording both combine sampling technology with digital editing facilities. This new type of technology may be heralding a tapeless future in the recording world with multitrack sampler/recorders having the editing facilities of the most advanced sequencers.

Sound Programming

A knowledge of the range, timbre, waveform and playing styles of acoustic instruments is a good basis from which to start programming, and once you have become reasonably proficient at this, it is quite easy to analyse any synthetic sound/noise you wish to recreate. Try out as many synthesizers as possible, since they all have a characteristic sound just like traditional instruments.

Digital synthesizers, because of their modular design and lack of individual control over each editable parameter, can be awkward to programme. As a result of their complexity and the large amount of parameters involved in creating sounds, it would be uneconomic and unergonomic to put all of these controls on the synthesizer's front panel. Usually a few switches, buttons, wheels or sliders are provided to access and edit sounds and information. Visual representation of the parameters being edited is generally limited, making it difficult to get an overall picture of the sound (though, with practice, viewing the parameters will indicate how something will sound).

With the help of an additional piece of equipment called a 'programmer' such as the one available for the Roland D-50, the PG-1000, or a computer based software editing/librarian programme such as the Pandora Technologies DXccessory for the Yamaha DX/TX range, it is possible to have a complete visual picture of all the sound's parameters. It is worth remembering that just because there is a keyboard in front of you, you aren't limited to producing sounds traditionally associated with keyboard instruments. Even if there is a vast library of sounds available for your keyboard, being able to edit these controls could still be necessary to produce the sound you really want.

Analogue synthesizers are generally easier to programme than digital ones as they usually have controllers (slides, knobs, switches and so on) to change each parameter. The most basic building blocks for analogue sounds are oscillators, waveform generators, filters and envelopes. An oscillator produces a pitched sound which then can be shaped (into a sawtooth, pulse or other waveform) by the waveform generator; the filters control the brightness and resonance of the sounds and the envelope shapes its attack, decay, sustain and release. Analogue produced sounds are generally thought of as being warmer and fatter than their digital counterparts.

With a little thought, the simplest of sounds, such as a single sine wave with a delayed vibrato and use of the pitch bend wheel, could be more effective than a superficially more impressive digital sound. It is the context which is important; choose the right sound for the right part, whether it is something similar to a sound you have heard on a record or it is your own mega-creation. Don't forget the majority of older analogue synthesizers have no way of storing the sounds you have created, so keep a note of the positions of all the controls you use.

Signal Processing

In its most basic form, signal processing can be thought of as adding treble or bass to a keyboard or synthesizer sound. These days, modern keyboards come with various forms of on-board signal processing such as reverb, delay, digital EQ and chorus. The Roland D-50 was very popular when it came out because of its on-board digital reverb, digital equalization, and digital chorus, which instantly made its already good sounds even more impressive. Before the D-50, discreet 'outboard' units would have been used.

A modern, MIDI-using musician may have a rack which would incorporate a mixer, synthesizer modules, sampler and some forms of signal processing, and life is becoming simpler as manufacturers now put their effects into multi-function MIDI controllable units such as the Alesis Quadraverb and Yamaha SBX 1000. For a more detailed view of signal processing, see the 'Recording' article in this book.

Synchroniz- ation

If you are using a sequencer the chances are at some point you will need to synchronize with tape. To synchronize means to have two or more devices (in this case a sequencer and a tape machine) locked together. This is achieved by having some sort of time code, such as SMPTE/EBU (Society of Motion Picture and Television Engineers/ European Broadcast Union), MTC (MIDI Time Code, a SMPTE-type code sent via MIDI), VITC (Vertical Interval Time Code, for use with video), or FSK (Frequency Shift Keying). The time code, which is generated either by the sequencer or by a time code generator such as the Friendship SRC/AT or the Roland SBX-80, is recorded on to a track of the tape machine. This is usually an outside track such as number 24 on a 24-track machine, or number 8 on an 8-track unit. The tape then becomes the 'master' and the sequencer is the 'slave'. This means that once you select a starting-point on the time code on the tape, the slave sequencer will always start playing at this point (e.g. if you are using SMPTE you may choose $00:00:10:00:^{00}$ as a starting-point, which is ten seconds in to the time code). SMPTE time code is a 24-hour clock, consisting of hours, minutes, seconds, frames and subframes.

There are four frame standards. In Europe we use EBU code which is 25 fps (frames per second). In America 30 fps is used for synching sound to black and white television pictures, but the speed for colour video signals is 29.97 fps (this is usually called 30 drop-frame). For films, 24 fps is the world-wide standard. As you may have gathered, SMPTE time code originated in the USA as a means to lock sound to picture. Once you have SMPTE on tape the SMPTE reader then locks the slave to the master frame by frame. With the widespread use of sequencers SMPTE was adopted by the sequencer manufacturers as an already established format. When composing soundtracks for TV/ film/video with a sequencer, it is now very easy to synchronize your sequencer with pictures. You can look at the picture of the video or film you are given which should display SMPTE on the screen so that if you need music to start when a door slams, all you have to do is co-ordinate your sound with the SMPTE code at the required point, for instance 01:49:26:13 (one hour, forty-nine minutes, twenty-six seconds, thirteen frame). Usually you would do this type of work with a cue-list, logging the SMPTE points where you want music or events such as sound effects to happen. Then you could write these points in to your sequencer to make your sampler or keyboards/drum machines play on cue.

If you run out of tracks on the tape machine while recording your music, you could run your sequencer in time with the tape so that the sequencer could be playing all the parts that you didn't have tracks for on tape. This not only by-passes the need for degrading each sound's signal by recording it on tape, it also allows you to record sophisticated, multi-layered music with only 16 or 8 track tape machines. FSK was used by manufacturers before they adopted SMPTE, but its main disadvantage is that you have to start from the beginning every time you input a musical part because it has to use the starting-point of the music as a reference point. SMPTE locks frame by frame, so you can start the tape at any point and the SMPTE reader will synchronize the slave to the master very quickly.

There are other forms of synchronization such as ENA, DIN SYNC, and TTL. It isn't worth going into any depth on any of these as MIDI sync (when you control one MIDI device by another via MIDI Time Clock information) and SMPTE/EBU are now the standard. It is possible to synchronize almost any units of electronic music technology. For example:

(*a*) drum machine + drum machine, in order to combine sounds; (*b*) tape + tape, to obtain more tracks e.g. 2 × 24 = 46 tracks (1 track on each machine is used for SMPTE); (*c*) sequencer + sequencer, to make more MIDI available and more memory.

There are devices such as the Kahler Human Clock (now incorporated into the Aphex Studio Clock), The Bokse Humaniser, and the C-Lab Unitor and Human Touch which all allow a previously non-sequenced recording to be synchronized to a sequencer. This is done by connecting an output such as the kick drum from the tape to the device which then creates a MIDI sync reference. This also means that a live drummer can control the tempo of a sequencer, which means you can have sequenced parts played in a live situation but with a human feel.

Technology is there to be used, and although it can initially seem daunting, if you can come to terms with it, it can be worthwhile creatively. If you are working in a commercial music situation, you cannot avoid being involved with technology to some extent, and as prices come down, the facilities which you can have for a relatively small amount of money mean that every serious musician should have some kind of composition/programming device which they can use at their convenience.

Due to the constant and rapid rate of change in music technology, and the appropriation of ideas from areas such as telecommunications, the terms of reference of this article will inevitably date within a matter of months. As a result, we suggest you watch out for the following possible future developments: the integration of audio and synthesizer products with every device being connected via digital ins and outs; new forms of storage media for digital information (such as for storing sampled sounds); bigger and better workstations; sounds created by 'physical modelling', a method by which you create a computerized acoustic model of an instrument; and developments in MIDI and MIDI networking.

Further Reading

Audio Media
Craig Anderton, *The Electronic Musician's Dictionary* (AMSCO).
John Chowning and Dave Bristow, *FM Theory and Application* (Yamaha).
Steve de Furia, *Powerplay DX* (Hal Leonard Books).
—— and Joe Scacciaferro, *The MIDI Implementation Book* (Terro Technologies Publishing).
—— —— *The MIDI System Exclusive Book* (Terro Technologies Publishing).
Terry Fryer, *A Practical Approach to Digital Sampling* (Hal Leonard Books).
Guidebook for MIDI 84–8–A4. This is free from Roland.
Home and Studio Recording
Studio Sound and Broadcast Engineering
Introduction to MIDI Programming for the Atari ST (Abacus), with lots of information on MIDI programming for computers.
Howard Massey, *The Complete Guide to MIDI Software* (AMSCO).
—— Alex Noyes and Daniel Shklair, *A Synthesist's Guide to Acoustic Instruments* (AMSCO).
R. A. Penfold, *Synthesisers for Musicians* (P. C. Publishing).

The Horn Section

DAVID BITELLI and **RAUL D'OLIVEIRA** are two of the best-known saxophone and trumpet players currently working in Britain. Together and separately they have toured the world and recorded with several superstar artists. They both continue to play a wide range of pop and jazz. This article covers the role of brass instruments in pop music which is useful to brass players and to musicians hiring in a horn section. There is also a thorough discography of notable pop horn performances and a chart of possible instrument combinations. The main body of the article has been written by David and Raul, but they have individually contributed a section on the saxophone and trumpet respectively. Norton York has added a similar commentary on the trombone.

The term horn or brass section usually means any combination of trumpets, saxes, and trombones. The modern, high standard of horn playing has largely progressed alongside the development of jazz. In early jazz, the horns carried the melody, rhythm and even the bass line. But R 'n' B changed the horns' role into an accompaniment for singers. The guitar bands of the late 1950s and onwards brought the end of horns in white pop for a while (as in John Lennon's 'Jazz is dead . . .'), and there is still some antipathy between rock guitar music and horns. That doesn't mean these instruments don't mix—listen to any good Zairean soukous band or the Janis Joplin group at their best. Currently, there is minimal use of solo or ensemble horns in the three-minute pop formula, while some musicians and producers have become obsessed with the electronic replication of the brass function at almost any cost. However, for everyone involved in music-making, the horn section can provide an exciting, rich and versatile musical resource.

Basic Approaches

The brass should be an integrated part of the music, not stuck on as an afterthought. Two or more players can act as one unit, working contrapuntally with the percussion, bass, guitars, keyboards and backing singers, complementing the performance of the song. To do that, the horn section has to be aware of what everyone else is doing and of where the song is going.

1. Live Playing

As a horn player you may be called upon to replace someone in an established group or you may be included from the group's outset. If the group 'covers' existing material in a particular style (such as New Orleans, R 'n' B, reggae, zouk or salsa), you would have to be familiar with the style you are playing either from your own studies or by being coached by the other band members. The horns are usually included from the start of most groups, with the exception of most pop bands in which they are often a late addition. This usual pop set-up can be a difficult situation—will the other players 'move over' to make room for the brass in the arrangements? A balance has to be struck between the impact of the brass lessening from its overuse, and the wastage and boredom from its underuse. However, horn players who want to solo all night should either form their own jazz band or invest in some 'music minus one' type recordings and wear them out at home!

Rehearsing Even if you are copying someone else's recording, try to adapt the recorded version to your group's live line-up so it is appropriate for your audience. What sounded great on record (overdubbed three times and padded by a 30-piece string section) may not work on stage through a cheap PA. The 'head arrangement' approach is common (i.e. not written down and everyone chipping in with ideas). This is a good process, though it can be rather slow. Think of melodic 'hooks', punchy stabs, solo sections, backings to solos, and riffs. Try to compliment and not to obscure the vocal— comment between the vocal phrases or groove along behind. Tape your rehearsals to help learn or improve the parts. Once the basic melodic and rhythmic structures have been fixed it may be helpful to organize any inner parts at a keyboard. Also, the horn section may not always consist of regular members. If you write out the parts, a substitute can be routined by the brass players without having to call a rehearsal for the whole band.

In the pop industry a horn player may be called in at a later stage of a project's development, for short tours or one-off showcase gigs. For these, it is worth obtaining recorded versions of the group's repertoire before the first rehearsal, transcribing their songs, and writing basic 'maps' or structures. Try to become familiar with the band's songs and their harmonic progressions, and sketch in your own ideas if that is appropriate. As you do this, check the key of each song with the singer as the tolerance of many cassette players may leave the keys 'in the cracks'. With all this done, your team of horns will give good results very quickly, taking up less, expensive rehearsal time. However, it often takes a good while to memorize a whole show because brass players frequently play small, fragmented and seemingly unrelated pieces throughout a song, unlike other musicians who have to grasp the whole entity. If rehearsal time and money are limited, the discreet use of music stands at the gig can be a solution!

Combinations The type and number of brass players used depends on the style and budget of each project. Independent movement (sub-sections) isn't usual for combinations of less than five brass players. For pop and soul music, trumpet and tenor sax has been the cheap and cheerful standby for many years, giving simple harmonies, octaves and some unisons. A trombone adds weight as it is the real meat of the section, while a second trumpet is essential if high trumpet parts are desired. A further addition could be a baritone sax. R 'n' B bands may use two tenors or other 'tenor-heavy' combinations. A loud rock band or pop outfit requiring only two or three screaming sax solos during the show should probably look for a player who will 'go electric' and also double on keyboard and backing vocals. Two trumpets and tenor, or trumpet, alto and tenor are good funk combos. For mid-range trumpet work and a reedier sound try trumpet, alto, tenor and trombone, giving the alto the option of leading the section with quite a light sound.

Two sax combos are often dwarfed by today's high volumes, however this is a beautiful sound in soukous, merengue or in R 'n' B (two tenors or tenor and alto). Classic Afro-Cuban music groupings are one or two trumpets (in septeto or conjunto) up to large formations of brass in which the trumpet and trombone are important solo instruments. However, Willie Colón uses a beefy all-trombone sound as a characteristic of his Afro-Cuban music. For reggae, alto and trombone is a classic format—the traditional 'Studio One' approach being simple but quite jazzy in its feel (such as Don Drummond and Tommy McCook). Tenor and trombone is a good versatile sound pioneered by the Crusaders (Wilton Felder, Wayne Henderson) but it can lack impact in loud electric bands.

Playing together The art of playing together starts with listening hard to everyone else, so you know exactly how you should play *every note*. Be aware of the other horn parts, what the rest of the band is doing and your place in the overall picture. Whole band and section rehearsals should be used to decide phrasing and dynamics. You should be aware of which are short notes, how hard each note should be attacked, the exact length of long notes, where to bend or smear notes, and the use and intensity of vibrato and other effects. Don't rely on being pushed or driven by the rhythm section—the horns should have their own engine. Be flexible in your approach to intonation. Playing at high volumes not only damages the ears (tinnitus is incurable) but seems to distort the perception of pitch.

Gigging The control of a band's overall blended sound is very often out of musicians' hands and in those of a sound engineer, especially in larger venues. Horn players can help an engineer by being consistent in their distance from the microphone. There are various schools of thought as to how far from the microphone one should play. In a loud context you will probably end up with the microphone down the bell. Microphones attached to the bell or 'bugs' are another option, the former being better for section work. However, all this is really down to trial, error and funds. Trumpet players should probably move back a little for those real screamers, and in for the low register or flugelhorn work. A similar approach is obvious for other instruments.

Monitor sound is also a continual problem unless you are working with a regular team of PA engineers. Being in control of the monitor desk isn't worth all the coffee in Columbia: the engineer is criticized by everyone. Due to inadequate on-stage monitoring, brass players often have to end up playing by 'feel', convincing themselves that their sound really is reaching the audience.

Before going on stage it is good for the horns to tune up by playing a couple of ensemble passages. If the stage sound turns out to be a mess, at least you have 'programmed' your embouchures to play somewhere near the truth. The acoustic properties of the venue may change drastically between the sound check and the performance due to the arrival of the audience. A monitor check with the PA switched off is a good idea for checking the on-stage sound as if the audience were there. An obvious point which is often overlooked is provision of adequate and consistent light if sheet music is required.

2. Recording

What works on the gig doesn't always work in the studio, and vice versa. Studio work is very exacting, requiring a thorough control of the instrument, sensitivity to musical demands and great patience. Every aspect of recording is usually expensive—time *is* money. A good horn sound is a combination of sympathetic players with good, blended sounds, playing parts that work on their particular instruments, into the right microphones for the right room. Many engineers and players have their own pet instrument/microphone combinations but there can be no rule. A good engineer would probably come into the recording room and listen to the sound as it leaves the instruments. Many don't and unfortunately aren't used to recording acoustic instruments.

Pre-production It is usually better for one of the horn team to be involved in the pre-production of a recording project. Ideas from demos can be sketched out, changes made from the live versions of songs, instruments may be added or subtracted and voicings can be altered. The arrangement on paper for the recording session doesn't have to be cast in stone, but it is a good starting-point so that the chord sequence and format of songs are mapped out. Once in the studio all this work will save time. Inner parts, ideas, new material or phrasing all can be easily fixed, changed, inserted or indicated.

Although brass players can use a similar approach to vocal harmony groups, it isn't always appropriate as many good brass effects aren't typical vocal lines. Conversely, keyboard 'horn' lines from the demo also may not work when they are directly transcribed for brass. However, the need for 'something in the gap' combined with the use of keyboard ideas, re-voiced or otherwise altered, may turn out great. The horn arranger being asked to contribute his or her ideas will probably 'overwrite', knowing that extraneous material can be dropped easily.

It is important to plan the number of horn overdubs, taking into account the number of tracks available. The choice of instrumentation is of prime importance, depending on what is envisaged in the final mix. Compare Michael Jackson's 'Don't Stop' produced by Quincy Jones, with Larry Williams's team multi-tracked and far back in the mix, to Sly and the Family Stone's use of trumpets or flugelhorns on 'Running Away' on the album *There's a Riot Going on*. Some producers hire outside 'orchestrators' to transcribe their arrangements, whereas others do it themselves.

In the studio If you are a horn-playing member of a band, work with the engineer and the producer to get what you want for the group. If you are a 'hired hand', always bear in mind whose record it is and that the producer and artist take responsibility for the success or failure of the project. The finished product that the producer and artist envisage may be difficult to explain. So be patient and flexible, and remember who is paying.

Many good sounds can be achieved by experimentation, although the down side of this comes after three hours' sweat when you are asked to 'play it like you did the first time . . .'. Whatever you are asked to perform, go into the control room and check what are you doing—you really are under the microscope at any session. Be prepared for what you hear played back in the headphones to sound different in relation to the track on the control room monitor speakers. I don't know the reason for this, but any studio player will tell you it happens.

If the finished horn sound involves tracking (overdubbing), demonstrate a short section of the complete sound, quickly recording all the parts. Does that please? If not, it is easy to rearrange things early on in the session. Don't be afraid to spend three-quarters to one hour on the brass sound. Remember, it is quite common to spend three hours on a drum kit sound. Once a particular mode of performance has been approved it is usual to record that section of music wherever it occurs through the whole song. Due to 'dropping in', long riffs on fade outs, which would have been hard work in one take, have become possible. Good engineers are quick as lightning at dropping in even to repair just one note.

Recording a horn section involves 'spill' from one track to another because the individual players aren't usually segregated in the studio by soundproof barriers. However, for the sake of control and/or endurance, the baritone sax and any high note trumpet parts can be overdubbed separately. Varispeeding is another recording technique which affects brass players. It was popular in the 1970s and early 1980s, and involves slowing the track down by a semitone, recording at that pitch, and then returning the tape to the true pitch to give a very tight finished sound.

The studio headphone mix is very important, especially when you are playing to a pre-recorded rhythm track, as is usual for most pop sessions. Most studios offer two or more monitor mixes. Some players work with one headphone on and one off, so a mono mix is probably more useful than stereo. If you are recording 'live' with strings or other orchestral musicians, the pressure is really on because the wage bill is so much higher for the allotted time period. In these circumstances lead trumpet playing is a high stress occupation. Jingles require a different approach, as the length of the music to be recorded is considerably less than a pop song, at around 30 seconds. These sessions are often over in 30 minutes to one hour, while pop projects are the other extreme. In the many weeks of an album's recording, energy and spontaneity can often be lost in the endless search for precision.

Solos There are two main approaches: spontaneous and preconceived. Most jazz soloing for instance could be termed spontaneous, even though many great jazz recordings are edits of two

UB40

separate performances. Outstanding players such as Lee Allen and King Curtis, who could build long exciting solos on stage, have also recorded many succinct, swinging, simple melodic solos in just eight bars. Multitrack recording allows for numerous retakes of a solo, although this can be counter-productive. Sometimes artists or producers actually have a line in mind. (A famous example is the tenor line written by George Michael and played by Steve Gregory on 'Careless Whisper'.) A problem with this may be the range of the line in question—a melody played higher on tenor will sound different at the same pitch in the lower register of the alto sax.

Occasionally a production team really may be looking for you to write some sort of 'hook' to fill a gap in the arrangement. Common requests are: 'start on a high note', play like X on record Y', 'make it jazzy'. Many people in pop have a great musical ear for guitar or drum sounds but their record collection includes only a couple of items where other instruments are featured. So they might like the idea of a sax, trumpet or even a trombone solo, but they have no idea how to describe what they think they are looking for. Again, remember to be patient and flexible. Sound is of prime consideration. Good results often come as a result of a joint effort which refines the ideas which were played on the first or second takes. The finished solo may even be a composite of two or more takes.

Most soloists are individuals. An inherent conflict appears when player X is asked to perform like player Y. The bottom line is that player Y should have been booked in the first place: Junior Walker plays great; he plays like Junior Walker, not Clarence Clemmons.

The high note tenor solo in pop is clichéd now. Afro-Cuban music places more emphasis on the trumpet, trombone and flute. Trombone is a particularly important instrument in reggae. Effects can be added to horn solos in the mixing stage and all of this will probably be out of the soloist's control, although the fashion for ADTing (artificially double tracking a single sound) the sax solos fortunately has passed (for further details about ADT see the 'Recording' article).

Studio combinations Technology in all walks of life has put people out of work. Skills have been lost only to be rediscovered some years later. Making art or culture financially profitable in these times is difficult. Despite the visual media boom, there is less demand for musicians; no more than eight brass players could clean up the London recording pop scene at present. Part of the reason for this is that the engineer/synthesizer-playing team can put together most of an LP at home without any extra live musicians.

Overdubbing theoretically means that two players can sound like four, six, eight or even more. The process is time-consuming and a different end result is actually obtained from using eight individual players. Also, overdubbing many times can dull the sound or produce an artificial-sounding effect. If that is the desired result, synthesizers can also be overdubbed with the brass. A balanced, well-written four- to six-piece brass section, correctly recorded, can sound massive with no 'tracking' at all. Three-piece sections (such as two trumpets and tenor sax; tenor, alto and trumpet; tenor, trombone and trumpet) are usually overdubbed once. A four-piece section playing a four-note chord which is tracked once will obviously sound different to a four-piece section building up an eight-note chord over two takes. It is vital to plan during pre-production for the harmonies and registers which the horns are going to play in the overdubs.

One player tracked up many times (such as Tom Scott, or Jeff Daly with Showaddywaddy) is a different sound to a four-piece sax section. The latter has the input of four or five different sounds and intonations. However, tenor sax and trumpet tracked up can sound great, as played by Trevor Laurence and Steve Madaio on Stevie Wonder's 'Superstition'.

Individual Instruments

Saxophones

In the 1940s and 1950s sax players had to approach section playing with a view to blending with the sax sections of up to five saxes and also with four other 'sections' (trumpets, trombones, rhythm and vocals). The more modern method is to blend under the trumpet. Even though one function of the sax is to warm the sound of the horn section as a whole, the required sax sound is usually clean and quite hard. However, a sax vibrato will generally give the impression that the sax is leading the section.

For a solo a different sound and vibrato can be adopted. A very individual sound or vibrato combination must be kept under control in section work. Some players take a couple of horn mouthpiece set-ups to a session because the big-sounding bright set-up may be too harsh for the studio. A narrow lay and/or a softer reed will give better control of intonation and phrasing. Many top studio players have 'small' but high-quality sounds.

The right sax for the job is important. Even experienced arrangers may not be sure which one they want. Some players may take three or four instruments to the studio, all set up and ready to play. In fact, some top sessioneers will play all the saxes, clarinet, bass clarinet, flute, alto flute and piccolo, all to a high standard, while others find their voice (and their living) on just one or two instruments.

Tenor sax is the classic jazz and R 'n' B horn, although the approach has become quite stylized in the shadow of the mighty Michael Brecker. Alto sax is sweeter, unless you follow the Earl Bostic/Louis Jordan school. Currently, a more 'straight ahead', post-be-bop sound is fashionable. Baritone is generally used for the bottom end of the range, functioning between the horns and the bass guitar (though a notable exception is Ronnie Ross featuring on Lou Reed's 'Walk on the Wild Side' and recent Matt Bianco and Basia recordings). The soprano sax has a very plaintive sound. The instrument itself has been developed recently so its intonation isn't as much of a problem as it had been in the past. The great Sidney Bechet is sadly out of favour at the moment; however, the King Curtis curly soprano sound is probably more relevant to today's music. The more common approach is the Wayne Shorter/Loose Tubes style. It blends well with trumpets, flugelhorns, clarinets or synthesizers.

The trumpet

The trumpet has its roots in the classical orchestra, but its popularity really came from jazz. Louis Armstrong, Dizzy Gillespie, Miles Davis, Clifford Brown, Ruby Braff, Booker Little, Clark Terry, Lee Morgan, Freddy Hubbard, Maynard Ferguson and Wynton Marsalis are just a few of the many exciting players who have produced great jazz trumpet performances. It is the trumpet's sound which has made it the 'King of the Brass Section'.

The trumpet in Bb is not the only instrument used in orchestras and in pop. There are trumpets in A, C, D, Eb, F, G, and the piccolo which sounds one octave higher than the Bb trumpet, all with a distinctive sound. However, most orchestral pieces and pop arrangements use the trumpet in Bb, the usual range of which is:

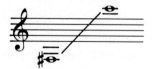

In this century composers have been writing higher and higher for the Bb trumpet, so it is quite common to achieve as high as this:

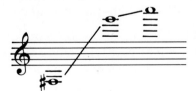

Chicago

This range is often left to specialist lead players, such as Cat Anderson of Duke Ellington's orchestra, who don't play all the time so they are fresh to come in on top of the whole horn section at climax points in the music.

The trumpet is quite different from most instruments. With a piano, guitar or drum kit, anyone can press a key, strum a string or hit a skin to produce a sound. With a trumpet, many people find it very hard, if at all possible, just to make a noise. This is because the trumpeter physically has to create the sound of his or her instrument. If you are attracted to the trumpet you are half-way to overcoming the strange sensation of a cold piece of metal touching your lips. Then the 'buzz', the sound of your lips vibrating together, will come without discomfort. Once you have held a trumpet, you know if it is the right instrument for you. There is an indescribable feeling of belonging when you play because you express through your trumpet what you may like to sing or say, but in a brilliant and positive way.

Naturally, young players don't produce a great sound on their first attempts, but with practice, perseverance and patience their tone will get fuller and richer. So start practising now! I advocate a solid technical foundation for any trumpeter. With the right guidance and steady practice nothing is impossible or too difficult to be played on the trumpet, as the solo works of Maurice André, Rafael Mendez and Wynton Marsalis have proved. However, the eager student should not pick up the trumpet and play until he or she is tired just because he or she feels like it. Soft long notes are a good starting-point for practice, with a full sound and a long breath. The other main points to develop are as follows.

The lips must vibrate to make the sound.

The muscles of the lips and the face must be trained for endurance.

The tongue must produce the various different articulations.

The fingers of the right hand each must be trained separately to gain complete, flexible mobility.

The air which passes through the lips, causing them to vibrate, must be trained to control the tone for soft and loud playing as well as for high and low notes.

Resting is of prime importance during practice. I advise resting for as long as you play. Don't overdo the playing. Five to ten minutes, alternating with the same amount of rest, is plenty. Then you should never bruise the lips and you will enable them to get stronger with every daily practice session. Practising in this way lets you work all day long without getting tired.

The first major pop group to use trumpet as an integral part of their music (in a section with a trombone and saxes) was Blood, Sweat and Tears in the 1970s. You can hear some of their best arrangements on their hits 'You've Made Me So Happy' and 'Spinning Wheel'. Chicago used the trumpet in a three-piece section with a sax and trombone on hits such as 'Make Me Smile' and 'Call on Me'. Tower of Power also helped to popularize the trumpet with their use of two trumpets and four saxes, and almost all of ex-trumpet player Quincy Jones's production work, especially with Michael Jackson, is worth listening to, as he uses some of the better known Americans such as Jerry Hey and Chuck Findlay.

The Trombone

The trombone is the power house of the pop horn section, although individually it has never been particularly prominent. Jazz, particularly the big bands of the 1930s and 1940s, often featured the trombone as a star attraction, but since the days of Jack Teagarden, Tommy Dorsey and Glenn Miller, the instrument hasn't reached the same levels of public acclaim.

Although the basis of the trombone's simple design has been consistent throughout its history, its playing techniques are still evolving. With the rise of be-bop, trombonists such as J. J. Johnson and Kai Winding helped develop new ways of tonguing (doodle tonguing) and lip slurring (fretting) in order to respond to and keep up with the faster, more intricate melodies and improvisations of their contemporaries on the saxophone and trumpet. Bob Brookmeyer began pioneering the jazz valve trombone during the 1950s and early 1960s, and since then a stream of trombone virtuosi have emerged mainly from the USA with new and amazing feats of flexibility and control. In Europe, Albert Mangelsdorf has experimented with every aspect of the trombone's playing technique, pushing the instrument's sound and range into areas previously considered physically impossible; and Americans such as Jiggs Whiggam and Bill Watrous are renowned for their ability to use circular breathing, and play and sing two or three notes at a time.

One result of these players' work is that pop trombonists are often asked to play parts which don't acknowledge the particular difficulties of having a slide, and of being a tenor instrument which can also be used in higher registers. In addition, pop trombone playing usually demands an adaptation of the instrument's classical or jazz technique, particularly in the lack of vibrato, loud volumes, the use of its higher notes and a wide variety of tonguings. Afro-Cuban trombone playing has taken some of these to quite an extreme, sometimes using an overblown sound in its all-trombone or trombone-heavy sections; the former has been a constant feature of Willie Colón's music.

The trombone's function in pop music is usually to support the attack and timbre of the brass section as a whole. In small sections, with only one trumpet or alto sax, it is often effective to use the trombone's higher register so that it works almost as a second trumpet or sax. In larger combos, though, the trombone's beefy middle register adds warmth and substance to the section. The slide can be used as a special effect; you can hear it in the popularization of the Afro-Cuban trombone style on Kid Creole's 'Annie (I'm Not Your Daddy)'.

In the 1950s and 1960s, the trombone didn't often appear in pop brass sections except for the orchestras on Motown and Phil Spector recordings. The 1970s saw the trombone's use develop in American bands such as Chicago, with its trombone almost leading the section, and the Crusaders. Also during the 1970s the trombone's potential was realized as an exciting solo instrument, which the solo on Diana Ross's 'I'm Coming Out' illustrates. One of the most well-known funk and soul trombone players is Fred Wesley of the JBs who can be heard in full flight on the JBs' own albums or while backing James Brown. As reggae developed and grew in popularity, the trombone became one of its characteristic sounds, and Rico has become the leading player of his generation; he is featured with The Special AKA, although he can be heard on pop albums such as Paul Young's *No Parlez*.

In Britain, a number of trombonists have established themselves as soloists and section players. Of particular note is Peter Thoms (on Thomas Dolby's *Hyperactive*), Annie Whitehead (with the Fun Boy 3 and on her own inventive albums), Malcolm Griffiths (in Nick Heyward's remarkably tight brass section on 'Take that Situation' among others) and Richard Edwards (with Working Week, particularly his stunning solo on 'Yatra Ta').

Chart of Some Possible Horn Combinations

I. Large Groups

5 saxes (2 altos, 2 tenors, baritone) 4 trombones 4 trumpets	Classic big band formation from the late 1930s onwards in jazz and swing (Ellington, Miller, Basie, Kenton, Gil Evans). Popular for the New York and Cuban Latin sound and ballroom samba. Augmented with strings e.g. Nelson Riddle/Sinatra. The 'Sound of Philadelphia' in the 1970s.

3–4 saxes (mixed) 3 trumpets 3 trombones	Small big band. Good for Afro-Cuban, R 'n' B (Ray Charles), blues.

II. 4 and 5 Horn Groupings

Trumpet 3–4 tenor saxes Baritone sax	New Orleans R 'n' B/rock 'n' roll sound (Fats Domino, Little Richard).
Trumpet Alto, tenor and baritone saxes Trombone	Another versatile 'little' big band. Good for jump jive (Louis Jordan), R 'n' B and jazz.
4 trumpets Trombone	Hard Afro-Cuban sound (Son Catorce).
2 trumpets 2 trombones Tenor and baritone saxes	Small salsa/Afro-Cuban sound (Tipica 73).
Trumpet Alto sax Tenor sax Trombone Baritone sax (optional)	Versatile, reedy pop, funk or soul sound (Earth, Wind and Fire, or James Brown).
2 trumpets Tenor sax Trombone Baritone sax (optional)	Useful, hard sound for pop, funk, soul, soca and zouk. Good for high trumpet work.
Trumpet 2 Tenor saxes Baritone sax	Reedy Stax, Memphis-type sound (Otis Redding). Good for blues and R 'n' B.
2 trumpets Alto sax Tenor sax	Mobile, reedy, good for high trumpets (Stevie Wonder, Earth, Wind and Fire).
3–4 trombones	Salsa (Willie Colón, Conjunto Libre).
3–4 trombones Baritone sax	Popular late 1970s and 1980s Brazilian (Nelsinho).

III. 3 Horn Sections

2 trumpets Tenor sax	Mobile hard funk or pop sound which allows for high trumpets.
Trumpet Alto sax Tenor sax	As above but reedier (Brecker Bros). Also good for African music and jazz.
Trumpet Tenor sax Trombone	Good for urban blues, R 'n' B, reggae and jazz, from swing to post-bop (Art Blakey)
Clarinet Trumpet Trombone	Trad. jazz, 'Klezmer'.

IV. 2 Horn Groups

Trumpet Tenor sax	Versatile for jazz, pop, soul and funk.
Alto sax Trumpet	Classic be-bop front line (Bird and Diz).
Tenor sax Trombone	Jazz (Mingus), funk (The Crusaders), reggae (Rico).
Clarinet Trombone	Good for the traditional side of French Antillian music.
Alto sax Tenor sax	Soukous, merengue.
2 tenor saxes	R 'n' B and soukous. In the latter the tenors are played high with close harmonies.
2 trumpets	Classic Cuban 'Conjunto' sound.
2 trombones	Salsa.

Discography of Horns in Pop and Rock Music

Artist	Song	Album	Comments
Don Drummond (trombone)		*Greatest Hits*	Reggae with Roland Alfonso (alto sax), Tommy McCook (tenor sax), Baba Brooks (trumpet)
Black Stalin	'Burn 'Dem'		1987 soca
Arrow	'Hot, Hot, Hot'		1984 soca, arranged by Leston Paul
Georges Decimus and Kassav	'Nwei Zouk-La-Se Sel Medi-kaman	*Dance Cadence*	Zouk compilation. A hit
Various		*Oye Listen*	Salsa compilation
Various		*Salsa Hits*, vol. II	Salsa classics from Fania catalogue
Son Catorce		*Son Catorce*	Cuban
Conjunto Libre		*Ritmo, Sonido, Estilo*	1983 New York.

Roberto Torres		*Roberto Torres y Su Charanga Vallenata Vol. III*	Columbian/New York Vallenata
Francisco Ulloa		*Merengue*	
Various		*Super All Star*	New York mambo jazz
Various		*Festival of Merengue*	
Gal Costa		*Fantasia*	Samba-influenced Brazilian pop, arranged by Lincoln Olivetti
Juao Bosco		*Bandl-hismo*	Trombone arranger Nelsinho
Various		*Sound D'Afrique Vols. I and II*	Good African compilations
Salif Keita		*Soro*	American-influenced African pop
Fats Domino	'I'm Ready' 'Jamba-laya'		Any hits compilation
Little Richard	'Keep a knocking'		Any hits compilation
Various	'Roberta' by Frankie Ford 'Rockin' Behind the Iron Curtain' by Little Shelton. 'Sea Cruise' by Bobby Marchan	*The Ace Story*	R 'n' B compilation
Ray Charles	'Halle-lujah' 'I love her so'	*The Ray Charles Story*	1955—anything from mid-1950s to mid-1960s

Louis Jordan	'Caldonia'		1956—with Ernie Royal (trumpet), Louis Jordan (alto sax), James Cleveland (trombone), Sam 'The Man' Taylor (tenor sax), Budd Johnson (baritone sax) arranged by Quincy Jones
James Brown	'Cold Sweat'		This, or anything from the mid-1960s to mid-1970s
Chicago			Any early 'greatest hits'
Sly and the Family Stone	'Running Away'	*There's a Riot Going on*	Classic Sly, very influential in black pop music
Otis Redding	'Fa-Fa-Fa (Sad Song)' 'Can't Turn You Loose'		Any hits compilation
Ann Peebles	'I Can't Stand the Rain'		
Aretha Franklin	'Don't Play that Song' 'Respect'		Hits compilation. Classic tracks with King Curtis or Arif Mardin
Stevie Wonder	'Sir Duke'	*Songs in the Key of Life*	1976—classic 'tracked up' sections
	'Super-stition'	*Talking Book*	1972
B. B. King		*To Know You is to Love You*	Memphis horns
Billy Paul	'Takin' it to the Streets'	*Only the Strong Survive*	1977—Philadelphia sound
Earth, Wind and Fire	'Got to Get You into My Life'		1978—greatest hits
	'Getaway'		1976—greatest hits
Michael Jackson	'Don't Stop' 'Working Day and Nights'	*Off the Wall*	Produced by Quincy Jones, with the Larry William Los Angeles team

9 Songwriting

• •

TOT TAYLOR was a staff writer for Warner Brothers Music from 1980 to 1985. In 1981 he began a small independent record company, the Compact Organisation, which he ran with his partner Paul Kinder until 1986. Tot has had his songs covered by Mari Wilson, Mellissa Manchester, Slim Gaillard, Virna Lindt, Anita Ward and many others, and has written soundtrack music for films such as *Absolute Beginners*, *The Sicilian Connection*, and *The Shatterer*. He has also assembled music for soundtrack albums for the Ruth Ellis film *Dance with a Stranger* and Alan Bleasdale's *No Surrender*. Tot has toured and released six albums of his own in the UK, Europe and Japan and runs his own publishing company, Songmatic Music Publishing, which publishes his work and the music of nine other songwriters. Tot is one of the tutors on the London Popular Arts songwriting course. In this article, Tot assesses the position of the non-performing songwriter in the music business, as well as discussing the writing and selling of songs.

The Songwriter's Place in the Music Business

To earn a living as a professional songwriter in the early 1990s is a near impossibility if you live in the UK. Los Angeles, a few thousand miles west of Nelson's Column, is the songwriting capital of the world, and all the superstar songwriters of the modern recording era are based there.

Albert Hammond, Diane Warren, Billy Steinberg and Tom Kelly are names you probably wouldn't know, but between them they are responsible for 'Like a Virgin', 'Don't Turn Around', 'Nothing's Gonna Stop Us Now', 'Eternal Flame', 'True Colours' and many more transatlantic number one 'smashes'. The chances are you have heard of the songwriters of the 1960s and 1970s, the musical institutions of Bacharach/David, Lennon/McCartney and Goffin/King. Even the geniuses of the period between the wars are familiar—Rodgers/Hart, Irving Berlin, the Gershwins and Cole Porter. So why has the songwriter become a faceless, thinly bracketed credit underneath the title of a hit song?

Since the phenomenon of the 'singer-songwriter' went out of fashion, the songwriter's position in the power structure of the record business has been severely downgraded. Having been in the driving seat, the songwriter is now riding quietly in the back and may soon be out of the car altogether. Only the ubiquitous Stock, Aitken and Waterman, the very musical SAW, are known to Joe Public as songwriters incarnate, but even they needed to become producer, publisher and record label in order to break through the barriers put up by the record labels and entertainment media.

For the non-performing writer, the cover is that rainbow you are always chasing. You should be so lucky! Working under the old maxim 'everything begins with a song', thousands of demo tapes are mailed out everyday in little yellow jiffy bags by writers and publishers. They are sent to record companies, managers, producers and artists in the hope that one Whitney Houston or Anita Baker million-selling cut will send the writer on the way to a fortune. It will. It is rather like sending off an entry to a competition with a very vague correct answer. Most of these songs will never be heard by anyone, either ending up in the bin or if you're really lucky the A&R staff's secretaries will tape their favourite albums all over them. This is nobody's fault. There are just too many songs and not enough ears to listen.

Staff Writers

Publishers, particularly in America, have a wide selection of composers and lyricists on their books who often work in teams of three. These writers are paid a yearly advance to come up with songs in the style of anyone from Bobby Brown to Barbra Streisand. They work from a 'casting list'. This is a comprehensive and fairly confidential list of artists who are looking for material for future recording sessions. It includes a loose brief of exactly what should be submitted, for example, 'up-tempo, like previous hits, AA grade songs only, singles only, no "love-type" lyrics, no "message" songs'. The writers listen to the artists' previous albums and concoct something very quickly in the required style. This might sound like hackwork. It's not. These writers are skilled in any number of diverse musical styles, and after a few successes of their own will have A&R people running to them for new material.

You Just Write Songs?

Historically, songwriters have found it necessary to break into production in order to achieve and then control the recordings of their songs. The pioneers of this were writers like Leiber and Stoller,

Lee Hazelwood, and the team of Burt Bacharach and Hal David (who used Dionne Warwick's voice as the mouthpiece and image for their abstract pop hits). More recently, Patrick Leonard and Steven Bray have become a permanent fixture behind Madonna with their songs 'Into the Groove', 'Like a Prayer', and 'Express Yourself'. All of these were co-written with the artist, which is another trend in the story of songwriters trying to obtain covers. Many artists are no longer content simply to be offered a finished song. In part, this is because the audience feels that artists have more influence over their musical destinies if their names appear as co-writer on their records. Also, major publishers invariably sign artists as songwriters once they have had a hit, whether or not they have ever written a song in their lives before. One day they might!

In this 'modern' era when the public are as interested in the overall sound of a record as much as they are in the song, publishers are looking to sign producers who *write* and singers who *write*. Why they aren't chasing songwriters who write may seem baffling. But in Britain we have only a handful of artists who don't always write their own songs and who aren't controlled by a production team (Cliff Richard, Shakin' Stevens, Alison Moyet and Paul Young spring to mind). So those jiffy bags have very few targets in the UK. In a recent interview, a major British publisher was quoted as saying 'this is not a good company for songwriters'. What he meant was that songwriters now have to be a songwriter/artist, songwriter/producer, or songwriter/engineer to stand a fair chance of a publishing deal and subsequent record sales.

Producing Demos

Another big change in modern songwriting is the production quality of demos. I have heard demos of well-known songs which sound much better than the hit record. Ten years ago I would half-heartedly record a song with a simple piano or guitar backing. I would sing it myself and naïvely mail out a couple of cassettes to someone's secretary. Now I spend a week working on each song so it will end up sounding something like a finished record. Then I duplicate up to fifty cassettes which are mailed out systematically and followed up on the phone over the next few weeks. I woudn't dream of singing on the demo myself. Like many cover writers, I use a team of 'soundalike' singers to half-impersonate the style of the target artist. Despite all this, the success rate of all songwriters writing for other artists is tragically low. For every twenty or thirty songs a songwriter works on, the chances are only one will end up being recorded, and even that may be by an unknown artist on a record which will probably stiff.

Madonna

Beginning and Surviving

Like anyone else in the music business, songwriters survive by doing sessions, arranging, producing, and writing music for films, TV and commercials. These all drag you further away from your original vocation, which was to write a good song (to everyone in the record business a hit song is a good song). If I called up a producer or A&R person with a new song, their first comment would be 'is it a hit?'. My answer should be that with the right artist, promotion budget, producer, airplay, video and sales, it's a hit. I have never believed in that saying 'if it's good it'll get through eventually'. We all know songs and records which have been pushed into the public's face and after more pushing have finally stuck. Similarly, we all have our favourite artists who no one else has heard of. On the other hand, there are an awful lot of 'hits' at the bottom of the ocean.

I began piecing bits of songs together when I was 14 (not a particularly early start), playing around with a piano and a guitar at the same time. In the twenty years since, I have ended up working in almost every area of the music business. I became a player, band member, a writer of musicals, and a publisher. I started and ran several record labels, assembled soundtrack albums, and wrote music for films, TV and cinema commercials, and anything else that has come along which didn't drive me crazy (some of the former did). I was in good company though. Both George Gershwin and Irving Berlin started off as song-pluggers. Burt Bacharach spent years as musical director for Marlene Dietrich, and Joe Jackson began as leader of a Mecca danceband. Eventually, I became a hit songwriter, whatever that means. But the hits were no better than the others. They just got lucky.

Along the way, I have trashed record and publishing deals and achieved about 150 assorted covers which keep me financially afloat through MCPS and PRS income. Although these have their ups and downs, they more or less carry on forever, as long as my songs are selling and getting played. But songwriters have to remember that their songs are simply dreams until someone records them, and it is always easier to apply a DIY attitude to this than to wait around for an A&R executive to pick up on your song.

Writing Songs

When I started my ideal was to write musicals, and I decided to write pop songs in order to finance the production of the musicals. Most people assume that records is where the money is. That isn't strictly true. The Rodgers and Hammerstein estate (which controls all the rights to *The Sound of Music*, *South Pacific*, *Oklahoma*, *The King and I*, and many others) makes much more money annually than almost any pop star. And they haven't written anything for a while!

My inspirations were Irving Berlin and the Beatles. Fred Astaire and *Revolver* took turns dancing on my record deck. I was impressed that all these musicians had an enormous quality of output. They seemed to off load songs rather than write them. Their songs sounded so natural and organic, they didn't hint at the work and imagination which had gone into them. None of these writers were trained or understood anything about the theory of music, so I didn't see why I should either. But it takes skill to make a song sound easy. Although Berlin wrote 'There's no Business like Show Business', 'You Can't Get a Man with a Gun' and 'Doin' What Comes Naturally' in one weekend, it took him several days to come up with a middle for 'Blue Skies', which ended up being a simple four-bar phrase repeated. In my teens I listened to every song in the catalogues of the songwriters I admired, watching how their styles developed and in some cases as their talent diminished through the years. Gradually I learnt about form, chord sequences, melody, lyrical sound, metre and all the little bits of knowledge which could give you the ammunition to become a songwriter. That and 'the gift' of course.

Songs begin in so many different ways, but in every interview I read with songwriters, they all say more or less the same thing: 'when I started, I would play around with a chord sequence I liked, then work up a melody across it and fit the title into the most appropriate place inside the song'. Like many songwriters, I carry a book of titles and ideas around with me, and I have a bookcase full of cassettes with good and bad bits of songs in case I get stuck and need to dip into past inspiration to knock something together quickly. That's songwriting too. I have never understood inspiration. Often I am on a bus or walking along and a complete song with music, lyrics and a title comes out of nowhere and pops into my head. Then it's a case of rushing into a bank or somewhere there might be a pencil handy to write it down before it pops out again. Those instantaneous songs are often the best, but now I am more likely to be sitting at my synth, with a drum machine ticking over and a computer programme running, trying to come up with something for an artist who has never heard of me, but will soon be the recipient of my little C30! Recently I have begun 'co-lab' trips to America. This is an idea propagated by publishers to bring various songwriters together from different publishing stables to share skills, ideas and plugging contacts. By collaborating, the publishers and writers hope to maximize the chances of coming up with a hit song.

The process whereby the germ of a song slowly turns into a record is long, drawn-out and very stressful. Almost all songwriters who are seriously working towards cover songs use a computer. I have a standard Atari set-up with music software linked to a series of very sophisticated synths, drum machines, samplers, modules and reverbs. With this, I can programme nearly all of a song's arrangement before using a fairly up-market demo studio to record guitar, vocals, live cymbals and for the mix. This way, I make every decision about the shape, structure and sound of the finished demo. I usually begin with a vague chord 'wash'. Then I spend about a day programming the bass and drums. I take a break every few hours so I don't lose track of the whole sound. Finally, I add the 'sweeteners', bells, brass, strings, sound effects and various samples—anything to present the song in the best light. Some demos are recorded in writers' home 48-track digital studios, so I have to be as competitive as possible.

Lyrics

When I write a song, I nearly always have a rough idea of some of the lyrics, the title and the main ideas. Probably, I spend a few days getting the words right, using one of three rhyming dictionaries and a Thesaurus. A rhyming dictionary is not cheating. If I am writing a letter, I may need a dictionary. If I'm working on a song, I need rhymes. The big daddy of rhyming books is the Clement Wood (as used by Stephen Sondheim and Cole Porter). Generally, I use Frances Stillman's *Rhyming Dictionary and Poet's Manual* or the new *Penguin Rhyming Dictionary*, which is the best little book I've seen for quick reference. I don't like imperfect or half-rhymes, or soft words sitting on an emphasized part of the melody (and vice versa). So I spend a lot of time changing little phrases in my lyrics, even when the demo singer has come to the session, very often removing small words like 'and' or 'but'. However, the lyrical demands of some modern pop are a long way from the ultra-sophistication of Cole Porter and Larry Hart so a different set of rules apply. Some people say to me that they find the lyrics of many of the great show songs 'corny'. I never did. I never found them very 'poetic' either, but always extremely 'lyrical'. The composers who did write with poets and playwrights such as Maxwell Anderson, Langston Hughes and Ogden Nash often ended up with a slightly jarring musical accompaniment to very lightweight verse. If you listen to Berlin, Ira Gershwin, Al Dubin and Cole Porter you will hear 'lyrics'. Many current writers seem oblivious to the clichés of fantasy/reality, funny/money/honey, telephone/alone, and together/forever, which is fine for the lesser demands of the Top Ten but maybe not good enough if you want to write something to be proud of and which you can bear to hear again in a few years time. Most songwriters would agree that the state of song lyrics is at an all-time low. But they have been saying that for at least thirty years—and they're right.

Music

Melody has become more broken up and now consists of very short phrases which sit on top of the relentless thwacking beat so it can accommodate catchphrase titles such as 'The Only Way Is Up', 'Physical', and 'Fame'. Although pop music has generally become less melodic, people still use the same tricks. When Harold Arlen wanted to denote distance in 'Over the Rainbow', he used an octave leap upwards on the opening word 'somewhere'. When David Bowie aimed to illustrate space on 'Starman' he used the same device. Chord formulas are still patterned around the 1–4–5 blues changes, perhaps with their relative minors 6–2–3 as variation (diminished and augmented chords are rare, see Stevie Wonder, Billy Joel, Donald Fagen and Peter Skellern). More recently, the two-chord trick has proved successful as a chord riff, on 'Billie Jean', 'Like a Virgin', '1999' and just about every other rap, house or hip-hop track in the charts. Stock, Aitken and Waterman did bring a return to melody and chord runs, but most people attribute this to their songs being combinations of other people's material stuck together. I am disappointed that most current songs are unmemorable, but perhaps the audience prefers to forget them anyway. Now, the rhythm is everything and any modern songwriter will need an extremely good knowledge of how to programme a drumbox, how rhythm works and which rhythms are most danceable. In the 1960s it was the snare drum backbeat popularized by Motown, but from the dawn of disco, Hi-NRG and SAW right through to rap and the Pet Shop Boys, the 'onbeat' bass drum (on every beat) has dominated, with feet tirelessly responding to it.

Working with a Band

On the occasions I turn off the computer and work with a band, they may want to contribute ideas to the song's arrangement, so I generally do a very rough demo of the songs for them. Then I book a day's rehearsal to go through the songs a few days before they are recorded. At this rehearsal, the first thing to do is find a key which suits the singer. It is important to do this with a microphone as people's voices are generally higher 'on mike'. We also try out different bass lines, beats, and synth sounds, and select where the guitar chords will be placed within the rhythm. If the producer wants me to do a brass or string arrangement for acoustic instruments, I always write it out on manuscript paper, as players who have studied formally don't take kindly to songwriters whistling the lines they want them to play (though I've done this too!). Often the drummer is the creative musical force behind the band, so I may work with him or her on the emphasis and placement of the bass drum, snare and hi-hat. The bass frequently simply follows the bass drum, adding some fills, while the guitar initiates the chord changes. That usually takes care of the backing track. If I am not producing the final record, it is probably a good idea for me not to come to the recording session. Two sets of ideas don't make great records. The producer will have his or her own ideas about the song and must have the final word on the finished production.

Different Versions of a Song

The structure of verse, chorus and middle may change drastically throughout all the stages of a song's life, from its conception to its recording. The producer almost always wants to change the form, maybe placing the chorus nearer the top of the song, or taking the whole thing up one key to 'brighten' it. At the record company, the A&R executive often wants to change or shorten the song. This may result in an edit which removes the odd bar of music during which nothing is happening. Further down the line, the promotion people may want a special 'radio edit'. So, once out of your hands, the song may well change its shape several times.

The last development in the life of your song is often when the artist or the producer may want to alter some lyrics, or add some chords or new sections. They will want a credit and a share of your publishing for this. At this point, tact and diplomacy can mean the difference between your song appearing on the record or you ending up with 100 per cent of nothing. This can be a difficult problem, but you need to assess the pros and cons of your decision, remembering that in a business where fortunes are made very quickly, financial rewards can be spread over a very short time. It can be very hard not to get cynical and still remain enthusiastic about your vocation.

The End of the Songwriter?

I have always found writing the song, the dream part, easy. It is the blood and sweat of getting it to the next stage which makes life hard. In the mid-1960s Carole King and Burt Bacharach were guaranteed a string of covers on almost everything they wrote. Today we have several respected songwriters in the UK such as Peter Gabriel, Kate Bush and Elvis Costello. But I don't see people rushing out to record any of their songs. Meanwhile SAW are the most successful hitmakers of all time. I have never thought that success or hits had anything to do with whether you are good at what you do. Some of my favourite songwriters are people you will never have heard of. I always know when I've created something of value. But that, as always, is my subjective opinion. In the eyes of the record business there are only 'HITS', and every letter is a capital. Most come and go in three weeks, and two years on no one can remember a thing about them. If you do a little checking on the back covers of your albums and CDs you will see that the production credit is the predominant one. The person who wrote the songs remains hidden inside a faint bracket. We're becoming an extinct species. Ever thought about writing an opera?

Further Reading

Leonard Bernstein, *The Infinite Variety of Music* (Weidenfeld & Nicolson).
Ira Gershwin, *Lyrics on Several Occasions* (Omnibus).
Moss Hart, *Act One* (Random House).
George Martin (ed.), *Making Music* (Barrie & Jenkins).
The Complete Lyrics of Cole Porter, ed. Kimball and Gill (Michael Joseph).
Richard Rodgers, *Musical Stages* (Random House).
Max Wilk, *They're Playing Our Song* (Atheneum).

10 Production

MICK PARKER is a freelance producer, engineer and keyboard player. He has toured and recorded with major pop artists and is a co-director of the Gateway School of Recording at Kingston Polytechnic. His article describes the position and role of the producer within the music business.

In popular fiction, when things are going badly wrong in the studio, the cry goes up: 'Let's get a producer on it!' This appeal for help seems optimistically to assume that a semi-mythical figure will appear and wave a magic wand over the tape recorder introducing what is generally known as the 'fairy dust factor'! In fact, if the band or artist have already started recording without having thought about why a producer is necessary to the project, then chances are that bringing someone to 'produce' the music at this late stage will be a complete waste of time and money.

There are many theories about what makes a good producer, but this article is more concerned with the practical side of producing a record and describing a recording project from beginning to end. This is an abstract example which could be a single, album or demo tape, and it will point out how the artist and producer relate to each other and where potential areas of conflict can (and do) arise.

Getting Together

I am going to assume that you have written some songs which you like. They may have been recorded at home on a cassette machine with just one instrument or in a small recording studio with a slightly larger arrangement. If a record company is sufficiently interested in your music to commit a reasonable budget to making a recording, the first thing to do (after the necessary signing of contracts, deals and the pictures in paper!) is to meet the person who will have overall responsibility for the entire project—the producer.

The producer will get a credit on your record sleeve, and this is one way he or she picks up work. For example, if a record company's A&R staff like the sound of a particular record, often they will find out who produced it. A coherent album will probably indicate a steady guiding hand at the controls. To the A&R person who is responsible for your record's production that shows that a particular producer can be safely put in charge of a recording project. Of course, chart success helps a producer's career more than anything else.

Some record companies will let artists meet two or three potential producers, because bands don't always get on with the first person they meet. This works both ways. Sometimes a producer may be called to a preliminary meeting with a band. After hearing the tapes, the producer may decide that this project isn't one in which he or she wants to be involved. However, once the artist and producer have met and decided that they can usefully work together (you develop a feeling for this), then they can get down to the details of making a record.

The Recording Process

Even though as a musician you may not be operating the knobs and faders, a working knowledge of the operations involved in recording helps to keep you in control. By and large all recording is undertaken in the same way so it is helpful to introduce a flow chart here.

Pre-production and programming→setting up→miking up→backing tracks→overdubs→vocal→mix→post-production→£

1. Pre-Production

This is a frequently overlooked part of the recording process, although it is the vital preparation to any recording session.

Does the artist have enough material to make a record? This may seem an unlikely question but you'd be surprised. Sometimes lyrics are only half-finished, or there's a middle eight still to be written in one song. Although ideas often evolve during recording, it's best to have songs as complete as possible.

How structured are the song arrangements? One reason for employing a producer is the 'overview' he or she can bring to a project. You may feel quite happy with a song that lasts six minutes and has four key changes but you may have said all there is to say in three minutes thirty seconds. In an ideal world, the producer provides constructive criticism of your songs and their arrangements and you both reach a compromise. Of course there is a balance to be drawn here. Some producers will take one or two hook lines from an otherwise bland song and proceed to rewrite it completely. Others will simply alter the arrangements. Like many areas of music, there are no rules, just different ways of working and you need to be aware of these.

Who plays on the record? Once the basic arrangements have been agreed (hopefully without too much bloodshed!) this is the next big question. Here real conflict can, and often does, arise. This can be the hardest moment, matching up your artistic ambitions with the producer's responsibility to your project both as music and as a commercial proposition. I once worked 'live' with a major artist for a considerable period of time and wasn't asked into the studio to make the album. It was a bitter pill to swallow, but with hindsight the producer was right and the subsequent record is still a classic. One way around this conflict is to send a band out on a short tour just before making a record. Often the extra rehearsals for these gigs really tighten up the band and help them to excel in the recording studio. Despite this, a musician still may not be playing up to scratch, and this is when the producer has to suggest a replacement as diplomatically as possible. It isn't like a gig where the odd duff note is forgotten in the heat of the moment. When a mistake is on your record, you will always wish you had sorted it out when you had the chance in the studio. Sometimes a producer will decide that none of the band are capable of making the record, except the singer. In that case, none of the backing band will be invited to the studio and a team of session players are brought in instead. Also, you may want a 'guest' player on your record. These are often session players or other 'name' artists who can add a special ingredient to your music with a solo or a characteristic vocal sound. There are no rules for deciding who makes it to the studio, but this needs to be sorted out in pre-production.

Which studio? Studios come in all shapes, sizes and prices. If this is your first recording then the producer's recommendations are worth taking. Some producers have their own recording studio where they do 'in-house' productions. Often these are for records to be released on their own label. Other producers use studios where they have been happy in the past. Sometimes, various sections of the recording are done at different studios depending on each studio's facilities. For example, a studio with a good live room may attract people who want to record a great live drummer (there are still a few left!), or perhaps another studio has a superb grand piano. However, these studios may not be appropriate for recording synthesizer parts which need a larger control room rather than a spacious live room.

2. Setting Up

If you're recording together as a band, make a point of arriving at the studio together and on time. You'd be surprised at how casual some people are about turning up. It is your money that is being spent, even if the record company is picking up the bill at the moment. Less wasted studio time means more royalties! On projects where a large drum kit needs to be set up, it is useful for the drummer to come in a day early in order to position the kit in the studio so that he or she likes the sound of it and establishes a rapport with the engineer. The rest of the band can set up around the kit if this is how they like to work—isolation screens can be put around the drums to prevent 'spill' from other instruments reaching the drum microphones. Or the other band members can play in the control room leaving the drummer alone in the studio. There are no rules about this, just do whatever feels most comfortable.

3. Miking Up

With acoustic instruments, miking up is as vital a part of the recording process as actually playing the notes. Incorrect mike positioning can make the best performances sound flat. If you've got the time, your engineer will certainly want to experiment with the distance between the instruments. This will involve some patience on your part. You may think nothing much is happening as the drummer hits the snare for the ninety-fifth time, but the engineer and producer will be listening carefully to the sound, maybe adding a touch of 'equalization' (boosting or cutting certain frequencies) or 'compression' (ironing out awkward peaks).

4. Backing Tracks

Once the mikes are all set on the instruments, the time has come to begin recording. All players in the live room wear headphones so they can hear each other playing. Playing with headphones on for the first time can be a strange experience, but it is usually necessary (especially for the drummer who is probably keeping time to a 'click' track).

This is when the producer and artist decide what will be recorded in each pass of the tape. To keep the authenticity of their live sound, some bands prefer to record all the instruments in one go, doing take after take until the 'right' combination of accuracy and excitement blend together. This can happen quickly, but after five or six takes, people often start thinking too much about what they're doing and some of the live spontaneity can be lost. A tea break may be the best answer to this one.

Other bands and producers will want to record the drums in the first take. To help the drummer perform well, some producers lay down rough 'guide' parts on the keyboards, voice, bass and guitar. That way, the drummer is sure of the song's structure. Although it is possible to 'drop in' (rerecord and replace wrong notes) on all instruments, this is harder to do with the drum kit due to the ringing of the cymbals. The drummer usually has to get it right in one take. This is where your rehearsal and pre-production should pay dividends.

Other producers prefer to put down guide drums from a drum machine to build the full track with the other instruments. Then the drummer plays when there is more music to work with, and this can give the track a better feel. Once again there are no hard and fast rules.

5. Overdubs

After the basic track has been recorded to the producer's and artist's satisfaction, the rest of the arrangements can be added. These are known as overdubs. Here, we add all the parts which were worked out during pre-production. The main restriction on this is the number of available tracks left on the tape, but part of the producer's job is to ensure that there are enough tracks to record all the musical parts. Conversely, just because there are tracks to spare doesn't mean they all have to be used.

Any instrument can be overdubbed. Guitar, bass guitars, piano and synthesizers are obvious examples. At this point extra musicians can also be brought in as some songs benefit from having brass, strings or backing vocals added. For these, the producer may hire an arranger and session musicians to play or sing the extra parts. The arranger will usually be contacted during pre-production. A little forward-planning helps here. If strings are needed on four songs, then all those songs should be overdubbed in one session. Twenty musicians coming and going four times is very expensive. You needn't worry about session musicians not being able to play the arrangements. These people are professionals who take pride in doing a good job and helping you, the artist. After all, you could prove to be a welcome source of future work. As any good session player knows, negative attitudes or slapdash playing carry no recommendation.

6. Vocals

Adding the lead vocal is usually the last part of the recording process. By now the producer and the band have lived with the guide vocal for a while and they need to concentrate on the essence of the song. This can be the most demanding time of all as the artist has to be relaxed to deliver a special performance. Sometimes, three or four takes are recorded and the best of each one is mixed into a final version. Or a repeated chorus can be sung just once, 'sampled' and rerecorded into different parts of the song. The most satisfying way of dealing with a lead vocal is to get one magic take which can't be faulted.

7. Mixing

When it comes to mixing the record, we have another choice of studios: whether to stay at the original recording studio or move. Some studios offer mixing desks with computerized assistance to the engineer (SSL, Neve, etc.). This helps to remember fader positions during a complex mix. However, during recording these facilities are of limited use. As studios with these automatic facilities tend to be expensive, the advantage of using a cheaper, non-automated studio for recording is clear. Once again, it is the producer's job to retain an overview during the mixing process. Mixing by committee (i.e. the band) isn't the easiest way to work—the drummer wants the drums louder, the bass player boosts the bass volume and so on. Suddenly, band friendships are severely tested.

Currently, mixing can be done onto various formats. We can use digital masters on audio tape, video cassette or, more recently, on DAT cassettes. Also, we can make analogue masters onto audio tape and cassettes, with or without noise reduction. For fidelity and clarity many people prefer digital quality mastering. However, analogue mastering can add a 'colour' to the sound which some people prefer.

8. Post-Production

The producer's job is nearly over. The recording has been completed and all that remains is to give approval to the test pressings before the music is made into CDs, vinyl discs and cassettes.

Engineers

Engineers seem to fall into two types. The traditionalist has a working knowledge of different types and uses of microphones (a producer often relics on a good engineer to choose the best mikes for the kit, voice, guitar, etc., as well as to recommend the best places in the room for setting up instruments). The more modern approach is associated with computers, drum machines, sequencers and synthesizers. Here, everything is directly plugged into the desk ('direct injected') and microphones are completely excluded. Some studios specialize in this modern method. As a result, they aren't generally the best studios in which to record acoustic instruments. The distinctions between the two types of engineering aren't as black and white as this. By and large, all engineers have the knowledge to deal with both areas of their job. Indeed, a lot of engineers have graduated to the producer's chair. After sitting in on a wide variety of sessions, they have an excellent insight into what makes a record happen. Often an engineer will be part of a team, including session musicians, which a producer uses for almost all of his or her work. Not surprisingly, some of these musicians also become producers after years of experience in the studio.

Recording on a Budget

Until now, I have assumed that your recording project is benefitting from some outside financial contribution. Obviously, this allows the artist and producer to make decisions that aren't limited entirely by cost. If you are an unsigned band who are financing your first studio outing, deciding where to record inevitably comes down to money. In this situation, you will have to accept that almost any session organized on a small budget will necessitate some musical compromises. With this in mind (and the general guidance on choosing a studio above), the best advice is to shop around. See if a studio will do a deal for a twenty-four hour 'lock-out' booking. Find out if the engineer's fee can be included in the studio time. Talk to the engineer and see if he or she is sympathetic to your music. Make sure the engineer understands your musical aims. Offer to redecorate the studio, clean the owner's car, or walk his dog! Do anything for a bit of cut-price studio time. You won't find that top recording studios go for this approach, but at the bottom of the market a little bit of barter can go a long way.

Home Recording

Another more recent alternative to buying studio time is to finance your own studio. The arguments for recording at home are persuasive. For example, if you can afford two or three days recording time at a reasonably cheap studio, you could probably buy your own four-track tape recorder instead. Of course, the equation isn't quite that simple. A tape recorder is no good without some sort of mixing desk and a little 'outboard' equipment like reverb or effects. However, the big plus to getting your own-set up at home is that studio time suddenly costs nothing. You can record for as long as you like, when you like. You might want to start a limited partnership with another musician or engineer friend to buy more equipment and expand the system. If you can add a sampler or one of the so-called 'workstation' keyboard /sequencers, you would have everything you need to create demos whenever you write something new.

The Future

There has always been 'popular' music. The fast turnover of new material and talent is by no means a recent phenomenon. Most popular writers of other eras are long forgotten today, especially those who worked before the arrival of the sound recording and storage facilities which we enjoy today. The electric guitar has been with us for over forty years, the drum machine for ten and new forms of sound synthesizers are still evolving, so the sound of pop music will continue to develop in the future. New technology and digital communications such as MIDI have had an enormous impact on how we have made music over the last five to ten years. Nowadays, quite sophisticated demos can be made at home on recording systems which didn't even exist in the 1970s. Some of these demos need only a little work to turn them into finished masters. Of course, the danger is that the use of technology overshadows the music which it is supposed to complement. All this technology can only ever be a tool of your creativity and it is your talent which produces the very essence of good pop music, the classic song.

Further Reading

There are no books dedicated to the art of production which I can recommend; however, Tony Hatch's book is a sensible overview of the music business with some emphasis on production.

Tony Hatch, *So you Want to be in the Music Business?* (Everest Publications).

11 DJing and Remixing

PAUL OAKENFOLD is one of Britain's leading DJs. He has worked around the world in clubs and supporting major bands, as well as promoting product for Def Jam, Profile and Champion record companies. Most recently Paul has been remixing tracks in the studio including the Happy Mondays' first chart success. He has also moved into the producer's chair for the Happy Mondays' debut album, and is running his own record company, Perfecto Records. As a successful DJ, remixer and producer, Paul shows that being good at playing a musical instrument isn't the only way to a career in the music industry. Understanding what a particular audience wants from music, and how to give it to them, can be far more important than perfecting your vocal or instrumental technique. This article is an edited version of an interview with Paul during a hectic few hours at West London's Eden Studios.

Everyone thinks they can be a DJ. They reckon it is simply a case of putting on a record, which it isn't. When dance music started to happen in 1983 the average DJ was putting on a record, talking after it and putting on another record. He or she wasn't important and DJs were two a penny. Then the American DJs started mixing, getting involved in the recording studio, and becoming important. They were the people actually in the clubs playing the music and they knew what the kids wanted. They had to, because if a DJ is no good he or she usually gets fired.

In the last ten years a lot of upfront DJs have tried breaking in to mixing in the studio, but most record companies didn't believe in them and wouldn't take them on. Now, a lot of DJs from all over the world are going into the studios, working with good engineers and getting the right sounds which they know will work in the clubs.

Remixes

Record companies contact my manager if they want me to do a remix. They send me the tracks which I vet carefully. I don't want to remix just anything. With my experience in the record business I know how to dodge record companies' strategies. For instance, there has been a trend to get DJs to remix old catalogue tracks in a modern way. Usually I am not interested in this because remixing an old track just makes money for the record company. Certain tracks which didn't make it in the clubs the first time around could be turned into club hits, and that is fine. But I don't want to take any old track, perhaps by a country and western artist, and strip it down to remix it for the clubs, because I'm not really doing the artist a lot of good. I might simply give them one hit.

Ninety percent of DJs can't work a mixing board, and they don't need to. When I am doing a remix, I am the ideas man and my engineer is the technical guy. I put all my ideas across and he makes them happen. If you've got the right ideas and you're in touch with the current popular music, you can rely on the engineer. Being a good DJ isn't down to the physics of sound engineering. DJing needs years of experience so that you know how to deal with different kinds of crowds, tempos and music, all to keep a floor going. Then you can put that knowledge into your remixing.

The basic deal for a remix is a flat fee from the record company, and at the moment DJs don't get any writing credits. This situation may change because of the fact that remix DJs change a record so much it ends up being all their production. When I do a remix, I usually spend a day getting my ideas together so I can come to the studio and work on what sounds right. I might only want to keep the vocals and maybe the tambourines from the original record, and then I build a whole new track which is in line with what is going on currently in the clubs. I try and work as much as possible on original ideas. If you steal a great lick or sound, and your record is a hit five months later, you will probably end up being sued left right and centre. I aim to stay away from all that. With my engineer, we make our own sounds with synthesizers and we use a few samples.

When I hear a record, I understand what is wrong with its structure. For instance, most DJs don't want the vocal to come in after five seconds if they are trying to mix a record. Straight drums instead make the DJ's job much easier. As a mixing DJ you need breaks, which means stripping the record down to drums and bass, with very little vocal. DJs use breaks in three parts of a record—an intro, middle section and an outro. These are designed for a DJ to mix in and out of a record in those sections. That is the basics. On a dance

12″, it is always useful to start with a strong intro which is still simple enough for a DJ to use for mixing.

Currently there are two ways of getting into studio remixing. You can start as a studio's tape operator or as the tea boy or girl and gradually progress up to being the engineer. Or you can work really hard at your DJing and aim to be as original as possible. Bring out your own personal taste in music. There are so many DJs playing the same music, you've got to have a distinctive musical personality— which is basically the sounds that you're in to.

The DMC

The Disco Mix Club is a world-wide organization for DJs. They have outlets for everything from record bags and special mixes to information about where DJs can get the best deals for equipment, or about who can give inexperienced DJs some tuition. Any working DJ can join, just as a mobile DJ to start with. DMC simply ask for some proof that you are working, such as newspaper cuttings, promotional material or a letter from a promoter or club manager. For a subscription fee each month DMC send their members a copy of *Mixmag* magazine, as well as three albums (two of mixes not commercially available, and one of previews of as yet unreleased tracks), and generally they try to nuruture young DJing talent. When an up-and-coming DJ sends them a tape with potential, DMC invite him or her to come and work with them on a management contract. Then they try and get a record deal for the DJ while helping him or her to develop creatively and technically in the DMC studios.

Magazines

There are three magazines worth reading. The DMC monthly magazine, *DJ World*, has a world-wide perspective on developments in DJing. *Mixmag Update* is a weekly information sheet which comes out for DJs and record company people telling them about new records to look out for, hot imports that have just come in, reviews on records, and tips about job changes or about radio stations which are opening up specializing in dance music. *RM* is home to the official dance chart which is compiled from DJs all over the country. This is a useful guide to which records are happening and which ones to buy. Also, there is a column which reports about new as well as established clubs. If you want your club mentioned, they will write about it.

Clubs and their Managers

The worst thing about running a club is that all the club manager wants is to make money. He or she doesn't care who is let in through the door as long as the club is packed. From the DJ's point of view, looking to build a successful club, you don't want to let in just anyone. You have to be choosy to build up the night and to attract the right people so your club lasts longer than average. If you open the doors to anyone you will just turn into another ordinary club. But you have to be careful with club managements. If you can get a manager who understands what you are trying to do, and believes in you, that is brilliant and rare.

DJs and Bands

I have a very good relationship with bands. Recently, I have been supporting bands in concert which is an area only a few DJs ever get in to. Major bands of today aren't looking for support acts. They are after someone to get the crowd going so when they come on stage the whole place is going mad. If you put on a support band everyone stands around and waits for the main attraction. I go on stage for a couple of hours to warm up the audience at festivals and on tours. When I do a studio remix I have nothing to do with the band or artist because if they come in they can be so precious about their material they stop me working properly.

Starting Out

When I was 16 I wanted to work in the record business. I applied to all the record companies, and that was a complete failure. It was and still is a catch-22 situation. I had no experience, and where could I get experience if they wouldn't give me a job? My next move was to go to New York because at that time the heart of dance music was in America. I passed my exams to have something to fall back on, packed my bags and hustled my way in the business out there.

Once I was back in London I began DJing with a mate of mine. We would go to one of our local clubs and persuade them to let us hire it on one of their quiet nights. We knew a lot of people who were into the music I was playing, so every time we would throw these parties, about once a week for about a hundred people in the early days, those hundred right people would set off a chain reaction by telling all their mates and before we knew it the clubs were always busy. It isn't that different to how some bands start out. We were doing our gigs around London, our crowd would come in, I was playing, and we were enjoying ourselves.

When you start your club, make up leaflets to promote the night with your name on it. That was all the promotion I ever had: 'Local DJ Paul Oakenfold'. Put them in clubs, pubs, bars, shops, or wherever, to get the people in who you want to attract. You must aim your leaflets right at them.

My DJing has always gone hand in hand with my work for record labels. With them, I am promoting or producing, and with DJing I am out there in touch with the kids finding out exactly what they want. That knowledge is what record companies buy from me in my remixing. After years of DJing all around the world, I have come to know what people want and I put that into my studio and club work.

I use Technics SL 1200 Mk2 turntables. They should be the standard in any club, simply because they are the best. They can be bashed around and are very reliable. They also have a varispeed pitch control, so that if one record is 118 beats per minute (bpm) and another is 114, you can control the speed of both records to bring them in line with each other. If a young DJ can afford it, it has to be worth buying his or her own gear. A good DJ has to practise, although success isn't necessary about being technically the best mixer in town. Originality and taste are more important once a DJ has reached a basic level of competence. It may take a long time to break through, but try. Nowadays clubs play more kinds of music compared with when I started. Then it was very narrow-minded—reggae, rock, soul or whatever. Although you will still probably have to specialize when you do your first gigs, up-and-coming DJs can currently use a wide range of music. I always try to incorporate a variety of good music into my show.

Every record company has a DJ mailing list and they send out anything from 3 to 500 records free. As a young DJ, you have to prove you are working enough in the right places to be worth being put on the mailing list. To start with, DJing is really hard, but you have to keep going. If you really believe in what you are doing, it will happen for you.

Magazines

RM (from high street newsagents, weekly)
DJ World (from the DMC, monthly)
Mixmag Update (from some dance specialist shops and from the DMC, weekly.)
Mixmag (from high street newsagents, monthly)

Organizations

The Disco Mix Club
PO Box 89
Slough
Berkshire SL1 8NA
Tel. (06286) 67276

12 Recording

· ·

DAVE FOISTER is in charge of recording at the Guildhall School of Music and Drama. Like many recording engineers he grew up playing with tape recorders, and this experience eventually led to his studies on the Tonmeister music degree course at Surrey University. Dave is also a regular contributor to *Studio Sound* magazine. His article provides a musician's view of the modern recording studio.

The modern, hi-tech recording studio is a potentially baffling place, and like it or not musicians need a basic understanding of its workings if they are to make the best of their music. Of the many obstacles to this understanding, the biggest is the large amount of jargon standing between the musician and the ideas which these often confusing words describe. Crack the jargon and you're half-way there.

Picking up the Sound

Before we can record, amplify, process, equalize, flange, or phase a musical performance, the sound made by the musician has to be turned into an electrical signal. A signal is simply the musical sound converted into an electrical voltage, and in most situations this conversion is done with microphones.

Broadly, there are two main categories of microphone: dynamic and condenser. Dynamic microphones operate on simple physical principles; for instance, one type, the moving-coil microphone, works very much like a loudspeaker in reverse. (A loudspeaker uses an electrical audio signal to move a coil of wire in relation to a large magnet. This coil is fixed to the loudspeaker cone which moves with it to produce sound waves. A moving-coil microphone has a diaphragm in place of the loudspeaker's cone. This diaphragm moves when sound waves hit it, and a coil attached to the diaphragm moves within a magnet to generate a signal matching the original sound.) Dynamic microphones tend to be robust, reliable and cheap. They are usually capable of withstanding high sound levels and are often resistant to vocalists' popping and blasting effects. On the other hand, the accuracy with which they reproduce the frequency range of the music—the frequency response—is usually limited and uneven, giving a coloured sound lacking extreme treble and bass.

By contrast, condenser microphones are generally expensive, complex and delicate. They contain electronic circuitry which needs a power supply in order to work at all. This is usually supplied from the mixing console using a system called phantom power. Despite these apparent drawbacks condenser microphones are used for most tasks in the recording studio because their sound quality is generally far superior to dynamics. A good condenser microphone is suitable for recording almost anything, whereas dynamic microphones often have flaws in their frequency response which are less noticeable on some instruments than others. This doesn't mean that condensers are used to the exclusion of all else; some sounds, such as toms, snare drums, bass drums, certain voices and guitar amplifiers, work well with dynamics, partly because of their more comfortable handling of loud sounds.

Condensers often offer a choice of 'polar pattern' (an expression indicating the direction(s) from which the microphone picks up sound). There are three basic polar patterns: omnidirectional, cardioid and figure-of-eight. An omnidirectional microphone responds uniformly to sound from all around it. This is useful for picking up room ambience as well as the instrument it is near, and makes it easier to record a musician who won't keep still. Omnis also tend to have the flattest frequency response and the least coloured sound of all condenser microphones.

A cardioid is the most common polar pattern, and is probably what most people mean by a 'directional' microphone. It responds mainly to sound in front of it, less to sound from its sides, and hardly at all to sound behind it. If this response were plotted on paper, the resulting diagram would be roughly heart-shaped, hence the name. The cardioid is useful for picking up an individual instrument while rejecting spill or stray sound from adjacent instruments.

The figure-of-eight microphone responds to sound equally at the front and back, but not at all at the sides. This pattern is often used for stereo pairs, placed as close together as possible at 90 degrees to each other, and it also has several specialist applications such as radio drama.

Other patterns of microphone, such as supercardioid and hypercardioid, are generally combinations of these three standard ones. There are also some specialized patterns such as rifle or 'shotgun' microphones whose very narrow directional properties have little use in the music recording studio. Another particularly unusual group of specialized microphones includes the PZMs (pressure zone microphones) and boundary microphones; these have a unique hemispherical pick-up, which is enhanced by mounting them on a large flat surface. This has several uses; for example, PZMs are often used for recording grand pianos, taped inside the lid. This gives a good overall pick-up of the piano sound with remarkable rejection of outside spill, since the lid effectively becomes part of the microphone.

Microphone Placement

Microphone placement is at least half the art of recording. Why spend hours messing with equalizers and outboards when the sound you want could have been achieved by moving the microphone six inches? It really can be that critical. This is a huge subject, learnt mainly by experience, and one of the rules (as in so many areas of recording) is that there are no rules.

The most common mistake made in the studio by musicians is the assumption that microphone positions for recording should be the same as for PA work on stage. This is rarely true. On stage the aim is to pick up maximum volume and minimum spill, and to avoid the feedback which occurs when a microphone picks up its own highly amplified output from the loudspeakers. This is generally achieved with extreme close miking, which inevitably compromises the quality and fidelity of the sound, because only *part* of the instrument's sound is coming from the point where the microphone is placed. The need in the studio, on the other hand, is usually for a natural instrumental sound. This is normally achieved by increasing the distance between the microphone and the performer. This gives the different elements of the sound from the various parts of the instrument a chance to develop and blend into the overall sound we expect to hear. Don't be surprised if, for instance, a saxophone microphone in the studio ends up two feet away from the instrument instead of stuck down the bell as it would be on stage.

The astute musician should never interfere with anything the engineer has done without checking first. Most engineers have spent as long learning their business as musicians have been learning to play their instruments, and the sight of a musician moving a carefully positioned microphone isn't likely to improve the happy atmosphere in the studio. Obviously there are occasions when an engineer is less than the best, or when a musician has a particularly clear idea of how something might be done, but an immediate assumption that the engineer is incompetent or that the musician knows best is no substitute for teamwork and consultation.

Some instruments produce their own electrical signals, such as bass guitars, electronic keyboards and drum machines. It is generally pointless to degrade these signals through an amplifier and then pick up the amplified sound via a microphone. It makes far more sense to connect these instruments directly to the recording equipment. Unfortunately, their levels and impedances rarely match those expected by a mixing desk, so it is usually necessary to feed them in to the console via a special interface called a DI (direct injection) box. The major exception to this is the electric guitar. The guitar's amplifier makes such an important contribution to the player's sound that it would be senseless to leave it out of the recording chain, and for this reason electric guitars are almost always recorded using miked-up amplifiers. The only alternative is to 'DI' the guitar via one of the various electronic boxes such as the Tom Sholz Rockman; these boxes simulate the effect of an amplifier on the guitar sound.

The Mixing Console

The mixing console, or desk, or board, is perhaps the most intimidating object in the studio. Its apparent complexity can cease to be so daunting when it is broken down into its component sections, and in particular when it is realized that most of it consists of a lot of identical channels. A channel is the complete strip of electronics required to handle one input signal, so a 24-channel desk can handle twenty-four inputs, a 16-channel sixteen inputs and so on. A typical mixer channel consists of an input section, an equalizer, some auxiliary sends, some routing switches (usually incorporating a pan-pot) and a fader.

The Input Section

This performs several simple functions. Firstly, it selects whether the signal coming into the channel is from its microphone socket or from its line level input; the line input is designed to handle much higher signal levels than the microphone input, such as those produced by a tape recorder or an effects unit. Secondly, the input section makes initial adjustments to the level of the incoming signal. This allows the desk electronics to handle the signal without introducing distortion (as would happen if the incoming signal were too loud) and without adding noise (as it would if the input level were too low). For instance, a quiet acoustic guitar is likely to need a fair amount of amplification before the desk can handle it adequately, while something loud like a bass drum needs much less, and may have to be attenuated (turned down) so as to avoid overloading the electronics. A switch to introduce some attenuation is called a pad, and pads are often also fitted to microphones and DI boxes.

The input section may incorporate filters for removing extreme low frequencies, called bass cut or high pass filters. These are used because many acoustic problems in the studio, such as spill, vibrations in the studio's structure and musicians tapping their feet, are most troublesome at these low frequencies.

The Equalizer

The *equalizer* (often abbreviated to EQ) is another bit of jargon almost calculated to deter the lay person. In fact, an equalizer is little more than a glorified tone control. Most have the familiar Bass and Treble controls, although these may be marked LF and HF (for Low and High Frequencies respectively). Most also have some form of middle frequency control, and the level of sophistication of this is often a guide to the standard of the whole desk.

The simplest mixers may have a straightforward presence control, for boosting or cutting upper middle frequencies to move a sound (particularly a voice) forward or backward in the mix. The next step up in flexibility is a control for selecting the frequency at which the middle control functions. If this can cover the whole of the middle of the audio spectrum it forms a swept mid-range control. The most sophisticated consoles also have a control for the width of the frequency band affected, from a narrow peak to a broad gentle lift or cut. This gives control over all three important *parameters* (boost/cut, frequency, and bandwidth or Q) and is consequently called a parametric equalizer. This is quite different from a graphic equalizer, which has a set of sliders each controlling its own fixed frequency band, and which is rarely fitted to a console but used as a separate unit along with the other outboard equipment. Some desks may have two or more bands of parametric or semi-parametric EQ in addition to treble and bass, offering tremendous flexibility. For example, a parametric equalizer has the versatility to enhance the click on a bass drum, to 'tune out' rings in toms, to even out uneven bass guitar notes or to add presence, sparkle or body to any instrument.

Many equalizers have a switch to disable the EQ altogether, on the basis that the signal should not pass through any more electronics than necessary. EQ isn't always needed, although there is often an unfortunate temptation to use it for its own sake. It may well be the case that the sound from the microphone or tape is exactly what is required, but that doesn't stop some people spoiling it with EQ in the belief that a 'proper' mix has EQ on everything. If the sound isn't right straight away, a good engineer should attempt to achieve the required result with microphone placement first, only using EQ to 'touch up' the sound and for special effects.

The Auxiliaries

Also known as aux sends, these are a common cause of bafflement. They are just an extra set of feeds, or outputs, from each channel, so that as well as going to a tape recorder with all the other channels a signal can be sent to another device. This other device can be anything from a reverberation unit to a foldback system. For instance, if a reverb unit were fed from Aux 1, then each channel with its Aux 1 control turned up would be sent to the reverb unit to have the appropriate amount of reverberation added. If an amplifier and several sets of headphones were connected to Aux 4, then the studio musicians would hear any channel which had its Aux 4 knob turned up, and the mix or balance they hear would be set by the Aux 4 controls. This system of supplying monitor sound to the musicians is called foldback. Some desks have an aux dedicated to this purpose marked foldback, and may have another marked echo send for feeding reverb units.

There is an important difference between these two feeds. Any signal going to the reverb needs to be controlled by its associated channel fader, so that the loudness of its reverb goes up and down with the volume of the main signal. To take an extreme case, if a signal were faded to nothing its reverb should disappear as well, not just carry on regardless. For this reason the signal should be sent off to the reverb after it has been through the fader, or 'post-fader'. On the other hand, if this were done with the foldback signal, the musicians' headphone mix would change every time the fader was moved, which would be distracting and confusing. Foldback signals are therefore sent from a point before the fader, or 'pre-fader'. Many desks allow some or all of their individual aux feeds to be switched between 'pre' and 'post' for increased flexibility.

Routing

The routing switches decide where the main output of the channel is to go. A multitrack recording console has several main outputs, called groups or busses, feeding the tracks on the tape. There may be four, eight, sixteen, twenty-four or even more groups and any channel may be routed to any group (and to the appropriate track on the tape) by pressing the relevant routing button. Any number of channels may be routed to a single group so they can be mixed together and recorded on to one track if necessary. It is also common to mix several channels to a pair of groups to be recorded in stereo on two tracks; this is often done with toms, for example. For this process the pan-pots (panoramic potentiometers) are used to position the signals as required in the stereo image. These controls 'move' the sound anywhere in the space between the two speakers.

There would also probably be a main pair of outputs on the console. These feed an overall stereo mix of the whole piece to a two-track recorder, either for live stereo recording or for the mixdown of a finished multitrack tape. These are marked either 'Mix' or 'L-R' to distinguish them from the numbered groups. Again, the pan-pots are used to set up a stereo picture.

Solo

If it is often necessary when recording several sources simultaneously to listen to just one of them to adjust its EQ or check for problems. Pulling all the other faders down from their carefully set positions is clearly impractical, and switching all the other channels off would be laborious and time-consuming. Each channel therefore has a solo button for listening to its signal alone, usually without affecting the signals being recorded, and there are various ways in which it can do this.

The most common is called pre-fade listen, or PFL. This monitors the signal in mono before it has been through the fader, which means the solo signal is heard even if the fader is down. AFL, or after-fade listen, monitors the signal after the fader, usually in its panned stereo position. The most drastic method is often called solo-in-place (SIP), which actually switches off all the other channels. SIP clearly can't be used during a take.

Somewhere near the solo switch there is usually a cut or mute button, which switches off all the feeds from that channel. At the very bottom of every channel is the fader, the channel's main level control, usually with a 'scribble strip' for marking which instrument is on each channel.

The Monitor Mixer

When building up a multitrack recording, it is vital to be able to hear what is already on the various tape tracks as well as what is being played in the studio. Just having all these signals blaring out of the monitors together at some arbitrary level would be hopeless. To make some sense we need to balance them sensibly against each other, set up a stereo picture, and maybe add some reverberation. For this reason a multitrack mixing desk incorporates a second small mixer, purely for these monitoring purposes, known as the monitor mixer. This provides a level control, a pan-pot, some auxes (for feeding foldback and reverb) and possibly some EQ for each track or desk output. The placing of the monitor mixer falls into one of two categories: a split console has the monitor section clearly separated from the main mixer, while an in-line console incorporates the monitoring system into the channel modules. This means, for instance, that track 4's monitor controls are somewhere amongst channel 4's EQ and auxiliaries. This inevitably appears more confusing to the new-comer than the split position, although many engineers prefer it.

The Master Modules

The mixing desk also has a master section, carrying such things as talkback (for communication between the control room and studio), a line-up oscillator for equipment calibration, master controls for the auxes, volume controls for the control room monitor speakers, and switches for selecting what to listen to, such as the main output, the foldback feed, a stereo tape machine and so on. There are also meters for checking the various signal levels present in the desk. These can be either mechanical vu's or PPMs or LED bargraph types.

The Multitrack

The multitrack tape machine is a fairly simple idea,.despite its apparent complexities. It records several separate tracks (up to thirty-two) across the width of its tape, each carrying its own individual instrument or group of instruments. It is possible to record on some tracks while listening to the ones already recorded so that the new recording is in time with the original tracks. In addition, the engineer can accurately control where recording starts and stops, sometimes to the extent of being able to rerecord a single note on an individual track.

At the most basic level, a complete live performance (with everybody playing together) can be recorded all in one go, with each instrument allocated a separate track. These tracks can then be mixed afterwards, and all the decisions about EQ, effects and balance can be made at leisure, rather than having to get all the engineering right and finely adjusted live on the take. Mixing is often done with the involvement of the whole band, although this isn't always a good idea—differences of opinion can be very expensive.

The next level of complexity is to build up a song from a basic backing track (perhaps just the rhythm section) by adding, or overdubbing, lead instruments and extra parts one at a time. This allows the luxury of being able to correct mistakes, or to play a solo several times until 'the one' is recorded. This idea is taken to its ultimate sophistication in pop and rock recording, where it is quite common to build up an entire song bit by bit, even recording the separate parts of the drum kit one at a time. This gives the greatest flexibility on the mix, since no one part is picked up on any other track.

Outboard Equipment

During mixing, either live or from multitrack tape, several extra effects and treatments are probably added, and the signal processors used for these effects are known generally as outboard equipment. Such processors fall broadly into two groups: one concerned with the level or volume of the signal, known as dynamic processing, and one creating effects based round time shifting and delays, which is time domain processing.

Dynamic Processors

Dynamic processing includes limiting, compression, gating and expansion, all of which rely on changing the signal level in real time to alter its dynamics in various ways.

Compression This is used to reduce the dynamic range of a signal or in other words to reduce the difference between its loud and quiet extremes. It does this by turning down the signal level during the louder passages. Many signals, particularly a voice, saxophone and rhythm guitar, produce a wider dynamic range between loud and soft than is usually required in a mix. In many cases, some notes get lost while others jump out as being too loud. One solution would be to push the fader up and down during the mix. This is occasionally done, and is known as 'riding the gain', but in most cases it isn't practical, and this is where the compressor comes into its own.

Much of the time, the compressor is doing nothing at all, until the signal rises above a predetermined level. When the signal crosses this threshold, the compressor turns its volume down so that, for example, a peak 10 decibels over the threshold comes out only 5 decibels above it. In this case the size of the excess peak has been halved, giving a compression ratio of 2:1. Increasing this ratio gives more compression, as does lowering the threshold.

The way in which the compressor goes from doing nothing (unity gain) to compressing is known as the 'knee'. An abrupt transition at the threshold point is a hard knee while if the compression is introduced gradually as the signal rises further above the threshold the result is a soft knee. On some compressors this can be varied. The compressor can be told how quickly to react to loud peaks (the attack time) and how quickly to turn itself back up to normal after compressing (the release time). These adjustments are normally used to remove unwanted 'pumping' or 'breathing' effects, but they can also introduce special effects of their own, such as the enhanced attack on a rhythm guitar achieved by setting the compressor to respond slowly.

Limiting If the compression ratio is very high, around 40:1 or 100:1, the effective result is that the signal can't rise above the threshold at all. This is known as limiting; a limiter is simply a severe compressor, often used to protect equipment such as amplifiers, speakers, tape recorders and broadcast transmitters from overload.

The gate A gate (also known as a noise gate) is used to remove unwanted background noises in between the wanted sounds. The classic application is a snare drum; the snare's microphone usually picks up a lot of hi-hat, top tom and other drums. If a heavy treatment such as reverb is put on the snare, it also ends up all over the other drums picked up by the snare's microphone. A gate solves this problem.

A gate is normally closed or turned off, passing no signal at all. When the signal rises above the gate's threshold, it turns on (opens) and allows the signal through. If (as is generally the case) the snare were the loudest thing on the track, the gate could be set to open when the snare is hit and stay closed at all other times, ignoring and therefore shutting off the lower-level spill from the hi-hat and other drums. For those occasions when the level difference between the wanted sounds and unwanted spill is so small as to make the threshold adjustment difficult, many gates incorporate adjustable filters in their trigger circuitry. These filters allow the gate to ignore low frequencies such as the bass drum or high frequencies such as cymbals, which means the gate can be tuned in to the particular sound which needs to be heard above the spill. This is known as frequency-conscious gating.

Like the compressor, a gate has controls for attack and release. There is usually a hold time as well, where the gate once open stays that way for a while regardless of the signal level. This avoids the gate flicking on and off during long sustained notes.

The expander An expander is similar to a gate except that the signal isn't shut off during the quiet sections, only turned down a little. It may also turn up the loud parts, thereby expanding the dynamic range at both ends.

Time Domain Processors

Time domain effects include reverberation, echo, delay, chorus, flanging, phasing and automatic double or triple tracking. All these effects involve the manipulation of the time relationships between different signals.

Reverberation and echo Although they are often confused, reverberation and echo are technically quite different. Echo is the kind of effect heard when shouting across a lake in the Alps, and a distinct repeat of the shout comes bouncing back from the opposite mountain. Reverb, on the other hand, is the bloom added to a sound, for example in a large room such as a cathedral. With reverb, no separate echoes are heard, but the sound bouncing round adds an extended sustain to the original. The effect used on old rock 'n' roll vocals is echo, with clear repeats audible behind the vocal line. Nowadays vocals are almost always treated with reverb. Echo in the strict sense is rarely used today, apart from as a pastiche period effect.

Reverb used to be simulated using springs or large metal plates, or even special rooms known, confusingly , as echo chambers. Nowadays the effect is almost always achieved using digital reverberation processors. With these computer-controlled devices it is possible to define the size of the imaginary room, how long the reverb lasts, how bright it sounds and so on. Producing an echo effect is much simpler and merely involves delaying the sound by a small amount and then adding the delayed version back in to the original. This used to be done with tape, utilizing the physical distance between the record and playback heads of a tape recorder (taken to extremes with the old WEM Copycat), but again this is now usually done digitally.

Delay, ADT, chorus and flanging If an echo-type delay is lengthened it becomes simply delay—when, for example, a guitar line is heard again half a bar later (in the style of Mark Knopfler). If a delay is shortened it can give the illusion of two instruments playing together and this is known as automatic (or artificial) double tracking, or ADT. The illusion is enhanced if the delay isn't constant but shifts up and down slightly since this introduces slight changes in pitch which make the effect more natural. If ADT is shortened still further, and maybe additional short shifting delays are added, the rich, thick, swirling effect known as chorus is produced.

If the shifting delayed signal comes extremely close to the original signal, and even becomes synchronized with it at times, the result is flanging. This is the unmistakeable sweeping, whooshing sound which was rather overused in the late 1960s and early 1970s, sometimes known as skying since it sounds like an aeroplane flying through the music.

Currently all these and more are produced using digital techniques, and many signal processors can provide several of them, sometimes two or more at one time. Most modern outboard equipment incorporates some form of MIDI control, from simple patch changing as on the Midiverb II to complete mappable control over every parameter as on the AKG ADR68K. For instance, it is quite common to be able to increase the amount of reverb by playing a keyboard harder, or to have reverb time increasing on higher notes. Some devices also produce their own MIDI events; some gates can send MIDI 'note on' messages when they open, and this can be used, for example, to trigger electronic drums in time with real ones.

The Patch Bay

All the studio's equipment has to be connected together, often in many different ways, and it would be ludicrous to have to mess around with the plugs in the back of all the various devices every time they need to be reconfigured. This is why every control room features a panel like a telephone switchboard, known as either a jackfield or a patch bay. All the inputs and outputs of every piece of equipment in the room are connected to the patch bay and then can be conveniently interconnected using handy short leads which always have the right plug on the end.

The Master

The final mix, with the studio's wondrous effects and treatments all over it, needs to be recorded in all its glory on a stereo tape machine for eventual transfer to CD, vinyl record or cassette. Very often this mastering machine is digital. Expensive digital mastering systems have been available for some years. The comparatively low price of the Sony F1 system brought digital recording within the reach of most studios, and the more recent advent of DAT (Digital Audio Tape) has meant that even home studios can produce digital masters. Many top studios have digital multitrack machines, but for the most part these are still prohibitively expensive, and analogue is still widely used. Also in common use in leading studios are hard disk recording systems, which can offer stereo or multitrack digital recording with many of the facilities provided by sequencers, plus fast, powerful editing and signal processing.

Analogue and Digital Recording

Analogue recording works by aligning magnetic particles on a tape so that the 'shape' of the resulting magnetic pattern is a close representation, or analogue, of the waveform of the original sound. This suffers from several problems, the most important of which are distortion (when the signal is too loud) and noise (which is always present on the tape and becomes a nuisance when the signal being recorded is too quiet). Unfortunately the usable window between these two problems (the signal to noise ratio or dynamic range) is much smaller than the dynamic range of live musical sound. This window can be extended by using noise reduction such as Dolby or dbx, but even when stretched to its limits, the available dynamic range is often not quite adequate.

Digital recording, by contrast, makes no attempt to record a representation of the sound. Instead it chops up the incoming signal into tiny slices (most systems slice 44,100 times a second), measures the size of these slices, turns its measurements into binary numbers (strings of 1s and 0s) and records these numbers. On playback the numbers are fed through the reverse process and reconstituted into the original sound. As the recorded data consists simply of a series of 1s and 0s, the analogue bugbears of distortion and noise don't arise; the system only needs to know whether a 1 is present or not. The difficulty with digital equipment is the enormous amount of data to be recorded (around 1.5 to 2 million bits per second). To cope with this, video recorders are often used for storage as they are designed to deal with this kind of density of information. The limits are set by the sampling rate (the number of slices per second) which have to be at least twice the highest audio frequency required, and by the number of bits used to encode the binary numbers—each bit gives 6 decibels of dynamic range. This means standard 44.1 kHz 16-bit systems such as CD, DAT and Sony's 1630 or F1 have a flat frequency response up to 20 kHz (higher than most people can hear) and a theoretical 96 decibel range which is ample for almost every purpose. Some of the so-called problems of digital recording come down to it being so accurate that it faithfully reproduces technical shortcomings in the signal which in the past would have been happily masked by noise. Digital—especially now it is so widespread thanks to CD—means the engineer has to get it right. Direct to disk recording is now becoming more accessible to professional and semi-professional studios. The leading equipment in this area is currently Akai's DD–1000 (a dedicated direct to disk recorder), Digidesign's 'soundtool' (for the Apple Macintosh and Atari computers), the AMS Audiofile, and the Synclavier.

Home Recording

Not so long ago, the subject of home recording would have required a separate chapter all to itself. Home studios used to be lash-ups of domestic and semi-pro gear which created their own rules and operating difficulties. As the price of high technology has plummeted more recently, the dividing line between professional studio equipment and home recording gear has become more and more blurred, so that the same items are often found in both environments.

Most home studios are four- or eight-track, and many include DAT mastering. The differences between this and a pro studio lie in the number of tracks, the generally unsuitable acoustic ambience (acoustic treatment is one of the most expensive parts of fitting out a studio) and in the tolerance of the gear. Pro equipment is built to be hammered 24 hours a day and its higher quality of design and construction makes it hard to overload and less noisy. Home recording gear often needs to be handled more gently and carefully, particularly in terms of signal levels. On top of this, different working methods are needed when there is a shortage of tracks. A four-track portastudio doesn't offer the luxury of separate tracks for each instrument, so a lot of submixing has to be done in the course of recording a piece. This is achieved either by recording several instruments at a time on to one or two tracks, or bouncing tracks. Bouncing means recording, for example, three tracks separately, then mixing them together and recording the result on the fourth track. This frees up the original three tracks for new overdubs. This requires care and a crystal ball, since the balance recorded in the bounce can't be altered afterwards. Working this way demands that the portastudio engineer is far-sighted enough to judge how those three tracks are going to be placed in the final mix. It is this kind of lack of flexibility and shortage of options which generally differentiates home recording from the professional studio. As always the bottom line is cost.

Applying the Technology

Modern recording offers a vast palette of possibilities, so much so that it is all too easy to let technology swamp the music. It is also very easy to fail to bring out the music's full potential by not being aware of the creative scope on offer in the studio. The musician who can achieve an understanding of the possibilities and harness the studio's technology to his or her imagination is the one most likely to achieve artistic satisfaction from recording. Commercial success is an altogether different ballgame, requiring a combination of talent, luck, originality and a host of other factors more tenuous and often more sordid than mere knowledge. Over to you.

Further Reading

John Borwick (ed.), *Sound Recording Practice* (Oxford University Press).
Home Studio and Recording
Music Technology
Sound Engineer and Producer
Sound on Sound
Studio Sound

Part 2 The Business

· ·

13 Doing it the Right Way

· ·

HORACE TRUBRIDGE is the Musicians' Union Careers Adviser, previously having been the project co-ordinator of the Hackney Agency for Music Marketing Action (HAMMA), London's only free music business advice and information agency. As a founder member, songwriter and saxophone player, Horace played in the 1950s-revivalist band Darts from 1975 to 1985. In the early 1980s he also ran an independent record company, worked as a session player and appeared in West End shows.

From my experience in many areas of the music business, I offer my 'gameplan' for a band's success. If this is followed, it should let bands progress as far as their creativity will allow. This involves a lot of hard work. But although graft is indispensable, it is no replacement for raw talent. Along with luck, this is the scarce commodity which no one in the music business can manufacture and which everyone in the industry is looking for. I wish you lots of both.

The Right Stuff

The British music business is extremely competitive and only the bands who are prepared to commit themselves totally to their careers will succeed. When you are forming a band, try to make sure that everyone involved shares the same commitment and dedication. You don't want to work hard for a year establishing your act, get offered a tour, and then find that your drummer won't give up his milk round. Many bands break up because of personality clashes between musicians. For instance, if there is a conflict between the vocalist and guitarist, you can't ignore it hoping that it will go away. The chances are it will blow up into a huge row, or even a fight, just as you are about to go on stage at the Marquee. If you all get on well and are prepared to make the same sacrifices to succeed, you might just be 'the right stuff'.

Equipment and Band Economics

Adequate equipment is essential. So often there is an imbalance in the quality of a band's gear. For instance, the keyboard player may be using £5,000 worth of state-of-the-art technology while the bass guitarist is playing through a tired old AC30. This shows that this band isn't working as a unit. The keyboard player obviously cares more about advancing his or her career than the future of the band. To buy the equipment you need, open a band bank account and put in whatever you can afford every week. Probably, some band members will contribute more than others. As long as proper written accounts are maintained, everyone can be paid back when the band begins to make money. Also, keeping band accounts is useful to familiarize you with the practicalities of money coming in and going out. If you never lose sight of this information, you should be able to guard against extortion by unscrupulous industry entrepreneurs. Finally, try not to go wild with the amount of equipment you buy, because you can use money for other things. For example, if you hadn't spent so much on a 'super duper' multi-flange guitar pedal, you could have made a profit by having more band T-shirts on sale at your gigs.

The Band Sound

Every successful band has its own sound. Whatever music they play, you always recognize the band's unique style. This is the elusive quality which record companies look for. To develop your band 'sound', you have to identify it. If you rehearse in different rooms, setting up the equipment randomly, then it will take you a very long time to achieve this (the chances are you never will). It is worthwhile to choose a rehearsal room which suits your music, and stick to it. The first time you use the rehearsal room, spend as long as necessary setting up your equipment until each member of the band can hear themselves and everyone else clearly. Then draw diagrams showing exactly where the gear is positioned, where the musicians and vocalists are standing, and what the levels are on the amps and the instruments. From now on, every rehearsal should be arranged and set up in this way, so that your band will sound the same every time you rehearse. With this method, you should be able to identify your band's strengths and weaknesses quite quickly, and to write and arrange accordingly.

Tape every rehearsal on a portastudio or cassette machine, and distribute copies of the tape amongst the band well in advance of the next rehearsal. This gives each musician time to practise so that you all arrive at the rehearsal ready to try out new, revised musical parts. Taping rehearsals also reduces the likelihood of arguments about who played what at the last rehearsal. If you need someone to do the taping, either make it one musician's responsibility, or try to find

The Smiths

someone who would like to mix your sound at gigs. At this stage you don't need an experienced sound engineer. Enthusiasm and a willingness to learn are far more important, because working with a portastudio and a mixing desk in the rehearsal room will teach a novice engineer a lot about sound mixing. The advantage of this is that when you start gigging, you have someone out front who knows your songs, and who can either mix your sound or at least keep an eye on the house engineer.

The Team around the Band

Ideally, your basic team should be a roadie and a sound engineer. Your sound engineer should mix the out-front sound at every gig and attend rehearsals regularly to keep up with new material. Your roadie should organize transport to gigs, getting your equipment in and out of venues and also attend to any on-stage problems which may come up when you are playing. You may also have a manager who organizes the arrangements for gigs as well as developing new areas of work like contracts for recording, publishing, with an agency or for merchandising. If all goes well, you may eventually sign an agency deal so that you have someone booking your gigs and possibly arranging tours for the band. If you reach the stage where you are playing national tours, then you will also have a lighting crew, more sound technicians and maybe even wardrobe staff.

As soon as any contracts are offered you will have to engage a lawyer to negotiate on your behalf. And when the money starts rolling in, you will need an accountant to handle all of your financial affairs. As a general rule, it is a good idea not to choose the same accountant as your manager.

Style and Image

The UK has the most fashion-conscious record buyers in the world. Although some bands achieve success without considering their clothes and haircuts, these aesthetic qualities have an important influence over a band's commercial potential. Often, bands are naturally pushed into the style and image that is associated with their music, like heavy metal, gothic, hip-hop, punk and ragamuffin. All of these have an accepted code of dress which the people who buy these records also adopt. If your band's sound is less strongly defined, then you may need some help to dream up a style and image. Libraries are a good source of inspiration, and by browsing through the books and magazines on fashion you may get some ideas. Try the local charity shops as well. Many bands have taken on a style of clothes which they bought second-hand.

Making the Demo

Once you have rehearsed, you will need to record a demo, especially as many venues won't consider you for a gig unless they have heard you on tape. Ideally, you should record the three strongest songs in your set. Go to the best studio your budget will allow and remember that studios will often drop their price if you haggle. The most common mistake that bands make on their first recording session is to be underrehearsed. Usually that results in a lot of wasted time and money as you sort out problems which should have been dealt with before you opened the studio door. Also, uncertainty on your part can lead to the risk of you surrendering all control over the session to the engineer, who will be more than happy to move into the producer's chair. Try to meet the engineer before your sessions. Play him or her your rough rehearsal tapes of the songs you are going to record. Then you can explain the results which you want from the session and the engineer can advise you on any extra equipment which you may need to hire. This gives the engineer a chance to hear your music and assess how to record your band. All of this saves valuable and expensive studio time. Never combine mixing tracks with recording sessions. If you try to do it all in one go, you will almost always be dissatisfied with the result. Probably, you will end up paying for a remix. If you can afford it, spend two or three days recording your tracks, take away a rough mix and then go back to the studio after a week or so. Then you have time to fix on a definite idea of how you want the final mix to sound.

Getting Gigs

The main thing to remember when looking for your first gigs is that promoters, bookers and pub landlords aren't bothered whether you are going to be the next U2. Apart from a few notable exceptions, all they care about is feet through the door and selling beer. With that in mind when you approach them, stress that this is one of your first gigs and you are going to get all your family and friends along to support you. This should be enough to convince someone to give you a chance. However, you can't rely on your family and friends forever. You are going to need to develop a following if you want to move on and play bigger and better venues. Some bands think that just playing gigs will be enough to attract a following. The trouble with this attitude is that there are just too many bands around for that to happen. To give your band a better chance, you will have to do some marketing.

The secret of attracting more people to your gigs is to get your band's name better known. Currently, most people won't go and see a band who they haven't heard of. Similarly, people tend to assume that if they have heard of a band, then they are probably worth going to see.

If you can come up with an interesting band 'logo' or visual image, that can be a cheap way of self-promotion on stickers and badges. Just think of how many people will walk past and subconsciously absorb your band's name on a sticker which is on a high street lamp post, even if it only stays there for a couple of days. If only one of those people is wondering what to do on a Friday night, thumbs through the listings, spots your band's name, and thinks 'I've heard of that band, they must be worth seeing', that sticker, which cost you less than a penny, has been very cost effective.

T-shirts are worthwhile and can be very cheap to produce. Everyone wants an original T-shirt, and they are walking advertisements for your band. Also, you could put your regular fans on a mailing list, writing to them every month to inform them of your next gigs and urging them to bring more of their friends along, in return for a back stage pass to Wembley when you play there! Contact the local press and encourage them to write about the band and advertise or review your gigs. Put together leaflets listing your forthcoming gigs and distribute them around colleges, street markets, other people's gigs, and trendy clothes shops. If none of this works, maybe the band is just no good.

Doing the Gig

It is essential to have written confirmation from the booker or the venue of all the arrangements about your gig. The most important of these are the gear 'get-in' time, sound-check start and finish times, on- and off-stage times, the guest list allowance, the food and drinks allowance, dressing-rooms, PA and lighting details, and the fee.

Arrive punctually to be ready for the sound check at the agreed time. If you are in the support band, you will almost inevitably have to put up with delays in your sound check as well as other inconveniences. In this situation, it hardly ever helps if you start shouting or losing your cool. The best approach is to be patient and philosophical. If you arrive late, raise merry hell, and insult the stage crew you will certainly be remembered. However, if you are charming and efficient you may actually get booked again by the venue! Similarly, all sorts of things often go wrong on stage, and the golden rule here is not to communicate mistakes to the audience. The chances are that the punters only know an error has been made if the drummer decides to smirk at the guitarist, or the guitarist turns away from the audience to have a good laugh at the keyboard player. If you learn to keep your emotions in check until you are all back in the dressing-room, then at least you will leave the punters thinking that they have seen a professional band who might not be quite ready for a week at the Hammersmith Odeon.

Spare guitar strings, picks, and drumsticks should always be on hand so that any equipment breakdowns can be solved quickly and efficiently. When you finish your set, get your equipment off stage quickly. If you leave your gear on stage, you may find that someone else has moved it for you, and they won't be as careful as you. No matter how badly your set goes, if you have a professional attitude to your work and a friendly disposition, you will find that people will want to work with you again.

Doing a Showcase

The purpose of a showcase is to perform in ideal conditions to an audience mainly of music business professionals whom you have invited. This can be expensive and you are always gambling with the possibility that the people who you want to hear your music won't come. Usually showcases are paid for by management companies in an attempt to 'open the bidding' on a new act. Due to the cost and unpredictability of showcases, few bands without management arrange them. If you want to chance it, the first thing to do is book a venue. This will cost you anything from £200 to £1,000, depending on the hall's size, equipment and location. It is impossible to guarantee that anyone you invited will turn up, so you could try to guard against wasting your time and money by sending courtesy cars to pick up the more important people. If you go to those lengths, you are obviously taking a big financial risk. There are a number of showcase venues around London, most of them connected to studios. Often, showcases take place in the afternoon. To create more of an atmosphere, you could invite some of your ardent fans to indulge in the free drinks and snacks which are generally provided for the guests, along with a band publicity pack. This should contain band photos, a demo tape and a biography. Successful showcases can create substantial industry interest in a band, but if you are going to pull out all the stops, you have to spend a lot of money with no guarantee of a positive result.

Get to Know the Biz

By now, you should have reached the stage when your potential as a successful recording artist is evident. In this situation, you may only need to wave your tape under the right A&R person's nose to be offered a recording contract. But who is the right A&R person? Currently, major record companies' A&R departments are a lot more efficient than musicians realize. If you are regularly attracting a big audience at your gigs, then you have probably been seen by A&R personnel, whether you live in Camden, Cardiff or Carlisle. If you have worked hard to develop a solid gigging career and no one is offering you a deal, the time may have come to approach record companies directly. Sending tapes to the A&R departments is almost a total waste of time. Instead, you need to wise up about how the industry works and which people in recording companies are the most influential when it comes to signing and selling musicians' work. Reading the popular music press helps build a picture of which record companies deal in the different styles of music, but only by reading the trade papers will you identify the key individuals in each company who should be invited to your gigs and sent your tape.

The trade papers are expensive, but you could ask your local library to order them. Then, someone from your band can take charge or reading them through every week, taking notes on anything which might be useful. This way, you can make up a 'hit list' of personnel within companies to whom you want to send your tape. Once you have mailed out your tapes, it becomes somebody's job to phone all of these people everyday until you make contact and you get some feedback. When you do speak to your target people, it is important to emphasize that all you want is the person's opinion and that you will phone back in a couple of weeks to find out what they think. This process rarely runs as smoothly as I have suggested. Often, it takes months of phone calls before you have completed your 'hit list', and I would suggest that whoever takes on this job should have a very carefree and optimistic attitude. Eventually, you should have collected the opinion of everyone on your 'hit list' and, if no one has shown any interest in your music, you need to consider their reactions very carefully. If certain criticisms have cropped up consistently, you must decide either to correct these problems or to soldier on in defiance of market opinion.

Protect Yourself

Young songwriters are often worried about record companies and other artists stealing their songs. The instances of this happening are few and far between. Nevertheless, it makes sense to take a few simple precautions. Always mark your demos clearly with the copyright symbols (a letter 'c' in a circle) followed by the year in which the songs were written and the writers' names. In Britain, copyright exists as soon as a song is recorded on to tape or written on manuscript. It is easy to protect your songs' copyrights. The best ways are included in the 'Copyright and Performing Right' article in this book. Any musician who is seriously embarking on a career in the music business should join the Musicians' Union. The union will fight your case through the courts if someone tries to rip you off, it will check over contracts for you and offer cheap instrument insurance (see the Musicians' Union article for details). If you are offered any work on television or radio you will need to join the union.

The Buzz

The most effective way to attract record company interest is to create a 'buzz'. Everyone has heard that there is a big buzz going around about one band or another, but what does that mean? Usually, a band creating a 'buzz' is doing very successful gigs and totally ignoring the record companies. If you go to one of their gigs, you will see row upon row of A&R men standing at the back in their black leather jackets, all ready to make an offer to record the band. Don't think you have to be based in London to create a buzz, as recent history has shown that new music movements rarely originate in the capital. You are probably much better placed in your home town or nearest city. The main ways to produce a buzz are by being brilliant live and by winning over the media. If the popular music press start raving about you, people will flock to your gigs. If you are a great live act, they will keep coming back and so will the record companies. You should always keep the press up to date with what the band is doing and where you are playing. It may be worth sending them your demos, as well as pictures and biographies, and hope that someone takes an interest in you. Like most of your career, starting a buzz depends on the success of your gigs.

Any number of things can create your buzz—a much touted line of original band T-shirts, well-attended 'happening' gigs, or something as basic as an unusual band name. It is by no means unheard of for a band to be offered a deal on nothing more than a 'concept'. Your job is to go out and create as large a market for your band as is possible for an act without industry representation. If you achieve this, then a record deal is just around the corner, and you will have earned yourself a strong negotiating position which should enable you to sign the deal you want and not the first deal that is offered. It is important to realize that a deal's merits should not be judged solely on the size of the advance and the royalties being offered. You may feel that only a major record company can offer your band the right level of investment and promotion. But you have to balance that with the way a major won't allow you the same freedom of artistic licence and influence over your promotion and development that an independent company can offer. There are innumerable instances of bands signing large deals to major record companies only to find that the aim of the record company is to try and push the band in a totally unsuitable direction. When that happens it is rare for the band to win the resulting battle and emerge unscathed. In fact, months of wrangling between the band's manager and the record company usually ends with the band being dropped, by which time the other record companies who initially showed interest have gone cold. As in any large money-making industry there are crooks and con men masquerading as successful industry figures, and there is an understandable temptation to sign a deal with absolutely anyone after years of rejection. That is precisely what these crooks play on. As a rule of thumb never sign a recording/publishing/production deal where you are expected to invest your money in the recording or promotion of your material. This is certainly not a mainstream industry practice and the instances where this has occurred have largely proved to be cases of cleverly couched extortion.

Single Release

Releasing a single is probably the most effective way to promote a band. Initially, you only need five hundred records, the total cost of which can be less than £500. Once you have recorded your music, the first step to releasing it is to make the cuts. These are soft lacquer discs which record your 'A' and 'B' side from your studio master tape (these discs can be either 7" or 12", depending on your chosen format). The next process turns these soft, lacquer discs into metal stampers, and all your records will be pressed from these. There are lots of companies who will take charge of this whole operation, including the printing and fixing of the labels. Alternatively, you can sometimes save money by using different firms for each process. Look in the trade press to find them. If you want a printed sleeve for your record, you need them before the discs are being made so that they can be delivered to the pressing plant and bagged up. Five hundred picture sleeves can cost from £200 to £500 depending on the number of colours and the thickness of the card.

It is worth trying to get a distribution company to take your record on. Their cut will be around 30 per cent of the 'dealer' price, which is what the shops pay for your record, bearing in mind that your record will only reach the shops if the dealer asks for it. That is where the plugger and press officer come on the scene. If you can't afford them, you will need to do both jobs. Send your record to every DJ and radio producer in the country who you think might give it a play, and follow up your mail-out with a phone call. Also, send your record to journalists on all of the popular music press and phone them as well. If you can get some coverage, that may encourage the dealers to respond to the media's interest in you. If that doesn't work, you can always sell the record at gigs and get back your investment that way.

Pluggers and Press Officers

If you can afford it, hiring a press officer and a plugger will maximize the impact of your record. A press officer should try and gain exposure for your record through the·media. He or she should have good relationships with music press journalists and also have contacts within radio and television. He or she should mail out your single with a press release and photo to all their contacts. The press release will include information about the music and the band which you hope will be used in reviews.

A plugger's job is to get your record played on the radio. BBC Radio 1 is the most influential radio station in Britain and it is every plugger's dream to get their records regularly on to Radio 1's 'A' list. However, there are many other radio stations around the country that can influence the success of your record, albeit only on a regional basis. Your plugger should contact all the DJs with whom he or she has a good relationship, trying to persuade them to play your record.

To hire a plugger and a press officer, will cost you anything from £100 a week each, depending on their track record. Unless you have a personal recommendation, you can find professional pluggers and press officers listed in industry handbooks and advertising in the trade press. Three weeks is usually long enough to see whether your single is going to be a national success. If your record starts to pick up air play and get reviewed just after three weeks, it may be worth keeping yor plugger and press officer on for a bit longer. If the record isn't happening in any of the media, it is probably best to cut your losses and pay the bill. When you approach pluggers or press officers, bear in mind that this is how they make their money, and the amount of enthusiasm which they show for your product may not be a true indication of the coverage which they can secure.

Indies

The rise and fall and rise again of independent record companies is a topic of great debate within the industry. What makes a successful indie label? Everyone has their own idea but history shows that certain elements are essential to the long term success of an indie. It may take several releases and many months before the company starts to see a return on its investments, so it is essential for an indie to have a relatively solid financial base to see it through the difficult early stages and to sustain the levels of promotion until an act on the label breaks. Some of the most successful of the small indies have achieved success largely by catering for specialist markets (generally ignored by the majors) and developing a good reputation for its product with the fans of particular styles, so much so that some indie labels enjoy instant sales of a new release on the strength of the quality of their past product. This is called niche marketing which is a familiar concept in all forms of retailing. Situation Two, 4AD, Creation and Factory are good examples of this practice. These companies realized at an early stage that there is no point in trying to compete with the majors in releasing daytime radio or 'Top of the Pops' material, and that it would be better to find acts who have

Depeche Mode

proved popular on the live circuit but who are considered too left field for the majors. This approach has paid dividends for some indies and has helped to establish the following companies as real market forces: Mute with Depeche Mode, Rough Trade with the Smiths, Stiff with Madness, and more recently Silvertone with the Stone Roses.

Whether you sign a deal with an indie label, or release your own records, the success of your records will depend on the amount and quality of their promotion. A distributor won't take your record unless he or she can see a demand for it. Likewise, a dealer won't want a record taking up space in the racks of his or her shop unless he or she thinks the public will ask for it. People aren't going to request your record unless they have heard of it, and finally, they won't have heard of your record unless it has been promoted properly through the usual channels of TV, radio, music press, national press and live shows.

Your record doesn't have to be picked up by all these routes for promotion, but if you enjoy Record of the Week in *NME* at the same time as receiving good reviews of your live shows and the occasional play on Radio 1, this should allow you to make impression on the Indie charts or even the national top 100. This would be considered a success for a first release from a fairly new act. It is rare for an Indie band to take off big on the strength of a first record. The process is more gradual than can be the case on a major. The timing of your promotion in relation to your record's release date is crucial. The idea is to try and develop a steady build up of air play before the record is released so that on the week of release there is a good demand for the record and this reflects in your chart position. The real trick is then to sustain a high enough level of air play, press and TV to allow the record to 'cross-over' and appeal to people other than the band's fans. When this happens it is time to celebrate and consider all the various offers raining in from the major labels.

Don't Delay, Start Today!

I want to underline the biggest mistake which I believe bands make when they are starting out. Bands spend too much time chasing A&R personnel and other industry figures, and not enough time chasing punters, developing a following and creating a 'buzz'. If you can do those three, then the music business will soon be chasing you.

Further Reading

These are some sources of useful information about who's who in the industry. Those listed with addresses aren't always easily available in the shops.

A. Jenkins and O. Smith (eds.), *The Town and Country Music Guide* (Penguin).

Music Week magazine (bi-weekly)
The British Music Yearbook (Rhinegold Publishing).
The Making Music Handbook (Track Record Publishing).
The Music Week Directory (Music Week Publications, 40 Long Acre,
   London WC2E 9J2).
The White Book (Birdhurst Ltd., PO Box 55, Staines, Middlesex TW18 4UG).

14 Rock Journalists and How to Use Them

· ·

DAVE HILL began his career as a contributor to the *NME* in 1981, moving swiftly on to become music editor at London's *City Limits* listings magazine. By 1986 he had reverted to freelancing on several national newspapers and magazines before joining the newly launched *Independent* as rock critic. He now works as a general freelance feature writer for the *Guardian*, *Independent on Sunday* and *Arena* among others and has published several books including a biography of Prince.

Who Do They Think They Are?

There was a time when rock journalists were easy to characterize or, at least, to caricature. Wan and red-eyed, and nearly always male, they wore rebel chic regalia and communicated in either a hyperactive babble or a laboured monotone. They could be found, posing madly, directly adjacent to whatever was going free at any bohemian hostelry in town. They wrote for a small range of specialist titles, some of them bright and poppy, others resoundingly self-important, and all of them perfectly arcane to anyone outside a specific, like-minded clientele.

In this, the rock hack fraternity unerringly reflected the culture it documented. As a bizarre amalgam of egalitarianism, rebellion, idealism, moral sloth and wanton self-indulgence, rock generated the literati it deserved, from the early-1960s generation of giggly pop scribes (who pushed the old-school showbusiness correspondents aside) to the 'serious' boy obsessives who stumbled from the 1970s' underground, wielding big neuroses and even bigger words.

The post-punk era has made these convenient stereotypes if not redundant, at least seriously limited. Even apparently subversive convulsions like punk ended up encouraging rock's incursions into all sectors of modern consumerism, and so the music's press coverage has altered accordingly. Today, the specialist pop and rock rags no longer have the subject to themselves and only the most conservative publications on the news-stands fail to acknowledge that some sub-section of the now sprawling rock field is of interest to their readers. Indeed, the music industry can reasonably claim its market to include anyone from 5 years to 50, taking in both sexes and every social class. As a result, it is hardly surprising that everything from *Patches* to the *Daily Telegraph* employs at least one rock correspon-dent, from a teenage school-leaver in doorstep Nikes and a back-to-front baseball cap to some affable dilettante with a plum in his mouth and old school tie. Elvis has a lot to answer for.

Where do I Begin?

Aspiring rock artists should remember one golden rule when dealing with the press: there are no rules. Winning the favour of this curious breed is largely a lottery. Those with any degree of power and influence are already deluged with promotional material, atrocious records and pre-release cassettes, the vast majority supplied by the generously resourced press offices of major record companies. Only the most conscientious (and, frankly, those with nothing better to do) dutifully plough through everything that flops out of a jiffy bag and on to their desk. The few communications which do receive full attention normally achieve this through a combination of chance, inside information and relentless harrassment. As an unknown you can't rely on the first, and very likely have no hip London friends or business connections to facilitate the second. That leaves only the third, and even then any serious nagging offensive requires careful planning and execution to stand a chance of success.

First, select your target publications. The national dailies can be dismissed quickly, especially the tabloids. Unless you can promote yourself as a bit-part player in some concocted yarn involving Madonna, outlandish sexual indiscretions, wilful substance abuse or, better still, all three, they aren't going to be interested. At the snob end of the market, the *Independent*, the *Guardian*, and the *Observer* offer the most serious critical coverage of the rock world, tending to employ writers with some previous pedigree. However, editorial priorities are inevitably slanted against the exposure of new acts. When it comes to profiles and interviews, familiar names usually get the nod over the up-and-coming, partly because they are the ones the powers-that-be have heard of, and partly because the famous and/or notorious are what a less obsessive and more catholic readership wants to know about.

This inclination to celebrate the established rather than unearth the unknown is also echoed by many of the specialist titles. *Smash Hits*, easily Britain's biggest-selling pop magazine, is completely geared to reflecting the mainstream. You need to be either in the charts or heading that way to earn space in those gossipy pages. The same goes for its imitator, *Number One*, and also the reams of general interest glossies aimed at girls and women. In the end, the print media offer only very limited avenues to the exposure of bands and artists without industry backing or friends in the right places. What hope there is resides primarily in the same section of the news-stands as it has for several years—the 'serious' and 'specialist' music press.

Covering the broad territory of rock and pop *New Musical Express*, *Sounds*, *Melody Maker* and *RM* (formerly *Record Mirror*) are the longest-established weekly titles. Still blessed with a scent of what used to be called the counter-culture, they are also the most responsive to music generated from outside the mainstream corporate structure. Most of their readers are young, white and male and their interest in the music scene is intense. These four publications tend to reflect the range of musics which fit most neatly into the category of 'rock' (white music as opposed to the primarily black forms, 'soul', 'funk', 'reggae' and so on), although the emphasis varies from one magazine to the next. *NME*, for instance, has always included substantial coverage of black popular forms—soul, reggae, hip-hop—although this has not always met with their readers' approval. *Sounds*, on the other hand, is strongly orientated towards guitar-based white rock. Today's *Melody Maker* concentrates on pop's more adventurous independent fringes, while *RM* remains a likeable dog's dinner, differing from the others in its A4 format, its glossy colour pages, and content which veers from a left-field feature style to consumer-guides for club DJs.

All four are united by a healthy disrespect for dominant tastes and the remains of a reputation for exposing new talent before the industry finds it. The bad news for small-time acts is that this exploratory role has diminished significantly over the last ten years. In the period beginning just before the punk explosion and ending around 1982, the rock press played a decisive part in the making and shaping of a succession of trends from punk itself to Two-Tone, the so-called new pop phase and the emergence of quasi-mystical underground acts like Echo and the Bunnymen. The tight links between journalists and the flourishing independent label scene, local entrepreneurs and key grass-roots venues meant that they all helped to form tastes rather than simply reacting to them. However, as the industry became more organized, the rock papers have declined in importance. This is reflected in the pre-eminence of the smart, highly professional and rather conservative rock monthly *Q*, launched in 1986. With little of the didactic or combative attitude which characterized *NME* during the late 1970s, *Q* concentrates most successfully on giving its affluent, young male readers what they already know they want. Currently, *Melody Maker*, written by a verbose array of excitable young ideologues, is the most dissenting and innotative of the four general titles and the one most inclined to put some avant garde confection like the Sugar Cubes on the front page before anyone else has heard of them.

The other group of music papers which aspiring acts should look to are those catering to some very specific style and its devoted audience. The most successful title of this type is the heavy metal bible, *Kerrang*. Founded by a breakaway group of journalists from *Sounds*, it has gone on to outsell its progenitor and, though primarily star-oriented, considers it has a duty to reflect the grass-roots scene as well. It is an obvious place for young hard rock/heavy metal acts to make themselves known. In a similar way, exponents of anything fitting the nebulous description New Acoustic Roots (and its variants) should keep a keen eye on *Folk Roots* magazine (monthly) for potential sympathizers; jazz practitioners should get the studious *Wire* (monthly) and those operating in the more popular black fields of soul, funk, rock or rap should follow the perennial *Echoes* (weekly, formerly *Black Echoes*) or *Blues and Soul* (biweekly). There is also a steady turnover of smaller, and often short-lived, black music mags reflecting underground phenomena like hip-hop. Regular perusal will make clear which journalists might be most sympathetic to your particular style.

Finally, don't forget the entertainment pages of your own local papers or the arts coverage of college magazines. Their patronage may not launch you to instant international attention, but they might help to raise the takings at your next gig in the Junior Common Room or village hall, simply by listing the date, time and place.

You now know who it is you want to impress. The next stage is to take a long, hard look at yourself.

Who Are You?

Except in the most arid and scholarly publications, your value to journalists can never be measured simply in terms of the quality of your music. So before you embark on your campaign of harrassment, put yourself in the shoes of your prospective target. First, ask: 'Why should he or she want to write about me?' Second, and just as important, consider: 'Why should his or her editor want to publish an item about me?' The crucial point is that having a great sound is one thing, but being a good subject for an article may be something else entirely. For that reason, it is worth thinking about what is interesting about you from a journalist's point of view before trying to woo him or her with your beautiful noise.

It is no coincidence, for example, that stars like Boy George and Morrissey enjoy so much front-cover exposure. It isn't only that they enjoy commercial success and critical acclaim, but because they are, in the jargon of the trade, 'good copy'—talkative, controversial, witty and opinionated on a whole range of topics. Journalists just pop them a question and let them get on with it. The subsequent article almost writes itself.

But you don't have to be as colourful a performer or as vivid a personality as these two to make an interesting subject. From the journalist's position, any sign that you have put some thought into your music, your look or your lyrics, is welcome. Stock responses like 'well, you know, we don't really think about it that much, actually', send the hearts of even the least demanding interviewer plummeting into their boots. So before you start trying to make contact with the press, try to figure out what is engaging or unusual about you. It could be your background, your experiences, the audience you attract or anything that smacks of idiosyncrasy. Whatever else you do, *please* avoid musicianly prattle about your favourite brand of guitar strings.

Such an exercise of critical self-analysis will not only help make you a more appetizing prospect as a subject, it will probably benefit you artistically as well.

The Leisure Process

Once you have decided which of your manifold assets to emphasize, you need to get practical. Rock journalists receive far more unsolicited material than they know what to do with. The bulk of it, though, is just standard major record company dross which is greeted with a yawn and propelled directly into the nearest rubbish bin. To avoid this routine ignominy, you need to turn the journalists' boredom to your own advantage.

1. Printed Matter

The staple mode of communication is the press release. This comprises, quite simply, one or more pieces of paper on which are typed details of forthcoming gigs, record releases or just general bits of news and information relating to individual artists. With new acts, a brief biography is also often included by way of introduction. Record companies generally send these out some time before an event or the release of a product in order to whip up a bit of advance interest from the press. The reasons for this are obvious. Firstly, the bare details find their way into the news sections of all relevant publications so the artist's fans can place orders at record shops, apply for concert tickets and generally help to build up the (ahem) 'buzz'. Secondly, it gives individual journalists due warning that they should plan any prospective coverage to coincide with the artist's activities, simultaneously responding to public interest and amplifying it further.

The trouble with most biographies and press releases is that they are boring—very, very boring indeed. The press officers who compose them aren't employed for their outstanding literary flair and their missives routinely come replete with weak jokes and dismal puns. What a joy it is to find a press pack that is genuinely unusual, interesting, witty, self-deprecating or even just plain mad. Since unknown, unsigned acts have no one to compose such epistles but themselves, there is a great opportunity to bring a little sunshine into a cynical hack's life. Economy is the key. Get to the point, tell people what they need to know and do it with as much style, clarity and substance as possible. The corporate communiqué can be set out on anything from regulation A4 paper with a staple in the corner, to grandiose box presentations containing 'sampler' cassettes or compact discs previewing the alleged highlights of a forthcoming release. However, any sceptical correspondent worth their salt will show far more respect for a personalized, do-it-yourself presentation with a touch of imagination rather than all the glitz in Hollywood.

2. Cassettes

Naturally, any prospective support from a journalist will depend most of all on what you sound like. Ultimately, if people don't want to hear you, they don't want to know you. Once again, many rock critics receive enough tapes—and, for that matter, video promos—to build a model village. As ever, the knack is to make yourself stand out from the corporate crowd. Obviously, the way you sound is up to you, but it is worth deploying all the resources you have to ensure a decent quality of recording and to present the cassette in an appealing way. It is a dull dictum, but true, that if you give the impression you care about what you do, then others are more likely to care about it too.

Again, economy is important. A C30 tape is usually quite long enough and, assuming your songs are of average length, three of the best will do nicely. And make them your most accessible. If they are listened to at all, it will probably be in the bath, on a car stereo, or in some other environment where the music is competing for the listener's attention. If journalists are going to like you, they will make their minds up quickly and it is a positive advantage if they like what they hear, but haven't got enough. It means *they* have to get in touch with *you* to ask for more. On the other hand, if they are unmoved by the first track or two, it is unlikely they will bother with numbers three to fifteen anyway. But whether they love you or loathe you, never expect to get your property back. Just think of it as a loss leader and keep your fingers crossed.

3. Gigs

Folklore insists that the best way to lure a usually male journalist to a gig is to offer him a drink. Certainly the kind of modern-day would-be Kerouac who survives entirely on the proceeds from trading-in free albums and indulging in the fine art of 'ligging'—tagging along to any show in town where the record company picks up the catering bill—is not extinct.

However, aspiring unsigned acts with a reputation to make aren't likely to be in a position to sweeten up the hordes of sceptical scribes in the West End of London who spend their days loafing from one free lunch to the next. In fact most young bands aren't based in the capital at all and it is a long-standing complaint of artists with their souls in the provinces that the concentration of the national media in London obliges them to abandon their regional roots.

That said, one of the best chances an unknown has of national music press exposure is in the live review section. There are several reasons for this. One is simply that you don't need to have made a record or done anything very much except earned a local reputation as a watchable band playing original material. This alone can make it worth a reporter's time to come along. Artists based outside London should certainly make it their business to locate each publication's local 'stringer' whose job it is to reflect the scene in their own city or town. Very often the live review section's smaller items are written by junior reporters who are more willing to make their way to obscure gigs if it means getting their by-line in the paper. Keep your eyes open for the names of new writers on the magazines you read regularly and try to make contact by letter or telephone. Convince them you are worth a look and, almost out of the blue, you might end up with 300 words in *Kerrang* or *Echoes* or the *NME*. If they are favourable words, it could be the first write-up of many.

4. Nagging

All the press releases and all the triumphant pub gigs in the world will amount to nothing unless you are prepared to nag. As a species, rock journalists are often dedicated free spirits, either too young or just too immature to believe that the normal responsibilities of life—good manners, for instance—might apply to them. This means that the thankless task of nagging is of an elevated importance in the unknown band's armoury of skills: the less notice they take, the more you need to pester them. When you have sent off your pristine cassette, your witty biography and your complimentary tickets, the next thing you need to do is make a follow-up call: 'Oh hello. I was just calling to make sure you received our tape/tickets/press release . . . Yes, it is in a turquoise envelope with a silver band insignia and a Grimsby postmark . . . You've found it? good. I'll call in a couple of days to see what you think. Bye.'

The voice at the other end may be sullen, bored and indifferent or else cheerily superficial, but don't let that put you off. Remember, in five years' time, most of these people will either be press officers (doing the same as you are, but with less loving care) or they will have been kicked upstairs to edit a page instead of writing on it, thereby saving readers from any more of their insufferable prose. Obviously, go with your instinct, but as a basic approach, try simply to be polite. Don't give them a sales pitch because there is nothing more irritating. Just make friendly noises and go away. This is the best way to lay amicable foundations for your more concerted efforts in the days and weeks to come as you try to prise a response out of your carefully selected target hack. Lastly, don't expect too much. If you can get them to absorb your material at all, that counts as an achievement. If they like it, that is rare. If, finally, you get any column inches out of it, buy yourself a drink, cut out the precious words carefully and make a pile of photocopies. Even if you have been made the target of naked literary abuse, it will make satisfying reading when you play your first sell-out show at Wembley!

Eye of the Tiger

For freshly signed artists as well as unknowns, encountering the press is a new and sometimes uncomfortable experience. Rock isn't the art form of the chattering classes and only a minority of its practitioners have any expertise in elucidating a rigorous conceptual rationale for their work. Meanwhile, those garrulous starlets who utter a quotable phrase almost every time they open their mouths are few and far between. This means that interviews are often an ordeal for inquisitor and subject alike.

The trick here is to know what you want to say and make sure that you say it. Politicians do this all the time, turning any given question into a cue for making the point *they* think is important and never mind what their questioner wants to hear. There is no need to go quite that far with the pop scribes of this world, but the principle is worth keeping in mind. Often, the journalists are far more neurotic and insecure than you are. After walking in and setting down their pocket tape recorder, they soon reveal themselves as inarticulate and badly prepared and the whole encounter is punctuated with long, awkward silences. On the other hand, some writers take a more interrogative approach, grilling their beleaguered subjects from a prepared list of queries ike a policeman in search of a conviction.

From a personal point of view, the best interviews are the ones which become conversations, discussions which proceed on an equal basis, that are informal but still retain some kind of shape. Ideally, all that needs to be said can be said in an hour, and if you think the journalist is genuinely interested in your work, try to give him or her as much time as required—it is appreciated.

It takes the co-operation of both parties to pull this off and all artists would be wise to give their general interview method some thought in advance. One obvious, important factor is to consider which publication the journalist is from. A sweet young thing from *Smash Hits* isn't going to be after the same kind of material as some cerebral haircut boy from *Melody Maker* or a hack from your local paper. Plainly, individual journalists have individual styles but ultimately they have to turn the result of meeting you into the type of article their publication requires. *Smash Hits* will want to know about your make-up or your boxer shorts, *Melody Maker* leans towards aesthetics and primal therapy and the local *Argus* might just want to know a few biographical details and where your next gig is.

It is also worth working out how to create the best conversational chemistry. Many bands feel that each member should be present at every interview. This is commendably democratic and can work perfectly well, but sometimes the intimacy of one-to-one conversation yields more interesting results for both parties. Usually, one or two of the band are more chatty, outgoing or just plain pretentious than the rest. These are the people to let loose on the press. Remember, your value to a magazine isn't only your prowess or popularity as a musician. People can enjoy reading about you even if they don't like your music and if enough of them do, it improves your chances of more coverage the next time you need it.

The End

Although the total press coverage of pop music increased dramatically over the last ten years, the quality hasn't improved and the power of music papers to make and break an artist has greatly dissipated. As a medium through which to secure your fame and fortune, even those publications for whom discovering new talent is an important role aren't the force they were. Record companies have become far more adept at monitoring and exploiting new acts, and their links with the smaller labels—who they once only heard about by way of the left-field rock press—are now thoroughly institutionalized. Though they would hate to admit it, the rock press was once the most important stepping-stone on the way from obscurity to celebrity. There are now other routes to follow.

But although, in career terms, it may currently be more effective to woo record companies rather than journalists, the rock press isn't a completely spent force, nor is it a worthless one. What decent journalists have that most people in the pop industry don't, is a proper critical faculty. Spiteful, verbose and stupid though rock hacks can be, they are at least sometimes driven by something other than the logic of the balance sheet. If you take your music seriously and arouse the interest of a committed writer, the resulting article can make a genuine contribution to people's understanding of your work and of popular culture in general.

With more and more people getting their pop information from our squalid popular press and with most modern magazines covering music using only the language of consumerism and gossip, it is increasingly difficult to feel optimistic about rock journalism's values. At its best it remains one of the few areas of the modern press where imagination, honesty and idealism, however fatuous, can still, occasionally, be found. A positive interaction with these characteristics can only be to the benefit of artists and their followers alike. It might even make you a star.

15 Management

· ·

ED BICKNELL is manager of Dire Straits who he says that he wanted to represent within five minutes of seeing them live. Before his management career Ed worked as a drummer, had been Hull University's social secretary and was a successful agent representing British and international artists. This is an edited version of an interview with Ed at Damage Management's London offices.

Managers and Artists

The most important relationship in any artist's career is with their manager. A manager tries to co-ordinate, push and stimulate everything concerned with the music business to get the artist's product in front of the public. To achieve this, the manager needs a knowledge of the record industry, music publishing, concert promotion, tax and of how to run a business; as well as how to keep the act's family happy. A complete job description almost defies definition.

The best I can do as a manager is a combination of threatening, cajoling and being nice to everyone who can help to give my act the best possible shot. However, the artist must play an active part in their business career. When the record is finished and the studio door is finally shut, the artist has to get out and sell. They have to do the tedious promotional work, the dodgy TV shows in Belgium and the interviews at American radio stations where no one knows who they are. It is a treadmill, but if an artist isn't prepared to do it, there are two or three hundred others just waiting for their chance. There are certain things I won't do as a manager. I didn't get into music to be a travel agent, have people's gardens done, or to arrange their mortgages. That is a trap which people get into with acts and it is very dangerous for both sides.

Managers are focal points in the music business. They co-ordinate the production and promotion of an artist's music, making it possible for the music industry to have a success. For instance, this can mean persuading record companies to spend money on adverts and employing pluggers. Even with a band like Dire Straits that can be quite hard, because there is sometimes a certain complacency surrounding a big artist's release. The music business marries art and commerce. However, the artist's aims may not be the same as a record company's. So the manager has to vet what big business wants musicians to do.

Managing a New Band

Ideally, the manager should be there at the beginning of a band's professional career because he or she is going to operate the various deals which are set up. Generally, it is best for him or her to have some input into the management and other contracts instead of inheriting them from a lawyer. Lawyers mainly deal with the theory of things whereas an experienced manager is concerned with practicalities. I have seen clauses in record contracts which are absolutely meaningless and which I would happily have traded for a defined amount of money for a tour support, video, or promotional commitment.

A manager has to create an environment in which a new act can get on with their music as free as possible of worry about business. The first thing to do is sort out the basis of the young artists' business. The manager has to organize their companies, hire them an accountant and a lawyer (if they haven't already done that), get them VAT registered, and do a lot of simple administration like applying for passports. This organization is very important because the business structure with which the act starts ought to be the one they have forever.

Next, the manager would want to find the act a record contract, even before getting a publishing deal. Most publishers won't pay artists any money until a record has been released in a major market because the publisher has no other way of recouping any investment. Currently, getting a record deal for a new act is difficult. This is partly due to the increasing technological influence on songs. A lot of records are broken but not many careers are established. There is a difference.

For a new artist to progress, the most important management role is allowing the act to develop its songwriting potential. Ultimately, it doesn't matter how well a band's guitarist plays, if an act doesn't have good songs they will go nowhere. That is what it takes to become internationally popular and to have a longlasting career. If a band don't write their own songs, the manager has to find the right

Tina Turner

songwriters. The best thing Tina Turner's management ever did was to find the songs for her *Private Dancer* album. One happened to be by our client Paul Brady, and 'Private Dancer' was written by Mark Knopfler. The only difference between Tina Turner today and a few years ago is her material. She has always been great, but she made a tremendous jump when she started recording decent songs instead of versions of old R 'n' B tracks. Songs are the lifeblood of pop music, and all the artists I have represented have been heavily involved in songwriting.

A manager has to believe totally in a new act. If that isn't why he or she gets involved, the manager shouldn't be doing the job. The manager must work to ensure everything is in place so that the band's product comes out in time for the public to make up its own mind. If the talent which the manager believes in is recognized by the public, then hopefully they will go and buy the record. But if the act doesn't get success, two things may happen: the record company will probably drop the act, though they may try one more record; and the finances of running the band will probably cause the act to go bust. The manager can manipulate some things to stave that off, but pop music is about being popular. You need to have hits. If musicians want to do jazz albums or make obscure folk records there are routes for that. However, a band would be doing incredibly well to sell 15,000 jazz LPs throughout the UK. For pop and rock artists, success has to be measured by records selling in millions.

Artists need time to develop. Once the rollercoaster of success gets going, the most common problem in pop music is the second album. An act can make a successful first LP which may have taken five or seven years for a band's songwriters to create. Suddenly, the music industry is demanding album number two within four months. To cope with this, the manager has to try and stave off time pressures without losing the momentum of gaining popularity. This is an extraordinarily difficult balancing act, particularly with new artists. After their successful first record, they can go into the studio without proper preparation. They might jam a bit and produce substandard material because they are trying to satisfy the record industry's mania for following up success. Often this situation doesn't allow the artist enough time to write good new songs. My attitude is that if a band manages to release a second album of poor songs four months after their first album left number one in the charts, it isn't worth the rush. If Mark Knopfler took five years to produce another record, and it was a classic, I don't have any worries. I have to allow the songwriting people within this operation to have the time and security of mind to get on with their art.

However, it can be dangerous when an artist becomes very established. He or she can go to seed having bought a mansion and put a million pounds in the bank. Part of a manager's responsibility, with new and established acts, is to keep the stimulus going which makes the artist want to write, record and perform.

Live Work

Live gigs are the most interesting and enjoyable part of my work. I have a great live band, probably one of the best in the world. However, there are lots of acts who can't work live very well. Despite this, it is amazing how many managers put inadequate live bands on tour. It is self-defeating. The problem with a lot of acts is that they don't realize their limitations. As a result, they go on tour without knowing how to produce a good live show. If I were taking on a new act, their ability to perform on stage would be second only to the quality of their songwriting. Of course, I am leaving out the personality element. If the manager doesn't get on with the band, the whole thing collapses. I have to like the act and their music. If one of these things were missing, I couldn't do it.

To set up a new band's live work, a manager needs to organize things like equipment, crew, trucks, boats and planes (given the constraints of economy), and get a decent agent and promoter. For a new act, I would have to pitch them at the right venue for their type of music. It is part of the manager's brief to make sure the artist isn't put into the wrong level or type of venue. For instance, people have booked white country bands into rap clubs. Having worked as an agent, I always take care of Dire Straits' concert bookings and I have made that sort of mistake with them. I booked them into a working men's cabaret club in South Wales. I didn't know what it was, and they had to play in-between bingo sets. Fortunately, they were professional enough to do the gig, but it served no useful purpose.

It is very difficult to marry up the sale of a record with a live show. An established live act will almost certainly play to people who have bought their records. This doesn't necessarily apply to new artists. As a band's career develops, by album two or three, most of the concert audience will own at least one of the band's records and probably all of them. In that situation, the band isn't using the live gig to plug their current record, like an appearance on the 'Wogan' show. Instead, they are establishing a relationship with the audience, not by promoting the current record, but by securing a future audience for the one they haven't even made yet.

As long as a band can physically and economically do it, I would want to take their music to the people wherever they are. Dire Straits have persistently played in Belfast, Tel Aviv and Auckland, not just London, Frankfurt, New York and Los Angeles. That has made their tours very long and everyone needs enormous stamina and commitment. If I were interviewing a new act, I would try to ascertain their sheer punishment factor. During a tour, the Straits' live show is three hours a night, but they travel for at least three hours a day, as well as doing interviews, a sound check, eating, and phoning home. As a manager I have to judge whether a young band's professional tail is wagging the domestic dog or the other way round. This is something a lot of people ignore. I need to find out how my acts view their lives. Do they want a family? If so, when? It is important to realize an act isn't a robot. There are plenty of people in the music business who would like it that way, but I have to bear in mind that people get ill, home-sick and miserable. For instance, touring is very boring. The show is great, but after a three-hour musical high, it is back down to sandwiches on the bus, trying to find somewhere to eat after 2 a.m., or getting into the hotel when the night porter has locked up. Touring is so important. I would never take on an act who couldn't perform live. It would have no interest at all.

Live work is the one area where the artists and audience meet face to face. In most other circumstances, the public is one step removed from the artist, holding a record or watching a TV show. At a concert, the band actually meet their fans. The Straits make a point of having autograph-hunters back stage in the dressing-room so they can stay in tune with their punters. There is an idea which creeps in, particularly among younger musicians, that after a few hit records they are somehow better than other people. They aren't. They happen to do something where there is an enormous organization geared up to pushing them on to a pedestal. I have never mollycoddled any of my artists. I don't use limousines and the Straits have only needed a security person once. If I meet a new act, I always try and assess their maturity in order to judge whether they might go off the deep end as soon as they have success.

Fan Clubs

Fan clubs are a situation where a band can't win. For most people, music is just a part of their leisure, although inevitably there are some who want more from it. For the very young pop acts, there are very large numbers of teens and schoolchildren writing to them. With the Straits we get a fair amount of mail each year, most of which is easily categorized. They want information about what the band is doing; or they want to know where they can get T-shirts, sweatshirts, concert tickets and other merchandise. To deal with this, we established an information service. This isn't a fan club. Members get newsletters, the option to buy tickets first and some fans have met the band. If I were managing an act like Bros, I would run a professional fan club. However, one of the problems with fan clubs is that they tend to operate for very young people. There is an exploitative element to them. You are unlikely to offend the teenage punter, but you may disturb their parents. This is a very narrow line. Often there are letters in the papers from parents who have sent off for T-shirts and pictures from a band's fan club, only to have their cheque cashed and to receive nothing for months. I believe that if an act wants to run a fan club, it should be a service rather than a profit-making enterprise. Ours regularly loses money, as do those of many other major artists. My attitude is that if somebody has taken the trouble to write a letter, they deserve a reply. To be very hard-nosed there is also a vested interest in running an efficient information service for a band. If we can write back to somebody, or send them the CD or shirt they want, we will almost certainly have them for life. Most people are amazed to get an answer from the band at all. So it is good business and public relations to try and answer these enquiries.

Finding Bands

Most acts who approach me fall into two categories: new and established. The new acts can be divided into those with and without a record deal. Those still looking for a record deal usually send a tape, some photographs and a biography. I play the tape and make my judgement. I don't know any more than other people what is likely to succeed. I just have to react to what I like and what I can believe in. After twelve years in management, I haven't yet had a tape arrive which I thought I could do anything with. Statistically, I get far more phone calls from record companies, lawyers and very occasionally from publishers telling me about a new act they have just signed. They send me exactly the same as unsigned bands except the tape is invariably a finished master of high quality. Again, I have only rarely heard anything which has interested me. With established acts the same thing happens. I often get calls from their lawyers, sometimes from their record companies, and extremely rarely from the artists.

For most major managers the problem is time. The music business works in cycles. Bands and their managers tend to have periods of relative quiet, maybe for six months, after which they are in a fever of activity. This means managers have to be careful when considering whether to take on a new act. If I were to begin to manage another major artist, and Mark Knopfler were to ring up and ask me to get the band back together for an album and a world tour, something would

Mark Knopfler

have to suffer. Probably it would be the efficiency with which my artists' careers are dealt with, and my brain.

In the UK, we have a tradition of management firms with only one or two clients. In the USA, there are massive companies which have fourteen or fifteen acts. They operate by using fourteen or fifteen tour managers with fourteen or fifteen acts going to fourteen or fifteen gigs in fourteen of fifteen trucks. Vast amounts of money are made and I find it all very boring. Having tried it both ways, I am more comfortable with the single act approach, and in the history of rock management, that has generally been the most successful route. Management is a very personal service. A new act's problem is that if they approach an established manager, he or she will already be representing at least one major act. New acts are attracted by First Division managers because we are visible and our addresses are in *Music Week*. What new acts really need is the embryonic version of these people. All of us started from a very low position. Quite a lot of top managers had been in the agency business. Although young bands can find the established people in *Music Week*, they are probably a waste of time. They may get to one of these people if they get a record deal without a manager, and if their record is a mega hit, but that is very unlikely.

With most young bands, the manager is often the guy who owns the van. He or she may even be the local greengrocer who hears a band rehearsing down the road in the village hall. Sometimes that works, though problems can arise when the band gets down to London. Suddenly the greengrocer/manager has to choose between a safe livelihood and dedicating often sixteen or seventeen hours a day to the hurdle race of the music business. The reason it worked for me and the Straits was threefold. I genuinely liked them as people, I loved their music, and I was in exactly the right place at the right time. If it had happened two years earlier, I couldn't have coped. However, when I first encountered the Straits, I was a successful agent, thinking about leaving the agency business. I didn't have it in mind to go looking for a four-piece group. Like most managers, I don't seek out groups, even at showcases.

The Artists, Their Money and Their Manager

Most top managers are very honest. Amongst these people, the idea of ripping off an act is offensive. Paul McGuinness (U2), Roger Forrester (Eric Clapton), Roger Davies (Tina Turner), Bill Curbishley (The Who, Judas Priest) or myself don't concoct ways of conning our acts. Most of us have been with our artists a very long time. We regard our work as a team effort. It may not be a legal partnership, but it ought to be one ethically.

My golden piece of advice is not to have the manager handling the artist's money. In the history of litigation in rock 'n' roll it is almost always about money. Any artist I represent could tell me I am useless, but no one will ever be able to claim I stole from them, because I have never had the opportunity. There is one exception to that with the Straits. For purely practical purposes, I deal with the artists' money for recording and touring expenses. It is too complicated to send large numbers of bills over to their accountant every day. To cope with this, I set up separate clients' accounts with the bank with some funding from the band's accountants. All the bank statements and back-up bills go to the band's accountants to be audited, together with a complete statement of income and expenditure. On the 248 dates of the 'Brothers in Arms' world tour, the entire accounts were only £4.04 out of balance. However, I don't handle the band's royalty income from records and publishing. Those cheques and statements arrive here, made out to the band's companies. We check the statements, file them and send them on to the band along with our commission invoice. Any manager who does handle the artist's money is taking a foolish risk, as well as letting themselves in for an enormous amount of unnecessary work.

Management Commissions

The commission arrangement shouldn't leave either side resenting what the other is getting. Traditionally, management commission rates have ranged from 15 to 25 per cent of the band's gross income. The manager's commission doesn't have to be the same on everything, and my initial rates with the Straits were set by their lawyer at the beginning of our relationship. At various times I have altered my charges on particular areas. On radio, television, sponsorship, sessions and producer work I take 20 per cent because those things are often rather fiddly, involving quite a lot of work and not producing very much of a financial return. The commission on records is between 15 and 20 per cent, while on publishing I got 15 per cent until Mark Knopfler voluntarily put it up to 20 per cent. On live work I used to get 20 per cent. They were losing money on their early tours so to help them I dropped the touring commission to 10 per cent. When the band became profitable on the road, it went back up. In fact, the Straits raised this an extra 5 per cent just before the 'Brothers in Arms' tour in recognition of the agency service which I have always provided. This sort of relationship is ideal!

When working out commission rates the most important factor is the artist's ability to pay. If an act is starting out and the manager immediately takes 25 per cent of their money, the band are almost certainly going to be in financial difficulties. That doesn't mean the manager shouldn't take a considerable share of the act's income at the beginning. The manager will have business overheads which make sure he or she can do the job properly. My office costs £5,000 a week to run, employing four people. That has to be paid before I or my partner get anything. There is no point in the act giving the manager only 5 per cent and then complaining he or she doesn't turn up to their shows. The manager probably can't afford to get there.

When a band starts out, they could pool everything with their manager. Also, some people do deals on the net income. There are co-operatives in which the manager gets the same as the band members and the manager's office expenses are treated as a band cost, along with the trucks, boats and recording. However, the subject of commission rarely crops up with major artists. I have probably discussed it less than five times in twelve years with the Straits.

Good Management

The manager is the manager because he or she takes the job on. As Colonel Parker said 'I'm Elvis's manager because I say I am, and Elvis says I am'. Most people get into management because they find an act they want to work with. They don't necessarily need to know what management is, they can learn all that. Managers have to believe in their act because the low points can be very low, even though the high points are exhilarating. If I have ever had any doubts about my work with Dire Straits, I pull out one of their albums and play it. That is enough, I am back up straight away. The manager has to be honest, competent and use common sense, while getting on with the artist. I have been lucky enough to have almost the perfect relationship with my act. We have a very similar Northern background, are roughly the same age and have the same sense of humour. Apart from the music, that has really helped us to stay together. The greatest compliment Mark Knopfler ever paid me was in a magazine when he was asked to list the members of Dire Straits. He said that apart from himself, the band would be John, Ed and Paul. I thought that was great. Working with Dire Straits has always been a vocation for me. The others have just been a job.

16 Booking Agents

. . . .

CARL LEIGHTON-POPE runs Prestige Talent agency, part of the Bugle Group of companies which includes IRS records. He began in the music business running a recording studio and in band management. Carl moved into agency at NEMS in the late 1970s and after a few years was instrumental in the formation of the PAN agency. In the 1980s Carl has managed several successful artists and has run his own companies, Bonair Records and Bonair Songs. This is an edited version of an interview with Carl at his Prestige Talent offices and in the back of a taxi *en route* to a band's showcase.

An agent deals with live gigs, concerts and touring. To that end, the agent meets with an artist's management and its record company to decide the best touring period. This is usually linked with an album release date. Together, we assess when the album should reach the market place, and from that the agent books the territories where the band is to play. From talking to local promoters we decide the level at which the band is to work. That is measured by the size and capacity of the halls in each territory. Deciding on the right level for a band depends on the policy ideas which characterize different agents. I favour the approach that if the band is worth 2,000 people in a town, then it is smart to book the 1,500-seat venue. If there are two or three hundred people left outside trying to get in, there is a certain excitement surrounding the gig. Other agents would choose a 2,500-seater for the same band. They put pressure on the record company and the promoter to sell those extra 500 seats. However, I believe that particular gamble is often lost by negative press coverage. Instead of reporting the number of people at the gig, journalists query the 2 or 300 empty seats in the hall and question whether the band is really gaining popularity. If there are 2 or 300 people outside, the gig is sold out, and that term still has a certain magic in the music industry.

The Ticket Price

Having decided the touring period and the size of halls a band will play, the agent's job is to work with local promoters to determine the ticket price. After agreeing the hall's capacity, this is the most important decision during the tour. To set the ticket price, the agent has to look at what is happening in the industry, what an average ticket price is, and what the touring artist is worth as an attraction. A ticket price directly affects a concert-goer. When it is set, the artist is immediately linked with an amount of money in the public's mind. In the UK, there is still something magic about the £10 figure. If an artist's concert can be priced at £9.50, people don't consider it especially expensive. The aim with pricing is not to sell your act cheaply and not to leave the audience feeling ripped off.

Having decided on the capacity of the venue and the ticket price, it is simple to multiply one by the other to 'gross the hall'. Most halls are one ticket price. If the ticket price is £10 and there are 200 people in the hall, that is a £2,000 gross. After VAT has been paid, the rest of the money is split three ways: to the act, to the promoter, and to the cost of the event.

Costs

While planning the gig, the agent works with the promoter and looks at the event's costs. These include security, staging, promotion, marketing, radio adverts, catering on the night for the artist, carrying the equipment in and out of the hall, the PRS percentage, the hall hire, as well as the printing and distribution of posters. The list is very long! Once these expenses have been fixed, the agent goes to the record company and tries to reduce the event's costs. The agent may suggest a joint postering campaign, advertising the band's album on the gig's posters. Another idea is to split the cost of radio adverts. The record is played during the advert while the gig's details are broadcast. The reason for reducing the event's costs is that the less money which is spent on the gig means that more money goes to the artist.

Having deducted the costs after VAT, 50–60 per cent of the money taken from ticket sales is left to share between the promoter and the artist. Depending on the reputation of the artist, the agent makes a deal to split this percentage of the ticket money from 70:30 up to 90:10 or 95:5 in the artist's favour. If the artist is a major attraction, whose concert tickets are certain to be at premium, a 90:10 deal is likely. In that case, the promoter receives 10 per cent of the net and the band gets 90 per cent. However, a 90:10 deal after costs also means that every expense is borne in that proportion. If the band spends a lot of money in the venue (with a big stage extension, an early 'get-in' to the venue, playing very late, or running up an enormous catering bill), all of these costs are paid mainly by the artist. Every pound spent on these extra expenses is one less pound which can't be split between the artist and the promoter. For each pound of these costs, the artist pays 70, 80 or 90 per cent in lost revenue, depending on the percentage split between the artist and the promoter.

The agent also has a vested interest in keeping the event's costs at a minimum. The agent is paid by commissioning the artist. Whatever money the artist leaves the venue with is the amount which the agent can commission. This is around 10 per cent. The exact commission figure is a matter for negotiation between the artist's manager and the agent. The art of making a good deal as an agent is to keep the promoter's costs down, while allowing him or her a sufficient budget to make sure the event is successful.

Guaranteed Fees

Most bands work on a guaranteed fee against a percentage. For instance, if the net gross is £10,000, and £4,000 of that pays the event's costs, there is £6,000 to split between the promoter and the band. The agent's trick is to persuade the promoter to guarantee as much of the artist's share as possible. This is the moment when the promoter has to demonstrate faith in the act's ability to do good business. If an 80:20 deal is negotiated, the £6,000 should be divided with £1,200 going to the promoter and £4,800 to the band. The ultimate deal is for the promoter to guarantee the band the whole £4,800. This proves the promoter's confidence that every ticket will be sold, committing him or her to paying the artist a fee as if the event is a sell-out, however many people actually attend the gig. When there is a certain amount of risk involved in an event, most promoters opt for paying the minimum amount of guarantee possible against a larger percentage for the artist. In this situation, the onus is on the band to sell all the tickets and to come out with the extra money. If the band don't attract a sell-out crowd, the promoter's risk has been minimized. Then the promoter only has to pay the band the guaranteed fee plus costs.

The 'Gross' Deal

The agent can also make a deal with the promoter on the gross and not the net figures. The agent would agree with the promoter that for every pound taken on the door, the artist will receive a certain percentage. As an example, this could be 50p of every pound. The agent and artist don't care what happens to the other 50p, whether it is spent either as the show's costs or as the promoter's profit. The promoter simply has to guarantee the artist's 50p. In this case, the agent only needs to see a ticket manifest (a government-stamped document showing how many tickets are printed for the venue) and a box office statement from the hall (stating how many tickets were sold) when checking the promoter's expenses. If 1,000 tickets were sold at £1, the promoter would take £1,000. If the deal were 50 per cent of the gross, the artist takes £500 and that is the end of the matter. If the agent cuts this type of deal tightly enough, the promoter is forced to think twice about spending money. However, if the deal were, for instance, a 90:10 split and not a gross deal, the promoter would realize that for every pound he or she spends on costs, 90 pence of that pound belongs to the artist. This could lead the promoter into spending more money on advertising than may be necessary because only 10 per cent of these expenses are his or her costs. But if the deal were a gross deal, then the promoter would look to save as much money as possible. The disadvantage of this is that some promoters underadvertise, underpromote, and undermarket the gig to try and put more pounds in their pockets by reducing their expenses. Here the artist can often suffer by not selling a lot of tickets, while the promoter loses money as well.

Promotion

The result of good promotion can be a sell-out. It is great to drive through a German city and see full colour posters for your band with a ribbon across the poster which reads: AUSVERKAUF (sold-out). This raises the status of the ticket in the public's mind. Kids walk along the street, look at the concert poster, see the band's name and read 'sold-out'. They realize they may have missed an event. By doing that, an advance ticket-buying market is created. The next time the band plays in that town, kids will run out early and buy tickets. They won't want to be the one in their class, group or gang who missed buying a ticket having known the show was sold out last time. This is just one way a band can build up its market in the territories it tours, from a 500- or 1,000-seat club up to a 10,000-seat arena.

Talent Acquisition

As an agent my strength is in my clients. I can't rely on people coming into my office and booking artists. In my early years, I set out to find a roster of acts who I would represent. One of my first artists came through a very old friend called Richard Ogden who now manages Paul McCartney. Then Richard managed a band on Virgin records called the Motors. Richard played me their record and invited me to the end of recording party. I met the guys, loved the songs and they asked me to be their agent. Richard wanted me to book thirty shows in the clubs and I did. I had also been very friendly with Jeff Jukes and Max Hole (Max is the managing director of Warner

Brothers and Jeff manages the Fixx and Rupert Hine, a very established producer). Max and Jeff managed a group called Camel. This band were doing very good business in the town halls. They had just done a big concert at the Albert Hall with an orchestra for an album called *Snowgoose*. They came to me because they were unhappy with their agent and wanted to change to me. Richard Ogden was working on the Motors with a lawyer in New York, Charles Levison, who later became the managing director of Arista records in the UK and managing director of Warner Brothers. While he was at Arista, Charles and I got to know each other well. I impressed him with my work on the Motors and Camel. He had Patti Smith on Arista who had released a big hit, 'Because the Night'. She wanted to do some concerts in Europe and I booked the tour. Andrew Bailey, an A&R man also at Arista, asked me to look after a young guy named Roy Hill. This is the typical career pattern of a lot of agents.

Apart from demo tapes, agents find new acts from four sources within the business. The main source is record companies. Young A&R guys are out every night looking at bands. They sign an act whose manager is inexperienced and asks for advice on choosing an agent. Record companies look at agency rosters, like mine, or those of Barry Dickens (Fleetwood Mac, Bee Gees, Bob Dylan) or Ian Fluke (Eurythmics and Simple Minds) and they choose the agent who is suitable. Two other sources are becoming more productive of new talent. One is lawyers and the other is accountants. These professional advisers to musicians have immense importance to the longevity of an artist's career and the retention of his or her wealth. Pat Savage and O. J. Kilkenny run a very successful accounting firm. They represent Van Morrison and U2. They knew Van needed an agent and suggested I speak to him. These recommendations go on all the time, but they are recommendations and that is all. The agent has to make the artist believe he or she can do the job. The fourth way of finding acts is from among an agent's existing managers. Jeff Jukes managed Camel in the 1970s and the Fixx in the 1980s. They are both clients of mine. If Bruce Allen signs another act, hopefully he would come to me after my work with Bryan Adams and Lover Boy. Managers are not necessarily as transient as acts. A successful manager may manage five or six bands in his career. If an agent does a good job with the first one, and builds a successful relationship with the manager, there is no reason why that agent can't deal with all of a manager's acts. However, if an agent is enjoying the wine with a Bryan Adams, he or she may be drinking the vinegar with a manager's smaller act who makes much more work than the bigger act, with absolutely no income. Here the agent is investing in the small artist,

Bryan Adams

trusting the manager's judgement that this act should go on to be the next big thing.

I look at the charts every week. If there is something interesting, I make a call to the record company and find out whether an agent is in place. If there isn't, I speak to the manager and arrange a meeting. I saw Bryan Adams on the front of his album. He was wearing a T-shirt and jeans and looked perfect for the UK market. I listened to the record. It was a rock 'n' roll record which is my kind of music. I called Bruce Allen, his manager, and we met in Germany. Bruce also managed a band called Lover Boy. I agreed to represent Lover Boy and Bryan Adams throughout Europe.

The younger acts are the major problem in the music industry. At Prestige Talent, we have three young agents learning the business from booking colleges and clubs like the Borderline in London. We need these people to be our filters and talent scouts, going out to gigs and finding new bands. However, 90 per cent of the bands we sign attract us either with recently recorded product or with a record due out on release. It is now virtually impossible for a major London agency to book gigs for many acts who don't have a record deal. The agent's problem with acts who are still looking for a deal is how to judge their potential for success. If an agent decides to invest in an act for the first year of its career, this band may not sign a record deal. In fact, they may split up, probably owing the agent money. Agents have to regard these young acts as an investment. The safer investments are ones with more people involved. If the agent knows that a publisher, a record company and a manager have all invested, at least he or she can feel there are a number of people needing this act to be successful.

Young New Acts

Bands can't make it alone. They must have a team of people to present their case to the industry. The industry doesn't like dealing with the artist direct because that makes it difficult for music business professionals to be as critical or as observant as they would like. The business wants to deal with a representative. Young bands have to find their own team (agent, manager, publicist and others) to put around them and to believe in their music. The most effective way of finding support is through gigs.

Any major music paper, such as *NME* or *Melody Maker*, lists the telephone numbers of music clubs and pubs and these places do book young bands. They put on new acts if they are called direct and are sent a rough demo tape. Some members of a band could go out in the evening and pop into a whole bunch of places to ask if they will give them a gig. They won't pay a young act any money, but they will let them play third on the bill on a Monday night or on a Thursday night when there aren't many people in the venue. Bands have to stay out there. They have to be seen. Nothing happens while you are rehearsing in a garage. Nothing at all. Record companies, managers or anyone in the music business can only notice your music if your band is at a venue playing in the public eye. For example, I have been at a venue like the Marquee club to check out a band for a record company and have also watched 30 minutes of the first act. Most often the support band are terrible, but they could have been great and they could have been you. You might have been up there playing and somebody like me or a young talent scout from a record company might have been in there to look at someone else, to talk with a club owner or having a drink. Maybe they would feel there was something interesting about your band. Our young bookers look at about ten acts a week. Most of these aren't signed, but if we look at them early and register our interest in the act, we hope the band will consider us to be their agent when they have a record deal.

As an established agent, I have to remember that our big acts of today were our little ones of yesterday. I look after several young bands. One of my successful young bands is Del Amitri, who are on A&M Records. This is a Scottish rock band (every album has to be categorized to some extent in order to sell it). After meetings with A&M Records and the band's management, we realized Radio 1 wasn't necessarily going to welcome this band with open arms. This posed a particular problem for an agent. Usually, an artist can be booked out on the strength of a record's popularity and radio air play. As the band's agent in this case, I had to work with the record company to circumvent the rigid Radio 1 Top 40 format. We opted to promote the band at a local level, and not nationally. This avoided putting full page ads in *Melody Maker*, *NME* and *Sounds*, and hoping somebody would read them. Instead, we booked the band into pubs and clubs all around the country, anywhere we could. Wherever there was a gig or a support, we took anything for Del Amitri. The moment we had a gig, that city was faxed through to the record company marketing people. They instructed us to tell the promoter that they would give some money towards the gig's adverts in the local papers. The record company told their sales rep to go into the town's music shops with T-shirts, get the local papers promoting the act and put the band into the local radio station. The following day the band was in another town, the day after that somewhere else. As the band were good enough live, we could build up a ground swell of interest at a local level which then translated into national success.

The Problems of Success

After young bands have had a couple of hit singles, with their album selling well, everybody wants to see them perform live. Everything is going right and the act have a very good chance of success. However, modern artists haven't always played live very much and 'paid their dues'. They haven't worked in the clubs and colleges, building themselves up over the years. Suddenly, they are put into a situation where the expectations of their performance are much higher than they can possibly deliver. That causes a problem. The record buyer who has fallen in love with the band, and goes to see them play, is often disappointed by a lacklustre show. It isn't the fault of the band. They have become wildly popular, with their record sales and media profile, without knowing how to work with an audience, how to project, how to sell their performance or how to deal with their emotions on stage. Why should they? Probably they hadn't been on stage more than half a dozen times before they were put under this microscope.

The Making of a Good Agent

A good agent really understands the route a band has to take and must have a great relationship with his or her promoters to persuade them to believe in an artist. Although the agent represents the artist, he or she also must represent the promoters' interests. A lot of agents don't subscribe to this idea. I believe that the more promoters to whom agents sell acts that lose money, the less people there will be around to do business with. When an agent is cutting a deal, he or she needs to leave something for everyone. The agent must ensure the promoter makes enough money, and that the manager doesn't squeeze the promoter's profit margin too much.

Getting into the agency business isn't as easy as it may seem. A lot of young agents and bookers come from colleges where they have started as social secretaries and begun to book bands. The advantage of this is that social secretaries deal with other people's money, so a few wrong decisions won't hurt their own wallet. During their work on a social committee they can build their relationships with people in the industry, like agents selling bands and record companies helping with marketing and promotion. To become an agent, these social secretaries simply have to reverse their roles with the agents who have been selling them acts for the previous few years. If an aspiring agent doesn't go to college or university, there is no reason why he or she can't apply to an agency and come in as a very junior person to work their way up. This business is open to opportunists and opportunity. Getting in can be quite difficult, but once you are in and you work hard, it will work for you.

Agency Fees

For a young band first starting work with an agency, the normal commission rate is 15 per cent. The agent takes 15 per cent of the band's earnings, which has nothing to do with the band's costs. If a band rents a van or hires a roadie, that is of no interest to the agent. The agent's percentage comes from the band's gross earnings at gigs. When an act becomes more established, or if it is a new band with good management and someone who knows the business, the agent may make a 10 per cent deal—the standard commission rate. There is a 'Mr 10 Per Cent' feel about being an agent and there always will be. However, if you become a superstar artist, the agent's 10 per cent quickly starts to dwindle.

17 Major Recording and Publishing Agents

BRIAN SOUTHALL is a consultant to various music business companies and a freelance writer. His career in music began in the mid-1960s, editing and writing the pop page of his local Essex newspaper. From there he moved to the trade paper *Music Business Weekly* and on to *Melody Maker* and *Disc* before joining A&M Records as press officer. He held a similar position at Tamla Motown before becoming the head of press at EMI Records. During 15 years with EMI he worked in artist development, marketing, promotion and public relations, and on leaving the company in 1989 he was the director of public relations and communications, EMI Music Worldwide. He has published a history of Abbey Road studios and wrote the BBC Radio 1 special, 'The House of Wax', two programmes narrated by Cliff Richard telling the 90-year history of EMI.

The Structure of a Record Company

Record companies throughout the world operate in the same basic way. They all try to achieve two simultaneous goals—success and profitability. EMI Music Worldwide is one of the world's big five music companies along with CBS, Warners, BMG and Polygram. It operates in thirty-seven countries around the world and in 1988 celebrated ninety years in the recorded music business. The activities of all its record companies, whether they are based in Europe, Asia or South America, centre around recording, manufacturing, distribution, artists and repertoire, sales, promotion, and marketing. In some countries, EMI record companies aren't involved in all these operations. Manufacturing, for example, is often carried out in one regional centre. However, the areas of marketing, sales, and promotion are at the heart of every record company. From wherever the music and artists originate, their recordings have to be marketed, sold and promoted, and this applies to international superstars as well as emerging talent.

The size of EMI's operation in any country is determined by the size of the local market, the availability of promotional outlets (i.e. radio and television stations), and the number of local artists signed to the company. The business of music publishing uses the same approach. The size of each national publishing company is determined by the depth of the international song catalogue to be promoted, and the songwriting talent available locally. The business of artists and repertoire, commonly abbreviated to A&R, is the most important part of any record company. Charged with the task of discovering, signing and developing artists, the A&R staff are the first point of contact with a record company for the new acts who are intent on becoming the superstars of tomorrow. Before analysing the role of the A&R department in both record and music publishing companies, it would make sense to look at the other areas which create a fully operational major record company: manufacturing and distribution, recording studios, marketing and promotion, sales, professional advisers, and the international division.

Manufacturing and Distribution

This is concerned with the manufacture of records, music cassettes and compact discs (generally known as 'product') in factories owned and operated by individual record companies. These factories are mainly concerned with manufacturing product for artists signed to the record company. However, they also do contract work for other record companies which don't run their own plants. All finished product, whether it is for EMI or another record company, is transported to a distribution centre. From there, it is delivered to shops or to the warehouses of other record companies. Telephone orders placed by retail dealers are processed at the distribution centre, and their requirements are 'picked' from the storage lanes and packaged for delivery to shops.

Under the direction of a senior executive, the M&D facility is responsible for maintaining appropriate stock levels of the raw materials with which to manufacture records, cassettes and CDs, including labels and inlay cards. Record sleeves, which are printed and produced by specialist printers, are delivered to the plant in quantities specified by the record company's own production department. Similarly, the quantity of records, cassettes and CDs to be manufactured is set by the company's sales and marketing departments. This reflects the probable initial demand for each release. With product that has a regular and consistent sales pattern, the factory is responsible for ensuring that the appropriate levels of stock are maintained. The supply of all product to shops is in direct response to retailers' orders, which are placed either with the distribution centre or with the company's sales force on their monthly calls.

Sales

The company's sales division consists of a national team of representatives who sell all product. As well, there is a strike force to concentrate on singles. This smaller team takes records to shops which have a high singles turnover and also carries the most popular current albums to top up a shop's supply of its best-selling products.

On every release, targets are set for the whole sales force by the sales manager or director, in consultation with the marketing division. Each month, the company's new products are presented to the sales people by the marketing teams. The sales staff show these new releases to retailers who decide whether to place an order. If the finished product isn't ready when the sales force make their monthly calls, advance cassettes, track details and campaign plans will be presented to the retailers instead.

Most major record companies have experimented with selling other music-related items such as T-shirts, posters, calendars and books. Almost all companies have decided that these items are best left to specialist manufacturers. However, record company sales forces do supply music videos to the limited number of record shops which stock them.

Recording studios

These are often owned and run by record companies. EMI Music, for instance, owns the famous Abbey Road studios in London and the Capitol Tower studios in Los Angeles. Artists don't have to use their record company's studios, but most companies encourage this. Studios owned by record companies can also be hired by any artists and producers.

Marketing

Within a record company this involves planning campaigns aimed at record retailers and the record-buying public, along with the press and promotion staff who deal with newspapers, magazines, radio and television.

After it has been decided to make a record, these departments, together with the artist's manager and the A&R staff, discuss the release date. Under the direction of a marketing director, artists will be allocated to a label manager, a press officer and a promotion person. Their responsibilities include ensuring availability of the master tape to suit the release schedule; overseeing the production of artwork for the sleeve's manufacture; preparing the appropriate campaign for the single or the album release; and keeping within the promotion budget which is prepared with the marketing director.

In addition, they decide the quantity of the initial pressing of their artists' recordings (for a new artist's first single this would be around 5,000); they liaise with the manufacturing plant to ensure further stock is available if it is needed; and they avoid producing stock which would probably never be sold. The label manager also organizes promotional material like T-shirts, badges, picture discs and special limited edition sleeves (in the right quantities to ensure maximum effect and minimum waste). Along with the press and promotion staff, the marketing department has to ensure that every potential record-buyer is aware of their artists' work.

Assembling the right creative material, such as publicity photographs, sleeve designs, poster and advertisement material, is important for all artists. This material emerges from a series of meetings between the label/product manager, the artist and their management. Often artists have an idea of the image they wish to create. For this, the choice of the right photographer and designer is critical. Some record companies have their own in-house designers. These are usually the smaller, independent labels. Major companies call on many of the world's leading photographers and designers.

The Promotion Team

The company's promotion team supplies records and promotional videos to all major radio and television stations, as well as arranging appearances by artists on particular programmes. Without radio play, a record can disappear without trace. The public will rarely buy a record they have never heard, particularly when it comes from a new or unknown artist. Regional promotion ensures that TV and radio stations throughout the country are supplied with all the material and information available. Club promotion reflects the importance of dance clubs and the contribution they make towards a record's popularity.

The Press Department

The press department is responsible for ensuring that records are sent to all major reviewers, as well as placing and arranging artists' feature articles and interviews in appropriate publications.

Marketing Records

Singles released by major, established artists often benefit from a substantial marketing campaign, with posters and media advertising. The cost of this is covered by increased singles sales and the eventual high sales of the album. Clearly, the more successful and popular the artist, the greater demands there are from TV, radio and the press, while the promotional video will also be sought after by the media.

The release of a single by a new act doesn't usually result in a major marketing campaign. While relevant trade and some consumer advertising will be placed, this early stage is more about attracting radio play and media coverage. On the radio, the company can get the record heard by the public. Newspaper and magazine articles create an interest in the artist. As singles usually make a loss for record companies, being 'tasters' for the album, any large marketing campaign would only increase this deficit.

A new band's first album ideally follows some success with a single. That doesn't always mean a high chart place, although it would be very helpful! Good reviews, favourable media coverage and positive response from radio all serve to create a 'buzz' for the artist and promote interest in the album.

For the album, the marketing department constructs a campaign with appropriate advertising in newspapers and magazines, posters on buses, in the tube, at railway stations and on advertising hoardings, plus support for any live dates.

Live work for an up-and-coming artist is vital. Although record companies aren't in the business of promoting tours (see the agent's article in this book), they will lend their support to ensure their artists' performances are in the right venues. Sometimes this back-up will be financial.

Releases from major acts have a bigger push and the marketing budget is much larger. As TV advertising campaigns cost hundreds of thousands of pounds, there must be a guaranteed sales return to justify such expenditure. For this reason the concentration on TV advertising is on compilation albums and greatest hits collections.

Packaging

The packaging of all artists' product is vital. This is debated and discussed between the artist, manager, marketing staffs and the A&R person in order to create and present a consistent 'face' to the public. It is unlikely that the record company would enforce their views on a new artist over publicity photographs, clothing styles, sleeve artwork or video plans. However, these are the very subjects that need clarification and agreement before a record's release or the setting up of any tour dates and making of a promotional video.

International Division

On the international level, major record companies operate a marketing and promotion division. Its responsibility is to create awareness, both in and outside of the company, of current artists' product.

Under the direction of a director (or a vice-president in the United States), the international operation co-ordinates the simultaneous, world-wide release of major artists' product; and it organizes the delivery of new and developing artists' records, promotional material and videos to all overseas companies where these recordings are considered for release. The decision to release new product in overseas territories is made by each local company, taking into consideration the musical preferences of their own market.

When a record is released overseas, the international marketing division works on the promotional opportunities which exist locally, ensuring artists are available to visit those countries where there is radio, TV and media interest.

Professional Advisers

Within each record company there are financial and legal departments who play an important part in the company's investment programme, like signing artists, acquiring labels and assessing manufacturing capacity. They draw up contracts, ensure appropriate legal protection for copyrights, advise on recording and marketing budgets and check that royalty payments to artists and producers are made in a timely and accurate fashion.

While the final policy on all major legal and financial matters is set by the company's managing director or president, the advice offered by these specialist executives improves the efficiency, profitability and overall performance of the company.

Artists and Repertoire

This is the usual first point of contact with a record company for an aspiring artist. As a result, many young acts regard the A&R staff as the ultimate decision-makers: career makers or breakers, heroes or villains.

More often than not, the A&R personnel are working to a brief. They may have noted gaps in the company's roster of artists which need to be filled. Major record companies, by the very definition of the world 'major', are intent on targeting different audiences with specific styles of music. To achieve that, they need a wide spread of artists.

Balancing an existing roster is of primary importance to a major company, whereas some smaller independent companies can and do concentrate on a particular sound or style of music.

The question most often asked of A&R people is 'What happens to all the tapes sent in?' The answer is simple. Unsolicited tapes are allocated to the various members of the A&R team. They review them and respond accordingly. Usually a standard letter is sent if the tape is unsatisfactory or inappropriate. However, if there is something of interest, one of the A&R team will make contact with the artist, assuming there is a contact address or telephone number on the tape (it is remarkable how many tapes arrive without these basic details).

The second popular question follows almost automatically, 'What are the chances of getting a deal from an unsolicited demo tape?' The answer is not encouraging. One in 5,000 is a rough estimate. Record companies receive between 80 and 120 tapes in an average week. As Nick Gatfield, director of A&R for EMI Records (UK) says, 'In three and a half years at EMI I have signed only one artist from an unsolicited demo tape.'

According to Gatfield there is one obvious way of reducing the odds:

It is all about presentation. Send in a good quality tape with no more than four songs. Choose the songs which show the widest range of your abilities, and put the best one first. Also, include a brief biography and, if possible, a picture. It is as plain and simple as that. Some of the tapes we receive arrive on dodgy cassettes, have various bits and pieces of other music on them, and we have to waste time trying to find the relevant bit of the tape. Frequently there is no contact number, so even if we like the music, we can't do much about it.

The material included on any demo tape, to gain the attention of A&R staff who are listening to tapes all week, should be strong, properly presented and preferably original. 'Cover versions can give an assessment of singing ability', says Gatfield, 'but not star quality. I believe that non-writing artists need a staggering voice and great charisma. We are really looking for original material performed in an original way.' Star quality is the ingredient which is almost impossible to define and most sought after by record companies. 'Essentially what I look for is a star, somebody with great character,' confirms Gatfield. 'Of course, it is usually the front man, the singer, who needs to have that special appeal.'

The visual presentation of a new artist is another area of interest to A&R people. Presenting songs on video is a real bonus for the record company. 'Producing a video is fantastic. Every piece of material we have helps to assess an act. We don't expect videos from emerging artists because they can be very expensive,' explains Gatfield. 'Leaving videos aside, I won't sign a band without seeing them perform live, if that is possible. People are going out to see live bands again, and gigging is an important factor in establishing new acts. Diesel Park West sent us incredible demo tapes, but I would not do a deal without seeing them perform live.'

The role of management in the first stages of a band's career should not be underestimated. As Gatfield says,

all artists should look for management very early on. They can certainly get record company interest without management. However once a record deal is signed the value of good management becomes obvious. In addition to the A&R department's other duties, we also teach and help new, inexperienced managers who bring acts to us. Inefficient management makes life very difficult for everybody, artists, record companies, agents and promoters alike. A band's early live dates may attract interest from management companies who already have artists signed to record companies. These are the people who open the doors which are closed to unsolicited demo tapes.

New artists without management could buy the annual directory published by the British music industry's leading trade magazine, *Music Week.* This carries a list of managers plus all record company addresses. However, managers have their own criteria before signing a band to their 'stable'. The easy part is identifying the manager you want. The hard graft may be persuading him or her to do the job. Like record companies, managers want to hear good demo tapes, see a good live show and identify the act as having excitement and potential. Of course, not all management companies and managers are based in London. Every city and many large towns have a management company which can open doors and who are in regular contact with A&R staff, anxious for news about outside London.

With or without management, Gatfield has a few words of warning for up-and-coming hopefuls determined to make an impression on record company A&R people.

Don't pull stunts. Don't turn up and play live on the back of a truck outside the record company. It was probably effective the first time, but now it is looked on as a desperate move, a last ditch attempt to gain attention. Don't arrive at the record company expecting, even demanding, a meeting. You won't get an appointment. Send tapes in, or leave them at reception. The A&R people will listen to them at their own convenience, which may be at midnight after a gig or on a flight across the Atlantic. A&R staff don't listen to a tape for the first time in front of a new artist. Finally, don't assume winning a talent contest is a passport to success. We avoid all invitations to judge or sponsor such competitions. They lack credibility. If an act is good, we aim to be aware of them already. We never offer recording contracts as prizes, although we are constantly asked to do so. There are enough places around the UK in which to play live, create a 'buzz' and catch our attention without competing with jugglers and animal acts.

As most new artists signed by record companies are introduced to A&R departments by established managers, or by music industry lawyers, artists should consider approaching more than just a record company when seeking a recording contract. This situation also raises accusations that the record industry is an incestuous business in which the old pal's act dominates at the expense of new undiscovered talent. Nick Gatfield disagrees. 'The music business is a small community which communicates by word of mouth. Any artist should seek out those people who can get them closer to a record company.'

The lucky few who are offered a recording contract must understand what they are signing. As with any legal document, a record contract contains clauses and phrases which are not easily understood by the layman. 'To ensure that artists are fully aware of all conditions and clauses we will offer a list of music industry lawyers for them to choose from if they need help with the contract. We will not sign any artist who doesn't have legal representation. This is as much for their protection as ours,' says Gatfield (see Mark Melton's and Mark Boomla's articles for details of the legal and financial aspects of recording, publishing and other contracts).

There are other ways for aspiring stars to catch the attention of a record company. According to Gatfield,

the music press is read avidly by A&R departments to find anything of interest. These papers do review unsigned, up-and-coming acts and this is a useful source of information. Also, anyone in the company can suggest names to us who may be worth checking out. In particular, sales people in the regions often notice or see promising local bands.

We check this information with our talent scouts. We have two people working in A&R who are rarely in our offices. They spend seven to ten days in a particular area, seeing bands, checking out the local press and radio stations, getting contacts for future reference. These scouts need to be aware of new fashions as they happen so we can react immediately.

Before detailing the terms of a recording contract, Gatfield insists that artists who have been rejected should keep trying. 'It is important that acts don't just send in exactly the same tapes time and time again. Go back and work at it some more. When you have something that is absolutely right, something you are proud to present, send it in.' Artists who had been turned down can't expect assistance from a record company which already has a number of signed acts needing help and attention. As Gatfield points out, 'I can't work on a host of acts who I am vaguely interested in, just in case one day they come up with something exciting. If there is something of real interest to us, but we aren't ready to do a deal, we keep in touch and might fund a demo tape or some rehearsal time.'

The Recording Contract

'Any artist thinking they have made it when they sign a recording contract is totally wrong,' warns Gatfield. 'That is when it really all starts.'

The Advance

As new bands get a pittance for live work, the record company put them on a wage which can be in the form of an initial advance. For instance, an album deal will mean 50 per cent of the advance on signing. This can be paid out weekly or monthly. The remaining 50 per cent woud be paid on delivery and acceptance of the album.

In football, the world's major players are invariably signed to the world's top clubs. In music, the world's top artists are most often with the world's top record companies. Contracts offered by major record companies are basically the same. Artists sign a world-wide, long-term deal, and the record company is committed initially to releasing one or two singles and an album. The record company, however, holds annual options to extend the deal up to five, six or even seven albums.

A Major Artist Deal

World-wide deal for seven albums

Advance (recoupable)	£1.5m per album for first four albums; £2.0m in total for the remainder
Recording costs (recoupable)	£150,000 to £250,000 per album
Video costs (recoupable)	£300,000 to £500,000 per video
Manufacturing costs	35p per cassette 50p per album £2 per CD
Marketing costs	£60,000 per album
Unit sales required for:	
Contribution break even	700,000 albums and 550,00 singles
To recoup advances	1.6m albums and 1.3m singles

Signing major artists is a highly competitive business. Often it involves a long chase in which the relationships between the record company personnel, the artist and the manager can be the deciding factor. This example of a major deal outlines the money paid to the artist as advances for a seven-album, world-wide deal, with recording and video costs recoupable. An essential part of such a major deal is that the album from an established artist is launched into the market place with a strong impact. This is the reason for the committed marketing budget. This amount confirms the record company's belief in the artist. In turn, the artist supports the album by undertaking promotional work and, where possible, touring when the album is released.

A deal of this size, done by a British record company and covering the world, requires success not just in the UK, but also internationally. The British market represents about 8 per cent of the world-wide record business. The USA has 33 per cent, followed by Japan (14 per cent) and Germany (9 per cent). However, there have been times in the recent past when 50 per cent of the artists selling and succeeding in the USA have been British. Also, UK-based artists have been regularly responsible for over 30 per cent of the world's record business.

Unknown Artist Deal

Worldwide deal for five albums

Advance (recoupable)	£30,000 to £75,000 per album
Recording costs (recoupable)	£100,000 to £120,000 per album
Video costs (recoupable)	£30,000 to £50,000 per video
Manufacturing costs	35p per cassette
	50p per album
	£2 per CD

Unit sales required for:

Contribution break even	110,000 albums
To recoup advances	350,000 albums

When signing a new artist the negotiating strength mainly lies with the record company. However, the offer of a first record deal should not result in a 'sign at all costs' attitude from the artist. An unsigned act which is being chased by half a dozen record companies does have some leverage in negotiations, but only as much as the levels of supply and demand will allow. In the end, a record company makes a judgement on the value and potential of a new band. The company is rarely persuaded to change that assessment, even in the light of competition from other companies.

The unknown artist deal reflects lower advances and reduced recording and video costs which sustain the emerging act through the development stage of their career. A new artist with this sort of deal should expect to receive a royalty rate of 10–14 per cent of the retail price. This figure would include any producer's royalty.

As recording and video costs can rise with the artist's gradual development, there will be an evaluation of every record's sales figures to ascertain why a record failed or achieved only marginal success. Then a decision can be taken about changing the artist's material, producer or musical style. Finally, this decision amounts to the choice of whether to pick up the artist's annual option.

While it would be unlikely for a firm contractual commitment to be made which binds a record company to produce a promotional video, it is a matter of fact that a promotional video will be produced to support an artist's first single. With limited production costs, this video would fall into the £15,000 to £30,000 range, as opposed to the six-figure costs incurred by the established major artists. The cost of the promotional video for a developing artist would be recoupable against both audio and video income received by the record company. The income to pay these video costs is usually minimal with new artists, so these expenses are often set against future video exploitation. This is income which increases as the artist gains greater success and begins to release such items as compilation videos comprising selected promotional videos, or full length videos of live concert performances.

After the Deal: What Next?

After capturing the all-important record contract, the artist is left to work with the A&R person who made their introduction to the company. 'In those early days,' says Gatfield, 'the A&R person is everything to a new act—they hold the purse strings and there is a very special relationship because it was the A&R person who offered them the way into a record company, which is very, very special.'

However, the days of moulding artists ('wear that, play this, look like this, get your hair cut like that') have gone. As Gatfield says, 'I would not want to sign an artist who demands much moulding. I am attracted to artists needing assistance to bring out the talent which is already there. Starting with the right material, the A&R staff try to encourage artists to write commercially and they introduce them to good studios, engineers, producers and other musicians.'

The whole process takes time. It can be a year from signing the deal that the first single is released. 'Those 12 months,' explains Gatfield, 'are spent preparing and fine tuning everything. I don't like surprises in the recording studio. I hope to go in with songs we are all happy with, the arrangements agreed and the musicians properly prepared. It is too expensive to start rehearsing in the recording studio.'

Having signed the new artist, spent time ensuring everything is right and finally gone into the studio to produce 'the' single, the record company puts its wares out for everyone to hear. How will the public like it? Will the radio play it? Will it be a record that clubs get behind, or will the act become favourites with the media and no one else?

The A&R person's job doesn't end with handing over the record to the marketing, promotion and sales teams. As Gatfield stresses:

In A&R, we are fully aware of the problems which exist in exposing new and developing acts, especially with the current state of British radio. We are always looking for the revolutions in music, people like Prince or Jimi Hendrix. But the nature of the media in this country isn't open to people breaking new ground. Radio certainly isn't. I believe that part of our responsibility in A&R is to introduce new artists and sounds to the market place. It is tough, but with top quality artists we have a responsibility to offer their music to the public, however difficult it is to let them hear it. Despite British radio's disinterest in new music, and the reduced influence of the music press, I believe real talent will eventually get through.

With good quality records and exciting live performances, artists can attract the attention of individual journalists and disc jockeys, even if they don't benefit from much daytime radio play. Hopefully, these opinion-formers will champion the act's cause and gradually the public will be interested enough to find out more.

The pure pop act also has its problems when it comes to exposure. According to Gatfield, 'there is so much competition for air play between a host of pop bands, new ones need to have something special and different to stand out'.

Gatfield is still surprised by the record-buying public's assumption that the first record they purchase by a new act must be that artist's first release. 'It is amazing how often they are wrong. Sometimes artists have been working for two or three years, releasing records unsuccessfully, although the public's perception is that their first hit must be their first record. Significantly, the more time that bands take becoming successful is often reflected by their longer stay at the top.'

Music Publishing

In music publishing there are also A&R people. They have similar responsibilities to their counterparts in the record business. The main difference is that in music publishing the company's interest is predominantly in the music and the lyrics—the written song or composition—rather than the recorded sound.

More recently, record company and music publishing A&R staff have been assessing much of the same talent from different standpoints.

This is because most of today's major recording artists compose their own songs. Similarly, most new and aspiring artists offer their own material for consideration. There are some artists who rarely write their own material (Cliff Richard is the classic example), and as a result, the specialist songwriter always has a place in music publishing companies.

The music publisher represents the writer and their compositions. The company's main duty is twofold: the exploitation and the protection of the 'work'. To achieve these aims, publishers collect all money due to the works in their catalogue. This is from record sales, live performances and broadcasting (including TV commercials and film soundtracks). In the UK, songs remain in copyright for the lifetime of the composer plus fifty years. So, the publisher has constant work for new and contemporary writers as well as established composers whose work has spanned decades.

Music publishing companies are always alert to the possibility of signing new songwriting talent. This is their main means of improving and updating their catalogue of songs. They discover much of this talent in the same way as record companies. Often, new songwriters are searching for a recording contract as artists. A music publishing contract may be offered to a developing artist after they have signed to a record company. However, publishing companies are also the recipients of demo tapes. Publishers' requirements from these tapes are the same as those of record companies: a good recording which is well presented. The former head of talent acquisition at EMI Music Publishing in the UK, Peter Doyle, explains this:

Presentation may not get you plus points, but poor presentation gets the sort of result which reflects the lack of effort put into the tape. During my time at EMI, we received up to fifty tapes a week. Sadly, most of them fell well below the acceptable level of quality. Although we did receive some sheet music, we mainly got tapes. The ideal tape would have no more than three songs, a brief, factual biography, a photograph and details of any live dates.

It may seem odd that a music publishing company would want a photograph, but Doyle points out that 'the look of an artist may be important to develop an act's recording career. If we sign an act without a record contract, we develop their music and their image so we can present them favourably to a record company.'

Many songwriting hopefuls never get that far. Doyle believes it is mainly down to the quality of the songs which are submitted.

The songs are often badly written. It is obvious the writers haven't paid enough attention to current popular songs and musical styles. Unfortunately, most of the material which is sent in comes from people who have no other way of getting in touch with us, or who are unable to seek the advice of professional songwriters or publishers. Essentially, they are amateurs with little experience. Regrettably, this shows in the quality of their work.

Like record companies, publishing companies have their contacts. Many of these are in recording studios. Producers or engineers who are working with a new artist, and creating something unusual or interesting, regularly tip off their contacts in the publishing business. Doyle confirms this:

Most of the good songs which I heard about came to me that way. People at a studio might call me, or tell the act to get in touch with me direct. Like any other business, it is all to do with contacts and getting introductions. People who could open my door were managers, agents, engineers and producers. It is difficult for unknown newcomers to find those people in the first place.

The question of management and legal representation for aspiring new-comers is just as valid in publishing as it is in recording. According to Doyle: 'no one is forced to have a lawyer or manager when they meet with a publishing company, but deals would never be negotiated unless artists were legally represented. We would help artists by suggesting a list of industry lawyers for them to choose from.' To begin with, pure songwriters don't need managers as much as performing artists. But when non-performing songwriters became successful, with their songs being recorded by major artists, and used in films or as TV commercials, then the need for a manager often becomes more pressing.

Contracts

The contracts on offer to music writers fall into two categories.

1. The non-performing writer could be offered a firm one-year deal with options covering the next four years. There would be an advance paid to the writer on signing the deal. In return, the writer would give a product commitment. This would be a promise to deliver anything up to ten songs in a year. The royalties paid to writers for recorded music, referred to as mechanical royalty rates, are based on a percentage of the retail selling price. This royalty is divided between the writer and the publishing company. Initially, the split is around 70 per cent to the composer and 30 per cent to the publisher. These shares will change with a writer's success, as an ever larger percentage will be paid to the composer, subject to negotiation. The rights to the writer's compositions will remain with the publishing company for between ten and fifteen years after the expiry of the deal. There is also the possibility of further income for the composer from sales of sheet music. This is only a possibility when the songs are popular enough to be published in this form. A royalty of between 10 and 15 per cent of the retail price of the sheet music could be negotiated for the composer.

2. The songwriter who is also a performer, and has acquired a recording contract, could hope to receive a firm one-year deal with options covering the next three years. There would be a product guarantee to deliver an album of material per year, which would be released under the separate recording contract. If the publishing company are actively involved in acquiring a recording contract for the artist, they would provide studio time for producing demos.

Doyle explains another aspect of the deal: 'the contract signed in the UK would be world-wide. The advances would be at a level which enables the artist to live and concentrate on improving his or her writing skills. The publishing deal is totally independent from any record contract. There certainly would not be any conferring with the record company to try and establish comparable advances.'

So what does the publishing company do for the non-performing songwriter? Doyle explains that

the publisher attempts to place the artist's songs with record companies, or with artists, to get them recorded and released on record. In the UK, publishing companies take on very few non-performing songwriters. There is more potential in the United States for that. Most British recording artists write their own material, so they are the composers who are signed to publishing companies. Despite that, a talented songwriter would, I believe, still get a deal in the UK. In general, the emphasis in Britain is on the performer/writer.

Doyle advises songwriters who don't perform and who can't sing: 'Don't try to perform your own songs. You are doing yourselves and your songs a disservice. Try and find someone who can sing. It helps publishers enormously in judging the merits of your song.'

Having signed an artist, it is in the music publishing company's best interests to help this act win a recording contract. 'When you are developing an act up to a record deal, you spend a lot of time with them,' confirms Doyle. 'At EMI we had our own recording studio. Our acts were in the building a lot of the time working on their songs, while we would help in the most appropriate ways to ensure the artist's continued development.'

The writer who is also a performer isn't the only one who gets help.

We advise our composers, helping to sift out the bad songs and to search out opportunities for our writers to compose "covers" for particular artists. While we aren't ruled by the charts, we do want our songs performed by the right people. However, a lot of money can be earned from non-chart songs which are regularly "covered", recorded, performed or used in films, television or commercials.

When a company runs a record and a publishing operation, there is some co-operation when signing artists. Some artists work with

EMI's music publishing operation and aren't signed to the record company, and vice-versa. Doyle says:

Material did come to me at EMI Publishing from EMI Records, and if we were interested in an act who were also looking for a record deal, we would pass the information through to EMI Records. Often, aspiring artists aren't as aware of publishing companies as they are of record companies. As a result, record companies frequently receive demos more suited to a publisher's attention. Artists interested in both publishing and recording contracts should send demo tapes to each company. They should not assume their tape will get passed on.

The story of Elton John meeting his songwriting partner Bernie Taupin through a small ad in *Melody Maker* is one of the music industry's most famous legends, but the chances of two developing talents—a music writer and a lyricist—being brought together to form a successful partnership aren't good. According to Doyle: 'in principle, a publishing company would marry up a lyricist with a music writer, but I have never found the opportunity or the talent to do it.'

Breaking through, making it to the top and finding real success is never going to be easy, despite the well-voiced criticism of pop music being 'tuneless rubbish'. Peter Doyle is a publishing man who admires the skill of the songwriter. 'It is a craft that has to be learned, developed and finally mastered.'

18 Independent Recording and Publishing Companies

STEPHEN TANNETT is managing director of IRS Records. After a short recording career with the punk band Menace, Stephen joined Miles Copeland's organization working his way up from a job in the company's warehouse. This article is an edited version of an interview with Stephen at IRS's offices.

Everybody producing music for sale to the public has the same problem: because making music costs money, selling product (records, tapes and CDs) is the only way to survive. So small and large record companies all try to bring their music to the market place for an audience to buy.

The structures of majors and independents are determined by the size of the repertoire each company handles. The staff of a major can be huge, but the nucleus of people who deal with a band is very similar in a good small company. The A&R person is responsible for the artist's relationship with the record company. At IRS, a lot of our A&R work is done by Miles Copeland and myself. Our press and radio promotions people can be our own staff or a freelancer, depending on the requirements of our artist. Our label manager gets the finished master tapes to the stage of putting a sleeve around it, while our marketing person decides when records are released, in which formats and how radio and television will be approached. These departments all exist in major and independent companies. However, if a small company doesn't provide for any one of these operations, it is unlikely that company can give its artists adequate service. Single-handed operations are very difficult. No one can be in more than one place at any time, and in the life of a single or an album, a record company needs people working in more than five places all at once. As majors handle much more product than independents, they have more staff, maybe two or three label managers, two marketing people, and three or four radio promotions staff. Our personnel at IRS reflect the number of people we need to do the job.

The advantages of a small company over a large one is a matter of swings and roundabouts. In independent companies, a band can talk to the people who count and who make the decisions. If a manager is in the A&R office at CBS, he or she rarely has access to anybody else in the company. His or her only links are the A&R staff and perhaps the marketing people. Unless the manager represents a big artist, he or she wouldn't work with the record company's senior directors. By contrast, when a manager comes to seem me, I can make things happen to sort out any problems. A small company will probably focus its attention on each artist's project more than a major label. This is because majors work on the priority system. If your band isn't this week's priority, you are probably going to be forgotten. It isn't quite that cut and dried, but if you are signed to a small company with any degree of commitment, you can be sure that the company and their staff are in their weekly meetings pushing to get results from your music.

Independent and Major Publishers

Basically, publishers make paper transactions. They don't produce a piece of vinyl to be sold in a retail outlet. Old-style publishing was based around retail sheet-music sales, but current publishing is a banking operation which involves taking a risk on an artist. Anyone can be a publisher by registering their songs with the various societies (MCPS and PRS). If their copyright music becomes a record and is sold, royalties become due. A publisher can collect that money just as easily as an artist, but a publishing company has the resources to offer the artist effective promotion services. Often, smaller maverick publishers are the talent scouts for the music business. They sign up new artists' songs, and franchise off their rights in that music to bigger companies when these larger firms become interested. In effect, the small publisher 'subpublishes' their songs through a big company like SBK or Warner-Chappell.

The small publisher collects money in the same way as a larger one, but a bigger publisher has extra staff to promote a writer's repertoire. If a writer has produced a song he or she thinks is a must for Cliff Richard, a major publisher is most likely to get that song where it needs to be in order to interest Cliff. However, a small independent may take on an unknown songwriter when nobody else is interested. In that case, the small publisher invests money to own the new writer's copyrights. This can be one time when a young writer has to compromise on some immediate ambitions in order to progress on to the next stage of securing a record deal or having artists cover his or her songs. It must be better to have a publisher supporting your music, however big or small, than still being yet another unknown songwriter trying to get your first break.

Finding New Talent for Publishing and Recording

At IRS and the Bugle group we are very lucky because there is an agency called Prestige Talent which books concerts for artists who aren't signed to IRS or any other record company. Like all booking agents, they have to be very hot on new talent. They need to find the latest popular artists who are going to sell concert tickets. IRS hears about a lot of young acts from Prestige Talent.

Other ways we find bands include: (a) being recognized in the industry as a company that is worth approaching (managers with new artists drop in to play a tape to me or any of the other A&R people); (b) demo tapes (they all get heard eventually, but to get your tape picked out of the pile for special attention is difficult); (c) seeing them play live on the London circuit. If you work very hard at making somebody in a record company come and see you, that is probably as good a way as any to get some indication of your music's commercial potential. After sending in a tape, with a biography, contact address and a photo, a useful approach can be to update the A&R department every time your band does one or a series of gigs. Send in a sheet of paper personally addressed to your target A&R person. The mail will come through to the secretary, and most of the time if it isn't a tape and is just a letter, the A&R person's morning mail will include your gig information. At least your band's name and date sheet is on the A&R person's desk and they have seen it. You can't lose from that.

Tapes are the last resort because they are the least effective way of attracting attention. They are a part of the process, although I have never signed an artist from a demo without seeing the group play live. You have to be creative to make your tape jump out of the pile. If your biography says 'we are a 3 piece rock group from Lancashire, we play soft pop and melodic songs', it doesn't show much initiative. If a band can work that little bit harder to be more original, someone somewhere should start to be interested in their music. I have been approached on many levels, from stripograms in the office to packages arriving at reception with worms and a message inside threatening even worse if I didn't see the band (I didn't). I did look at the stripogram group because I was so horrified at the thought that they might do it again.

Attracting interest is down to persistence. Drop by the record company, go to the reception, give your tape to the receptionist and try to persuade him or her to put your demo on to your target A&R

person's desk. You have to use these methods because there are fifty cassettes coming in every day and you need yours to be picked out and heard with particular care. If somebody can manœuvre your tape to the receptionist, who gets it to the secretary and then to the A&R person, it has to help your chances.

Everyone is overworked in this business. The A&R work in smaller companies, when there isn't somebody whose sole job is sitting and listening to tapes, gets done when it can be. If someone really works hard to get something to my attention, it will be heard that much quicker. It is easy to find out who deals with A&R in a record company, and it has to be worth the legwork to find the person specializing in your type of music. However it is more difficult getting an opinion about an act's music over the phone. The phone rings a lot and usually it interrupts a meeting.

Developing New Artists

Once I am interested in an act's music and I like their live performance, the first thing I want to know is where this new band sees itself going. Some artists expect us to make them stars. Others present what they do and what they want to achieve in their first year, for example, putting out an album and going on tour. This reassures me that the band are clear about what they are trying to do, and it is far easier for me to get excited by someone coming in with a plan and an idea.

A recent example of this approach was our six albums with REM. When we signed them, they had already made an EP by themselves. They asked us whether we would consider releasing this record. We decided to take it on. They didn't ask for any money, they just wanted a good royalty and help with promotion. From then on, they delivered an album absolutely on time for an August or September release six years running. They always had their own plans. They never complained that their music wasn't on certain radio stations because they understood the scope of their work. It made life very easy for us. We could concentrate on trying to bring their product to as many people in the market place as possible. We weren't also having to create the idea and the reason for the band's existence. They had those already.

If a band's young manager could come to me with an independently produced EP, with live circuit work pulling good crowds, success in merchandising T-shirts, and evidence of media interest, that would be a fantastic beginning. Then everyone starts to believe in this group. When a manager walks in with none of these things a record company is being asked to use a lot of imagination. Sometimes that

works. When Kate Bush was signed, she wasn't a live artist and someone had to envisage her potential.

After deciding we like a band, we would consider whether to make singles with an option for an album, or to go straight for an album. In an album deal at IRS, we would make the band an offer based on the percentage royalty points which we thought were appropriate, having worked out a budget to make a record. Almost always the company will pay the artist's recording expenses, give them a small advance and choose and pay the producer. In any album deal, we normally take options for six albums. When we are developing an artist on an international basis, success doesn't necessarily happen in the first or second album. We may have to wait until the third one. In that case, we want to be around for the big money in the fourth, fifth and sixth records. All of our artists are on long-term contracts. Normally, we don't pay less than 10 per cent to an artist. Smaller companies may try paying less, but a starting royalty of between 10 and 12 per cent is fairly standard.

Working with the Same Recording and Publishing Companies

If a recording artist comes to me without a publishing deal, I always insist IRS is considered for publishing as we can pay better percentage splits, do just as good a job, and help invest in an act's career at a vital time. For instance, an IRS artist may want to tour. We may only be able to afford to put up a certain amount of money to help fund them. The band may turn to their publisher, who is part of a different company, for some extra money. The publisher might refuse and there is little IRS can do to force that publisher to help the band. If the band were signed to the publishing company which is part of the Bugle group, I could ring them to try and force the publisher to invest even more money in the artist. That can make all the difference.

If we sign a publishing deal in conjunction with a record deal, we usually make the deals co-terminous. So, if we only make one single with a band, we don't keep the publishing on that act forever. In a publishing deal, the average splits used to be 50:50. Then it went to 60:40 in favour of the artist. Currently, 75:25 is very favourable, 80:20 is exceptional and 90:10 is fantastic. Most deals are done on the basis of 60:40.

Showcases

If a band has an A&R buzz, they may play a showcase at the Marquee or another London venue. They probably invite the 'fraternity' (the A&R staff from the major record companies) to the gig. The risk is that there can be a collective NO from everyone. One A&R person might tell another that he or she doesn't like the band, and the feeling can spread like wild fire. Suddenly, everybody rejects the group, even though they may be fantastic. In one go, the band have killed their chances with twenty-five different companies. At least if it goes wrong with just one A&R person out front, there are plenty more to approach.

If I were looking for a record deal, I would be pursuing individual A&R people, getting them to come and see my band. The band would have to be playing a lot of shows so they are available as often as possible for viewing. Then, if the target A&R person does come, there is a better chance of him or her making a fair analysis of the artist without being caught up in A&R peer pressure.

There is apathy within the A&R departments of major record companies. It is different for smaller companies like IRS. If we go to see a band, we don't just send an A&R person, one of our product managers or maybe the sales director might come as well. We want to know their opinion of the band so that if we sign the group, we hope everyone in the company will like the artist's work and try to promote it as well as possible.

Self-Reliant Acts

Independent companies are often the setting for bands who already have an idea of the sort of music they want to make, and where they want to end up. More importantly, independents can be the right place for artists who want to keep a degree of creative control.

19 Radio

. . . .

STUART GRUNDY is an executive producer at BBC Radio 1, with direct responsibility for evening and weekend programmes as well as special events. He began in radio with the British Forces Broadcasting Service as a producer/ presenter and moved to Radio Luxembourg as a resident DJ in 1965. Two years later he joined the BBC to help launch Radio 1. Through the years he has produced almost every Radio 1 programme, written and presented numerous internationally syndicated music documentary series and published books on *Great Guitarists* and *The Art of the Record Producer*. More recently he produced the overall sound coverage of Live Aid, and as a presenter one of his programmes, 'Three at 30, Marvin Gaye', won the 1989 New York International Festival's Gold Award for Best Talk/Interview Special.

Although many people would disagree, radio is without doubt the musician's best friend. To make the most of it, musicians need to understand how it works. Within the BBC, music is confined to three national networks, Radios 1, 2 and 3, with a limited amount being featured on Radio 5. In contrast, local radio is a mix of commercial and BBC stations. In the offing, with a probable start date of 1992, are three INRs or Independent National Radio stations. Although the new Broadcasting Bill stipulates that these stations will provide a varied diet of programmes, the best bet is that one will feature primarily classical music, the second will have a pop/rock music base, while the third is likely to be an American-style 'talk' station. As Britain's only national pop music station at present, Radio 1 is most likely to interest aspiring rock and pop musicians, so I will explain its workings and policies in some detail (although much of what is said about Radio 1 will also be applicable to Radio 2).

Radio 1

Radio 1 broadcasts for twenty-one hours a day, although shortly this will be twenty-four. Its programmes are presented by well-established 'personality' broadcasters, some of whom are very music-oriented. For them, music is their only consideration and they would regard themselves as fans and supporters of pop music. Other Radio 1 broadcasters see their job as being popular entertainers. Indeed, one famous DJ was recently quoted as saying 'I'm paid to provide the bits between the records'. Not only is that true, it is also nothing to be ashamed of. A lively radio station has a variety of on-air personalities, and not all of them will be as devoted to music as others. Even though some presenters use music merely as a vehicle for their own performances, it is worth remembering that they would all find it very difficult to do their job without the music base.

Although presenters are encouraged to take an active part in preparing their programmes, this work is basically the responsibility of producers. Currently, Radio 1 employs nineteen producers who supervise 147 hours of broadcasting each week. They are all answerable to two executive producers, a head of music department and a network controller. So, the station's management structure is quite bare and this helps it to respond very quickly to current events.

Every radio station needs a target audience. This helps to structure the content of its programmes as well as its public image, and until the mid-1980s, Radio 1 was aiming at the 16–25 age group. The received BBC wisdom was that young people went through a period of obsession with rock and pop, but that as 'sanity and maturity' prevailed, they would graduate 'like their elders' to light, popular music. Now, extensive research has proved that quite wrong. It is very clear that today's parents don't fit the mould that society defined for them twenty years ago. So, Radio 1 has widened its target audience to 16–35 year olds.

Radio 1 is heard by an average audience of over seventeen million every week. The vast majority of people listen during the day, and the station has a different editorial approach to its weekday daytime programmes and to its evening and weekend shows. Put simply, weekday daytime programmes are more centrally co-ordinated and structured than all other shows. The core of weekday daytime programming is the 'playlist', which has three major uses for Radio 1: it provides an overall sound or 'station feel'; it is an effective way to monitor how often the most popular records are played; and it makes a group responsibility out of a decision which may have far-reaching effects for individual musicians and the music industry.

The Playlist

The Radio 1 playlist has changed its shape, size and effect considerably over the years. Currently, there are fifteen records on its

A list and twenty on its B list (records on the A list are simply rotated more frequently than on the B list). Every week, the playlisted records are programmed by a computer to rotate around the different weekday daytime shows. Out of the seven or eight records played in each Radio 1 half-hour, four or five will be from the playlist. As a result, the A and B lists provide just over half of the records on daytime Radio 1.

As it is such an important programming tool, with such important consequences for musicians' careers, it is worth understanding how the playlist is chosen. Every Monday morning, the Radio 1 playlist committee meets in one of the BBC's basement rooms. This isn't for any covert reason, it just happens that most of the BBC's committee rooms are down there! At this meeting are Radio 1's daytime producers and a chairperson who is usually the executive producer of weekday daytime shows. Any presenters or other Radio 1 producers who want to contribute are welcome. The emphasis at this committee is on records which have just been released, or which are about to be released. Everyone arrives with a stack of singles which they think are worth considering for the playlist. Each record is played and every member of the playlist group is asked to comment. Once the strength of the new week's material has been assessed, the next move is to decide which records will be removed from the present playlist to make room for the new ones. This discussion may be based entirely on 'gut feel' or on more objective things like statistics of record sales or radio play.

But What Gets a Record on the Playlist?

This is a reasonable question often asked of all Radio 1 producers. The truth is that although there are general criteria, like whatever is 'interesting', 'acceptable' or 'fantastic', these change from season to season, month to month, and even week to week. The playlist discussion often dwells on a record's 'freshness' or 'originality'. However, so much of what is now being produced lacks these very qualities that it may be more useful to look at successful artists' work to find an answer to this question. If you listen to David Bowie, Elton John, Bob Dylan, Bruce Springsteen or Paul Simon, you immediately recognize their music. Often this is because of a distinctive vocal sound, but sometimes more subtle devices make everyone want to listen. For instance, a few years ago I studied Paul Simon's music quite extensively. I discovered that for quite a long part of their career, every Simon and Garfunkel recording used a set of distinctive and unusual percussion sounds. I believe that these helped to combine their characteristic voices with a small element of surprise which gave each track its own fingerprint. But even if you aren't another Bowie or Elton John, you still need to try and develop an original style. If you sound like everyone else, no one will remember you, even for five minutes.

These are general criteria and it is dangerous to be too specific. Have the courage of your convictions to play what pleases you. It may be that your enthusiasm gives that extra bit of life to your record. Also, remember that radio producers listen to over 100 singles a week. They get bored easily, so if you can't excite them in the first 30 seconds of your record, you are probably in the wrong business.

Chart position is one criterion which is used to consider a record for playlisting. But no chart placing carries as much weight as the sound of the record. A song may be at number one, but if it doesn't 'feel' right for Radio 1, it won't be playlisted. Andrew Lloyd Webber was reputed to be furious when Radio 1 declined to playlist Michael Ball's hit, 'Love Changes Everything'. It is a lovely song, but it definitely sounds right on Radio 2 and very wrong on Radio 1. Dance music, too, often doesn't work on radio. Why should it? Usually, it has been designed to be highly amplified in a night-club. Chances are that it won't make an ideal radio record any more than 'Candle in the Wind' would be a dancefloor hit at Stringfellow's. If you listen to the music on individual programmes you will soon get a fair idea of where the playlist is at each week.

There is no need to worry about the duration of a record. It used to be said that 'if you can't say what you want to say in three minutes, forget it'. But the three-minute song is just a left-over from when that was all you could fit on to one side of a 78 record. There have been many examples of long, classic singles, like 'Eloise', 'McCarthur Park' and 'American Pie'. At Radio 1, the producers aren't very concerned about a record's length. If a record is terrible, then a minute is too long! Also, lyrical parameters are as wide as current popular taste allows. It is worth remembering that we are dealing with 'popular' music. If you are the sort of band that wants an arts council grant, then you are probably too special or too precious to conform to the limits set by 'popular' taste.

The Radio 1 playlist is much maligned, but it is as honest and fair as any system. Despite that, it still puts Radio 1 producers into a catch-22 situation. If they playlist a band's record, then that band think the playlist is 'marvellous'. But if they leave that record out, suddenly the playlist is 'unfair, monstrous and corrupt'. Often musicians don't realize that a record can be played more on Radio 1 when it is off the playlist altogether. It happens all the time . Radio producers have to remind themselves each week that radio broadcasting isn't about selling records, but about entertaining an audience. Research shows that less than 10 per cent of listeners to Radio 1 are regular record buyers, so it would be unrepresentative of our audience's taste to be ruled by the movements of the singles' chart. Radio presenters and producers often get great pleasure from seeing the success of a record which they have championed. But they are generally happy just to programme and share the pleasant experience of listening to popular music on the radio.

Pluggers

Apart from albums, there are over 100 singles released every week in Britain, and only five to ten of them will have much commercial success. Any conscientious radio producer will try to hear and consider all of these. However, it is very difficult to make a final decision on one hearing. This is when 'pluggers' start trying to 'persuade' presenters and producers to play a particular record. I believe that in Britain an outstanding record will find its way into the system without much promotion, assuming that it has been distributed to producers. Pluggers exist to exploit the middle ground of those record releases which may be a hit, depending on whether radio producers and presenters are prepared to give them a 'run'. At worst, a 'plugger' merely ensures the delivery of a record to someone's office. At best, the plugger can be a creative link between the artist, management, record company and radio station.

Obviously, it is in a 'plugger's' interest to claim that it was his or her work which made a record into a hit, but if you employ a 'plugger' it is worth being sceptical when deciding what to believe. Nevertheless, radio producers set aside some time each week to meet pluggers. Producers will usually only meet pluggers who they know already, and rarely see any band's representative because they are probably far too close to the music to have any objectivity. If you are new, young, and underfunded then don't worry. Just make sure that a copy of your record reaches the producers of programmes that you value. Your work should be your most eloquent argument. If you can afford one, a good plugger can benefit both the artist and the radio station by acting as a fixer for guest appearances, or providing news and creative ideas; but like everything, some pluggers are better than others, and radio producers usually prefer to exercise their own musical judgement and not to pander to pluggers' suggestions.

Live Music Session Recordings

Radio 1 has always spent large amounts of time, effort and money recording live concerts and, in particular, recording full-scale sessions. In the beginning, much of this effort was used to create music to play on the air when the station's needletime was used up.

(Needletime is a limit on the number of hours of commercially available recordings which can be broadcast by radio stations. These limits were originally set by Phonographic Performance Limited, representing the record companies, and the Musicians' Union, to safeguard the viability of commercial recordings.) Currently, Radio 1 devotes over 5,000 hours a year to recording musicians in its own studios, as well as at live concert performances. The Maida Vale centre in London, for example, contains six music studios and has two of these regularly in use for pop and rock sessions. On average, there is one session recorded each day which is likely to result in four broadcast items or songs. The shape of a session is as follows:

1. The setting-up and miking of instruments.
2. The recording or laying-down of tracks and vocals. (Generally $2 \times 3\frac{1}{2}$-hour recording period.)
3. The mixing of tracks and vocals ($1 \times 3\frac{1}{2}$-hour period).

The only difference from a commercial studio is that the BBC's recordings aren't meant for release on record. They are simply a recording of a band's live or alternative versions of their songs, which are used for one or two broadcasts. This system of sessions lets certain producers develop young musicians' talent, and there is a lengthy list of internationally famous rock and pop stars who were helped by a Radio 1 session. John Peel has encouraged hundreds of musicians on his programmes with his attitude that puts creativity and originality above musicianship. It may be hard to accept, but the argument goes that it is easier for a creative and original performer to learn how to play his instrument than it is for a consummate player to learn creativity. Certainly the numbers of internationally successful British musicians who came out of art school, rather than music college, seem to confirm this. John Lennon, David Bowie, Eric Clapton, Jeff Beck, Pete Townshend and Bryan Ferry are just the tip of the iceberg.

The producers who supervise Radio 1 sessions tend to be musicians who are used to coaxing good performances out of young bands in a limited period of time. Artists are booked for these sessions by individual 'commissioning producers', who are responsible for the shows which feature sessions. At present, the programmes in question are those of John Peel, Nicky Campbell, Richard Skinner, Andy Kershaw and Mark Goodier, and the Friday Rock Show. The producers of all these programmes are inundated with cassette tapes from bands, so they may take some time before listening to them all. In every case, you have a better chance of being considered if you are able to put your performance on record. It is possible to make a single, and sell it at your own gigs, for quite a small sum of money (see Chapter 13, 'Doing it the Right Way' by Horace Trubridge). It is even cheaper to pool your resources with four or five other bands and put together a composite album. If you aren't willing to take a risk on your own music, then don't be surprised if others won't either.

If you are after a session, don't waste your time sending tapes and records all over the place. Target them. Find out which of the above programmes and their producers are likely to be most sympathetic to your style of music and remember the following:

1. A record is better than a cassette.
2. Only send in three tracks at the most (naturally your best).
3. Give some brief biographical information.
4. Include your address and telephone number.
5. Don't hold your breath waiting for a reply. It may take some time!

Sessions are often recorded with bands who already have a record deal. In organizing the session, the initiative will almost certainly have been with the commissioning radio producer who will have approached the record company or manager. Occasionally a manager or agent will suggest that a band is 'available for session'. However, this usually produces a zero response. As with their choice of records, producers like to rely on their own opinion when they book bands.

Other Ways of Attracting Radio's Attention

A local radio station might be worth contacting. Regional breakouts aren't unknown, and local stations with a university campus nearby often provide the most fertile ground. Sometimes artists attract attention by producing some original news angle. This is fine as long as the music stands up to scrutiny. Often groups get publicity by claiming that their record has been banned. This isn't a ploy to be recommended. All too soon, bands find that their wish has been fulfilled! One of the few successful publicity ploys involved Elvis Costello being arrested for creating a disturbance outside the Hilton Hotel in London's Park Lane. CBS Records were inside holding their annual international conference, and Elvis stood in the street performing a selection of his songs using a small portable amplifier, just as his debut single 'Less Than Zero' has just been released. This was a delightfully outrageous thing for a little label (Stiff) to do, just to annoy one of the biggest international companies. It gained terrific publicity, but it takes more than column inches to sell records, and I am sure that Elvis's continuing success has more to do with talent.

Local Radio

In its current form, local radio is shared between the BBC and the commercial companies of the ILR network. In the main, BBC Local

Radio has pursued a programming policy based on local news. But each station is autonomous and some are more music-oriented than others. BBC Local Radio isn't well funded, and you may be able to provide some bargain-basement programming for them, particularly if you are a solo performer. This would depend entirely on getting to know your local station and its personnel. In contrast, ILR stations are businesses. They have directors, sales directors and shareholders, and they broadcast to make money. Recently there have been a number of mergers between these companies which have increased this financial pressure. As a result, many stations are now programmed by one man and a computer. Like their BBC counterparts, independent stations control their own programming policy. Some care about developing local musicians, like Radio Clyde, while many don't. As part of their broad-based agreements with the IBA and the MU, ILR stations are obliged to spend at least 3 per cent of their net advertising revenue on live musicians. Many stations choose to spend this money on recording their station's jingles, while others prefer to involve themselves with promoting local concerts by international artists. Many stations still record local musicians in their own studios. But, as always, it is worthwhile finding out more about your local station.

To get the best help from the radio, try to find someone in it who might be sympathetic to your music. Listen to the radio carefully and choose your personal contacts accordingly. If you are lucky, the radio can help your career enormously. However, radio producers have the best music to choose from to entertain their audiences, and like its listeners, radio can transfer its affections overnight and without explanation. Good luck.

20 The Musicians' Union

STAN MARTIN is assistant general secretary of the Musicians' Union with responsibility for the media. After drumming as a semi-professional in the 1960s, Stan took a degree as a mature student at Birmingham University, leading to ten years' work as a careers officer. In 1979 Stan became the Musicians' Union's South-East district organizer, and subsequently the Central London branch secretary and co-editor of the union's award-winning *Musician* magazine.

Strip away the insincerity and the hype from the music business and see it for what it is, a jungle. When you work in rock and pop music, you are in the thick undergrowth. Like the real jungle, the music business holds a dual attraction for the entrepreneur: the thrill of a gamble and the chance of a quick large profit. Added to this is the reflected glory of being associated with a high-profile, media-exposed product and the prized magical ingredient of youth. It is a heady combination!

The music business has some straightforward, honest, 'invest some money and hope to make a profit' entrepreneurs. However, one of this industry's main characteristics is that it attracts the maverick. The tales of manipulation, creative accountancy and downright dishonesty starring some of these wayward entrepreneurs are numerous and well documented. The resulting debris in musicians' careers would be disastrous, but for the MU. The union acts as an industry police force and a rescue service for its members.

What is the MU?

Fiction: The MU only recruits and is only interested in professional, session and orchestral musicians.

Fact: The MU has 40,000 members, with offices and branches throughout the UK, and almost anybody who is either a performer or a composer of music is a member of the MU.

The MU's Image

The union often gets a bad press, and there are good reasons for this. The union came into existence to serve the interests of musicians. It protects them and ensures they receive adequate payment for their musical skills. The union is not a record company, publisher, radio or TV company, promoter, agent or management company. It has no shareholders or directors. It is run by musicians for the benefit of musicians. Given this, negative coverage from the popular music press, who rely on the commercial music industry for their survival, is excusable. It is less understandable when the union is caricatured in more seriously researched publications.

In some guides to the music business the treatment accorded to the union can be shallow and misleading. There is no intimation that the very existence of the MU benefits all musicians, especially the young and inexperienced. Nor is there coverage of the breadth and scope of the union's services. Indeed, readers can be put off from finding out more about the MU, which is the only organization providing protection and service solely to musicians. The aim of this article is to help you find out more about what the MU really does for musicians, day after day after day . . .

The MU as a Trade Union

As a trade union, the MU exists to protect its members and to maximize their rewards, just like all trade unions. The similarity ends there. Musicians' work and way of life is different to that of the members of most unions. For example, most musicians are self-employed. They don't work for one employer on a regular basis. Going to work for a young musician may mean days spent rehearsing, getting songs down on tape, producing a demo on a front-room recording unit, or playing at a pub gig. This is a unique lifestyle and because of this the MU is a unique trade union. Like other trade unions, the MU negotiates with employers such as TV companies so that when a band appears on '*Top of the Pops*' or '*Night Network*' the members of the band will be paid an MU-negotiated fee. This is just one example of the MU as a negotiator on behalf of musicians. There are many more, such as negotiating for musical employment in holiday centres or on ships. One problem is that most live gigs are one-offs. As the union can't negotiate separately with every club or pub in the country, the MU has established minimum rates of pay for these gigs.

These negotiations and setting of rates is only one part of the union's activities. Printed across the bottom of MU application forms is the slogan: 'Musicians' Union—Working for Today's Musicians'.

Of course, there are all sorts of slogans. Some exhort 'Smash the . . . '. Others inform. The union's slogan informs you that it is concerned with servicing the needs of today's musicians. The MU is not preoccupied with the problems of yesteryear.

The Music Business Adviser (MBA)

Today's musicians are often quite young and new to the business. Of the union's total membership, approximately half are under the age of 30. Since the advent of rock in the 1950s and 1960s, the union has been the only independent organization to give service, protection and advice to rock musicians. In the 1970s, the union appointed a rock organizer and developed a specialist contract-vetting service. But life was simpler then. Solo performers or groups were signed to major record companies. The independent record sector barely existed, and recording was the concern only of established studios. In the 1980s, the independents became a real force, recording technology is easily accessible, and bands are more energetic and enterprising in producing their own records and promoting themselves. The union has responded to these changes by appointing a music business adviser who has expanded the range of services aimed at rock musicians.

Free Contract-Vetting Service

On recording, publishing and mangement contracts, the MBA or our specialist solicitor provide union members with free advice and a contract-vetting service. Also, a pre-contract discussion can be arranged with the MBA on an individual or band basis.

Music Business Seminars

These are regularly organized in London and other centres throughout the country. Topics covered include: recording agreements, music publishing, management, merchandising, all financial matters relevant to a recording artist's career, the A&R process and department in record companies, opportunities for composers in the mechanical media field, and making and marketing your own record.

Speakers include music business lawyers, accountants, record company A&R staff, marketing directors, and press and publicity executives, Radio 1 producers, composers and members of independent production companies.

Sting

Other Services Provided by the MU

The services provided by the music business adviser are only part of the union's total commitment to servicing the needs of today's musicians. The union works for musicians on two levels: supporting the individual member, and providing a protective umbrella for all musicians, whether or not they are MU members.

Insurance

All members are entitled to £500 free insurance cover on their instruments and equipment against damage and loss. For insurance cover over £500, the MU Insurance Advisory Service will arrange the best insurance deal to top up the excess. The Insurance Advisory Service will also provide cover for all your other insurance needs, such as for your car or your personal belongings. The union's involvement in insurance stems from the difficulties musicians have experienced in getting car or van insurance. Even when they did get cover in the past, the premiums were punitively high.

Benevolent Grants and Sickness and Accident Benefit

Financial assisstance from the union's Benevolent Funds and from the union's benefit scheme is available to meet some of the needs which arise because of a personal accident or illness. If you are ill and unable to work as a musician, the union has funds to help you.

Standard Contracts

The union provides free contract forms for virtually every type of engagement. Currently, there are sixteen contracts available. The most popular of these is for a one-off gig between a band and a venue, part of which is reproduced here.

If the type of gig you are offered is so unusual that it is not covered by any of the existing contracts, an MU official will devise one to suit your needs, or add necessary clauses to an existing contract (for performing on the back of a moving open-back lorry, the contract might require clauses covering additional risks!).

Legal Services

This provides musicians with legal advice on all matters relating to musical employment. This might be legal assistance to recover unpaid fees or help with the negotiations after a cancelled engagement. These legal services include advice on band names, partnership agreements between band members, Social Security rights and entitlement, and music licences—anything and everything relating to music, even including: 'Can a freight company hold on to my instruments/equipment because the tour promoter hasn't paid the bill?'

STANDARD CONTRACT

Musicians' Union Standard Contract

For the engagement of a band/group for casual arrangements

An agreement made on the ....day of ....19 ....

between .... of ....

(address) ....

(hereinafter called the "Engager") of the one part

and .... of ....

address ....

(hereinafter called the "Leader") of the other part

Witnesses

1. The Engager engages the Leader to provide a combination of

.............................musicians
(number)

appearing as ....
(name of band/group)

to perform for: *dancing/cabaret accompaniment/stage show/background
music (*delete whichever is not applicable)

at ....
(venue address)

from .... am/pm

until .... am/pm

on ....
(date)

2. It is agreed that the inclusive fee for the engagement shall be £ ....
which shall be payable in cash/by cheque (delete whichever is inapplicable) on
the date of the performance.

Legal assistance is most commonly used to secure payment of unpaid fees, or payment for a cancelled gig. You know the situation. Your band is booked for a pub gig. You perform. There aren't many people present because the landlord forgot to advertise, even in the free listings papers. As a result, the landlord blames the band for the poor attendance and refuses to pay. He is a big man with two Rottweiler dogs, so you don't argue! The union would attempt to secure payment. If necessary, we will support you through the court process.

Information Leaflets

General leaflets are available to members about gigs, royalties, copyright and contracts. Also, there is a series of specialist leaflets on management, publishing, recording contracts, work abroad, and agents. These leaflets are written in a direct readable style. As an example, I have provided an extract from the 'Gigs' leaflet.

ALWAYS ESTABLISH HOW MUCH YOU ARE BEING PAID AND/OR HOW YOU WILL GET THE MONEY

Some examples of the arrangements that you might be offered are:

- Straightforward fee paid on the night.
- A small amount plus half the door take.
- The whole door take, whatever it is.
- A guaranteed payment plus 'Pass the hat around' or similar arrangement.

In some cases these arrangements may seem reasonable. In others they are clearly a 'rip-off'.

The Union believes that any musician playing for the public should be guaranteed reasonable money.

Directories

A directory of the MU members in each geographical area is produced every two years. Every member receives a free copy and these directories are also supplied to contractors, agents and venues.

Posters

Good quality, well-designed, blank posters are supplied free to members and venues. Many bands now take responsibility for advertising their gigs, and these posters encourage these self-help initiatives.

Diaries

Every member is given a free MU diary. This isn't intended for the profound jottings which occur in the back of the van after a gig (to be auctioned at Sotherby's when you are dead!). The MU diary is a musician's professional pocket information kit. It doesn't merely contain such valuable information as the date of Mothers' Day, the distance from London to Inverness, and how to control the bleeding of a wound. It covers legal and taxation notes for musicians, as well as advice on recording contracts and other session engagements. It lists the names, addresses and phone numbers of all the union's offices and officers, at national, district and branch level. So wherever you are in the country, you can contact someone local when you need the union's help.

The Umbrella Activity

As well as these individual benefits and services to members, the union provides an additional service to all musicians by its presence and its activities. As 'the police force of the music business', the union is heavily committed to 'crime prevention'. It promotes this policy in two ways. Firstly, by educating and advising musicians to avoid traps, and on how to secure the greatest rewards for their talents, the MU decreases the pool of prey on which music industry sharks can pounce. Secondly, pursuing untrustworthy promoters or record companies, if necessary through the courts and on to the enforcement of judgements, deters other business people from trying to get rich at the expense of musicians. When the union publishes a Special Notice in its magazine warning members about the activities of a promoter, record company or contact agency, this not only informs members, it also puts off other unscrupulous operators.

The value of these union activities isn't as easy to measure as the benefits and services to individual musicians, but they are just as important. The 'police' role of the union is performed by its full-time officials. As well as national officials such as the general secretary, assistant general secretaries, and the session organizer, who operate from the union's national office in London, there are full-time officials in every district of Britain. The MU's geographical structure gives every member easy access to the union's services and to the ear of a full-time official. These district officials are a combination of advisers, negotiators, lawyers and general trouble-shooters. They are familiar with every branch of the music business, whether it is chamber music or anarchic rock. They have a working knowledge of contract law and other legal areas which affect musicians, such as noise levels and music licences, so that they can give advice on anything and everything that affects musicians.

The least visible of the union's services is the constant activity which benefits all musicians indirectly. This includes: making written submissions to public bodies; lobbying MPs and Members of

Stone Roses

the House of Lords when legislation on anything connected with music, like copyright, is being enacted; representing musicians' interests in national and international forums on issues such as the collection and payment of royalties on behalf of performers and composers. An example of this activity producing direct benefits to musicians is the case of commercial (ILR) radio stations. In the 1970s when commercial radio was first introduced to Britain, the MU persuaded both the Government and the Independent Broadcasting Authority that the new radio stations should have an obligation to provide some musical employment, and not just fill every minute of air time with recorded music. The agreement which the union negotiated is that commercial radio stations must spend not less than 3 per cent of their net advertising revenue on the employment of musicians. Since the union negotiated this, union officials have 'policed' the radio stations to ensure their compliance.

Perhaps the most visible of the union's activities is the financial sponsorship of events such as the ICA/MU Rock Week held in May 1989. This is one example of the union 'leading by example'. The union teamed up with the Institute of Contemporary Arts to co-promote a Rock Week held at the ICA building in London. This was a showcase for a wide variety of young British musicians and bands currently working outside the mainstream of rock and pop. The bands which appeared were selected by the Hackney Agency for Music Marketing Action (HAMMA) on behalf of the MU and the ICA. The theme of the week was 'Dangerous Bands in Safe Hands', and this was an attempt to highlight the union's concern that live music promoters should be aware of their responsibilities to new artists, and provide them with opportunities for live work with fair conditions and rates of pay. The union is constantly looking out for ways like this to show promoters, record companies and the rest of the music industry the right way to treat musicians, and to remind the business yet again of their responsibility to put back into music just a small part of the rewards which they enjoy, thanks to the skills of musicians.

That is the MU in action. If you want to find out more, write to the Musicians' Union: 60–2 Clapham Road, London SW9 0JJ.

21 Copyright and Performing Right

BRIAN ENGEL is the membership representative of the Performing Right Society. Before joining the PRS, Brian worked as a singer (including being a member of the New Seekers), songwriter, actor, artist and toy inventor among other creative and business interests.

People seem to find it relatively easy to understand the term 'patent', but have difficulty with 'copyright'. This is probably because, put simply, the word 'patent' applies to a physical thing, like a new piece of machinery or electrical gadget, whereas 'copyright' applies to 'intellectual property', that is 'ideas' and 'creations'. In the UK there is no requirement for a copyright reference, no copyright number or anything. Copyright is exactly what it says: it is the right to copy. The minute you have written a piece of music (providing it is genuinely original) you create a copyright. However, you need to be able to establish and prove that it was you who created the copyright. Only then will you avoid difficulties which you would otherwise encounter in claiming any money owing to your copyrights.

The PRS

When you are starting out in the music business there seems to be an impenetrable jungle of initials to understand: MCPS, PPL, MPA, PRS, BASCA, BMI, ASCAP; the list seems endless! So what are they all for? In the case of PRS, the title is self-explanatory. The Performing Right Society is a society of songwriters and publishers (or 'copyright owners') which grants the 'Right to Perform' copyright music in return for an annual fee (or licence). The PRS was formed in 1914 and now has over 22,000 members.

As the UK is such a small geographical market, there is only *one* Performing Right Society. This works in favour of music writers, and because the PRS is the only organization which can license venues and media in this country, it is sufficiently strong to make sure its members' copyrights are appropriately rewarded for any performances.

Securing a Copyright

A music writer can protect a copyright in a number of ways:

(i) Put the music down in some physical form, like a musical score or as a demo tape. Date it and place it in the safe keeping of a bank manager or a solicitor (although these professionals often don't like doing this, as it is a lot of trouble).

(ii) Get the copyright 'signed' to a publisher. It is then the publisher's responsibility to see that you receive the money which you are due.

(iii) Put the song down into a physical form, as described above, and send it to yourself by REGISTERED POST. Keep the receipt and DON'T OPEN THE PARCEL. It is accepted in the musical business that this is the easiest and best way to secure your copyright.

As a musician it is worthwhile to deal both with copyright and performing right. If you are a writer, the majority of your income may come from performances of your music either on the radio, the television or at live concerts. Consider this: every time a writer/performer sells an album, their royalty earns them around 60p (assuming they are on 10 per cent). But each time their music is played on BBC Radio 1, they are paid about £50—simple mathematics explains the rest!

It is never too early to consider the copyright and performing right on your songs. As soon as you start writing original work, register the copyrights in one of the ways already outlined. Then you should be able to collect any money which your songs may earn in the future.

PRS 'Licences'

Anyone who 'uses' copyright music has to buy an annual licence from the PRS. These 'music users' include everyone from radio and television stations, clubs, pubs, restaurants, shops, concert halls, dance halls and any other place where there is either live or recorded music audible to the public.

The money which is collected from PRS licences is distributed to the society's members (the writers and publishers) in proportion to the number of times their works have been played. Of course, the amount which the society collects each year varies with inflation and the actual number of licences which are granted. In the late 1980s, the PRS regularly received around £100,000,000 for its members.

The Amount Each Member Gets

Each member's PRS earnings depends on how much money the society collects and how often a member's work is played on PRS-licenced media and premises. For a three-minute play on a British national radio station, the PRS pays approximately £50. For a similar play on a small local station the payment will be less. Often the writer doesn't earn the whole payment. Instead, these fees are divided between a writer and a publisher. So, if a songwriter has a 60:40 publishing deal, he or she would receive 60 per cent of the PRS payment, and the publisher would get the other 40 per cent. However, a writer doesn't need to have a publisher, and in this case the writer would receive the entire sum.

How PRS Pays Its Writers

Every radio and television station submits lists of the music which they broadcast to the PRS. To check the stations' information, the PRS also monitors their output. From this steady stream of data, the number of television and radio broadcasts of every registered song, tune, or any other piece of music, is constantly being counted by the PRS. Then, the amounts due to the society's writers and publishers are calculated and distributed either as a direct payment to a bank account or as a cheque. There are four distributions a year and these payments also include substantial royalties received by the PRS from equivalent foreign societies for the performance of PRS members' music overseas.

As there are many types of live performance venues, like clubs, discos, and major stadiums, there is a variety of licence fees payable to the PRS. For instance, a concert attracting 70,000 at Wembley would have to pay more than a gig at the Sock and Warthog in the High Street. Also, it would be impractical for the society to pay out each time a particular tune is played at every PRS-licensed venue. The administration costs would be endless and it would be difficult to prove exactly how many times a local pub rock group has played any one song. To deal with this, the PRS has developed a complex scale of payments for live performances. In short, the society requires a list of all music which is performed live *only at major venues and on the bigger tours.* A band doesn't have to concern itself with filling in PRS forms at their gigs until they are working in these larger venues. At this point, the venue or the promoter will raise the issue with the band or their management. The event's promoter will pay an agreed fee to the PRS for the works which are to be performed, and a payment is then made by the PRS to the writers and publishers for the works listed as being played.

For live performances at smaller venues there is no need for an itemized PRS form because no payment is made for each individual song. A fee is collected by the PRS from the management of the venue and this is put into a fund called the General Distribution Pool. This fund is paid out to all members of the society. For more details on this subject, consult the *PRS Yearbook* which all members receive annually.

Running the PRS

There is no 'owner' of the PRS. It is a non-profit-making organization which is controlled by its members. They are represented by an elected general council of music publishers and writers who are drawn from a cross-section of the music profession (classical, popular, rock, TV, films, advertising). Its administration is carried out by a staff of several hundred who work under the direction of the general council. The council makes all the decisions which concern the society's policy, but on major issues, the members' opinions are sought through ballots and general meetings.

Membership of PRS

A writer is eligible for membership in a number of ways. Membership may be given if a writer has had three works recorded for sale to the public which have been released by a recognized recording label (one which is registered in the *Music Master* catalogue). This doesn't have to be a disc—a cassette or video qualifies as well. A writer is also eligible if he or she has three works broadcast on the radio or the television. These broadcasts don't need to be records because live performances on local radio can also count. If you write a song that sells well enough to reach the top 50 in the albums or singles chart you are eligible automatically. Or if you have three works which are performed live in PRS-licensed premises at least twelve times over the course of two years, you can also become a member of the society. A songwriter *proves* these twelve live performances simply by supplying the society with copies of posters, press advertisements or tour dates—*anything* which confirms these plays. Providing that these gigs were at PRS-licensed venues, then an application for membership will be accepted for serious consideration. A publisher is eligible for membership when they publish fifteen titles, ten of which must have been commercially exploited (and they must all have been written by PRS writer members).

The Organizations which Deal with Copyright

MCPS: this is the Mechanical Copyright Protection Society Ltd. of Elgar House, 41 Streatham High Road, London SW16 1ER. Their telephone number is 081–769 4400. This society pays the copyright owners (the writers and/or publishers) for the *manufacture* and *sales* of the physical articles into which their music is made, like vinyl records, compact discs, videos, and cassettes. This is a percentage of the selling price of these music products.

PPL: this is Phonographic Performance Ltd. of Ganton House, 14–22 Ganton Street, London W1V 1LB. Their telephone number is 071–437 0311. This organization pays money to record companies and artists for the performances of their music on radio and television, unlike PRS which pays the writers. If a performer is also a writer, then this society would be worth joining. A quick phone call to either PPL or MCPS will establish whether you are eligible for membership.

Further details about the PRS can be obtained at 29–33 Berners Street, London W14P 4AA. Phone: 071–927 8345. If you think you should be a member, we will take up your case.

22 Deciphering the Legal Jargon

MARK MELTON has been the Musicians' Union's music business adviser since 1987. Before that he was involved in band management and ran an independent record company, New England Records. He has a keen interest in popular music and the developing laws and rights in respect of musical performers and songwriters.

This chapter will discuss the main long-term contracts which a potential recording artist is likely to sign. These long-term contracts differ from shorter or one-off agreements (for endorsements or live performances) because they almost always call for musicians' *exclusive* services. I will consider these five contracts:

1. Agreements between band members
2. Management agreements
3. Recording agreements
4. Music publishing agreements
5. Booking agency agreements

All of these are for a personal service. As such, they involve a high degree of trust, good will, confidence and faith in all parties' ability to do the job in hand.

Musicians must seek legal advice if they are offered any of these agreements, and their legal adviser should be a specialist in the music business. A solicitor in divorce law or conveyancing will not deal with the music business on a day-to-day basis and he or she will not be able to advise you fully on the terms of a music industry agreement. The best way to find a legal adviser is to ask musicians in other bands, write to the Law Society or, if you are a member of the Musicians' Union, request a list of music business lawyers from the union's national office.

Currently, music business solicitors are in the talent-spotting game, just like record companies, publishers, managers and agents. It is quite common for specialist music solicitors to offer their services free of charge to a band who approach them, who are broke and are creating a 'buzz'. Of course the solicitor will charge the band when a record or publishing deal is signed. As the top solicitors are highly regarded in the music business, sometimes this can be another way of getting a foot in the door.

For the five contracts dealt with in this article, there is no such thing as a 'standard' agreement. However, it is also unlikely that any company will draw up an agreement from scratch. Most companies (record companies, music publishers and large management firms) have what they refer to as their standard agreement. This is offered to all the artists they sign. The company may be reluctant to deviate too far from the basic terms of this agreement, but there are a number of things which are negotiable. Legal and business advice is extremely helpful in establishing exactly which areas in an agreement *can* be negotiated.

1. Agreements between Members of a Band

The first issue is when a formal agreement should be made between the members of a band. Ideally, some sort of agreement should be worked out fairly early on. This gives each band member a degree of security. If there is no formal agreement between the band members, and if the band has been working in practice as a partnership, I have always viewed the band as operating as if there were a formal partnership agreement. In that case, the following rules normally apply.

Joint Financial Responsibility

All members of the band are equally responsible for the band's financial affairs. If there are any band debts, all members share the liability equally. If a member leaves the band, he or she is only responsible for the debts incurred prior to his or her leaving. New members of the band are only liable for debts incurred after their joining.

Profits and Assets

Without anything in writing to the contrary, it is legally assumed that all members of the band equally share the band's profits and assets. This is always the case unless the purchase of equipment and other costs are undertaken privately by one or more members of the band.

Band Name

If there is no written agreement on the matter, all members of the band share equally in the rights of the name. This makes it difficult if the band is split in half with both sides wanting to use the band's original name.

Other Points to be Considered in a Formal Agreement

Band member leaving the band Often there will be a clause in a partnership agreement stating that if a band member leaves the band he or she is required to give a certain amount of notice. This can range from one to three or six months, depending on what the band feel is most suitable.

Band member being dismissed from the band This issue is always riddled with acrimony. There needs to be a unanimous decision from all members of the band (except, of course, the band member being sacked) before anyone is dismissed. Also, there is a need for a dissolution account to be drawn up so musicians know the state of the band's finances when a member either leaves or is dismissed.

The points about joint responsibility for assets, liabilities and profits apply whether a band member is dismissed or he or she leaves voluntarily.

Composer members Often only one or two members of the band write songs. In recent years, it has been more common for songwriting members to allow the band's non-songwriters to share in a percentage of their songwriting royalties. Otherwise, the non-songwriting members of the band would be considerably poorer than the others. By sharing songwriting income, the songwriter is recognizing that without the help of the other band members, his or her songs may not be generating any income at all.

Band bank account The partnership agreement may deal with where the band's joint bank account is held and how many signatures are required on the account to deal with the band's finances.

Band decisions A democratic approach would be that a majority of the band constitutes the necessary authority to make decisions.

Limited companies It isn't uncommon for a band to form a limited company. Usually this is because of tax advantages. However, in the early days of a band's existence it operates more often as a partnership.

2. Management Agreements

Of all the music business agreements artists are likely to sign (with the possible exception of the agreement between the different members of the band), the management/artist relationship is a contract for services at its most personal. As a result, both parties should always behave in good faith. The manager should take into account the artist's wishes and aspirations. The artist must undertake to act reasonably at all times if offered fair advice by his or her manager. Also, the manager is expected to use his or her best endeavours to promote the artist's career, while the artist should do nothing to jeopardize the reputation of the manager. Due to the 'Fiduciary' (trusting) nature of the relationship, honesty and integrity is to be assumed on both sides.

Below, I have dealt with the areas most commonly negotiable in a management agreement. These should be discussed by both parties before entering into the relationship.

Exclusivity and Territory

A management agreement is an 'exclusive' agreement. Most managers want to deal with *all* of an artist's activities in the entertainment business *throughout the world.* Neither of these limitations are necessarily negative for the artist. Musicians need someone to co-ordinate all of their music business activities, and it makes sense that this should be done on a world-wide basis.

Length of the Agreement

Most management agreements are signed for between three and five years. A maximum of three years is preferable for the artist. Each year, the manager has the choice whether to continue the agreement. These 'options' only work on behalf of the manager. With an established, respected management company it is unlikely that any band would secure an agreement for less than five years.

There are certain safety clauses music solicitors put into management agreements to give the artist an escape from the contract. This type of clause may demand that if the manager hasn't secured a recording contract to the artist's satisfaction within a period of twelve months from the start of the agreement, the artist should have the right to terminate the agreement. Other safety nets (known as 'performance clauses') can require the manager to secure a certain level of earnings for the artist throughout the agreement.

Ideally, the artist could terminate the agreement at any time. However, managers put a lot of time, energy and commitment into their artist's careers (as well as a substantial financial investment), so it would be unfair for the manager to be dismissed at a moment's notice, just because the artist fancied a change of management. The important thing is to achieve the right balance.

Commission

Management commission rates vary, but a current average is 20 per cent of the artist's earnings. The agreement must specify that this 20 per cent should be on money actually received by the artist, not on items such as bad debts, and that there should be allowances for exactly what the commission is chargeable on in certain circumstances. For example, most managers seek commission on gross earnings, whereas artists' representatives attempt to reduce the manager's commission to net earnings from the band's live touring. Currently, touring is an extremely expensive business. As a result, solicitors argue that managers should not take commission on what the artist is being paid each night, but on the money the band earns as profit after having paid for the PA, lights, accommodation and other expenses.

Non-Commissionable Items

The following should not be subject to commision by the manager:
  recording costs;
  promotional video costs;
  producer's advances and fees;
  tour support money (money advanced to artists by record companies to underwrite any losses from touring).

Expenses

Clauses in management agreements about 'who pays what' are often the most contentious. It is generally felt that the manager should be responsible for his or her own office overheads, telephone bills, secretarial services and so on. All other expenses come out of the artist's earnings. These can include equipment, artist's travel and accommodation, the engagement of a tour manager, any personal assistance for the artist/band, legal and accounting fees. The most awkward of these are the manager's expenses when travelling at the request and on behalf of the artist. It often pays the artist to try and put a ceiling figure on these expenses. This ensures that the manager seeks the artist's permission before spending more than a certain amount of money. Other clauses could refer to the manager travelling and staying in accommodation of the same class as the artist.

Collection of Money

The British music business seems to be changing its practices for collecting money. Previously, managers received all the artist's money, deducted their commission and expenses, and finally paid the balance to the artist within an agreed period of time. However, the American method is now gaining popularity. In this situation, the artist is responsible for collecting money (often through their own accountants), while the manager invoices the artist on a monthly basis for his or her commission and expenses. A manager who is efficient at plotting an artist's career isn't always the best person to look after the artist's financial interests or sort out VAT, tax and National Insurance. If all the artist's money is paid to the artist's accountant directly, these financial matters can be dealt with by an expert, leaving the manager free to develop the artist's career.

Some bands are extremely keen to sign with a respected manager who insists on collecting the artist's money. In this case, certain safeguards can be built into the agreement to protect the artist and speed up the accounting of money. If the manager collects the money, the artist may insist the manager sets up a completely separate bank account. This would be in the artist's name, with the manager as the sole signatory. No money from any of the manager's other interests could be mixed in with this account, and the manager should not be allowed to borrow money from it. All he or she could remove from the account would be his or her commission and expenses. The balance would be paid to the artist. Usually, this payment would be made four times a year, but for larger sums the process should be quicker. Finally, if the manager were to get into financial difficulties, and his or her creditors required payment, it should be clear that no money in this account belongs to the manager, and it cannot be used to settle the manager's personal debts.

Right of Audit

An important clause in a management agreement where the manager collects the money is the right of audit. This allows the artist to look at the manager's books, with reasonable notice. If the artist is to collect the money, then the manager will require a similar right.

After the Agreement is Over

Most managers want to take commission on any deals they set up for the artist. However, record contracts tend to last longer than management agreements (a management agreement might last for three years while a record contract may go on as long as ten). As a result, artists feel that if they have parted company with their manager after three years it is unfair if their previous manager continues to take commission on album sales for another seven years. Conversely, managers (quite reasonably) insist that it would be equally unjust if their rights to commission on projects which they have initiated were to cease the moment they parted company from the artist. Consequently, compromises have built up over the years. One of these is that when the two parties separate, the manager continues to take commission for a number of years, but only on those records issued or those songs written during his or her term of office. This means that an artist can take on a new manager who can take commission on all new projects, while the former manager continues to earn from all previous albums for a specified time. The exact details are negotiable and depend on the circumstances of each deal.

Getting Out of the Agreement

Both parties in a management agreement should have the right to terminate the agreement if certain things go wrong. Like any legal agreement, if there is a material breach by either party there should be a right for the injured party to terminate the contract. A manager's persistent failure to pay over money to the artist would constitute such a breach, as would constant failure to make him or herself available to the artist, or the wilful neglect of the artist's career. Both parties need the right to end the agreement if the other goes bankrupt or is forced into liquidation, or ceases to operate in the music business.

When things go wrong between artist and manager, it is often difficult to prove any of these contractual points. In that case, the four fundamental aspects of the manager/artist relationship are the focus of negotiation. Have both the parties acted in good faith? Has either party breached the fiduciary nature of the relationship? Has the manager at all times respected the wishes and aspirations of the artist? Has the artist acted unreasonably in ignoring the advice of the manager?

3. Recording Agreements

The record deal is certainly the most important of an artist's long-term contracts. The legal terms of this agreement will not necessarily govern the day-to-day relationship between the record company and artist, but it will set out the obligations of both parties, or 'who is responsible for what'. As with other long-term agreements, a record company demands an exclusive contract with its recording artists.

This is hardly surprising as establishing new artists is a costly and lengthy process.

How is the Artist Paid?

Royalties on record sales govern how much an artist earns from his or her recording career. Royalties vary depending on the perceived value of the artist to the record company. An average of 10 to 14 per cent of the record's retail selling price is the average for a new band. In pence per record terms, this means that most bands receive a royalty of between 50p and 70p per album sold. This figure is calculated on the assumption that an album retails for just under £7. However, the royalty is based on the retail price less VAT and a percentage of the packaging charge, to which record companies require artists to contribute.

Before these royalties are earned, the company want to recover the cost of recording the albums plus any other financial advances they have paid to the artist. For example, a new band signing a major record deal may well spend £50,000 recording an album and receive another £50,000 in personal advances (money to live on until royalty income is generated). If their royalty from album sales is equivalent to 50p per album, the band needs to sell 200,000 albums before they break even. This begins to explain why record companies require long-term agreements with artists and are looking for acts with world-wide potential.

Most new artists and bands aren't in a strong bargaining position. They may have to settle for royalties which are lower than they would prefer. Consequently, artists' representatives tend to build 'bonuses' into agreements with which record companies are usually quite happy. It isn't uncommon for a record contract to allow for a royalty increase of 1 per cent throughout each year of the agreement, and for this to be raised once certain sales figures have been reached (commonly, this might be for gold and platinum status albums). There are other areas such as 12″ singles, TV advertised albums and various mail order clubs which are all subject to negotiation between the record company and artist.

Once musicians' royalty income becomes greater than the cost of their recording time and personal advances from the record company, they start receiving royalty statements. Usually these arrive twice yearly, within ninety days of the end of June and December.

The Length of the Record Deal

Most record company agreements are on the basis of a one-year period plus a number of options. Major record companies normally require at least five or six options. Potentially these options tie the artist to the record company for up to seven or eight years. However, if the company elects to exercise its option at the beginning of a contract year, it must pay the artist a previously agreed sum of money as an advance against future royalties. It is important to set a figure for these advance payments which is realistic for the band to live on throughout the period of the contract. There is no 'average' advance figure, but major record companies are often willing to pay in excess of £50,000 to a new band, rising each year throughout the contract. Smaller independent companies aren't in this league. With an independent, it is vital to restrict the maximum length of the agreement to the shortest time possible.

Recordings

The artist needs to ensure the record company is committed to releasing a certain amount of product each year. Ideally, artists should see an album released in every twelve months of the agreement. Contracts should be structured so that if the company doesn't release any recordings during a certain contract year, the artist has the option to terminate the agreement and look elsewhere for a record deal.

The choice of material, recording studio and producer are always contentious. Currently, the balance of power over these decisions seems to have swung in the artist's favour. Most recording agreements allow for a mutual choice on all these areas between the artist and company.

Third-party producers often require a royalty as payment for their work. More often than not, the producer's money comes out of the artist's record company royalty payment. The most an artist can do is to limit the amounts which are paid to a well-known producer. I suggest this should be a maximum of 2 per cent. In this case, if the artist receives a 12 per cent royalty, and the producer requires a 2 per cent royalty on record sales, the artist is left with a royalty of only 10 per cent split between the members of the band.

Videos

Videos have proved spectacularly successful in launching many bands on a world-wide career. In the early 1980s, many British bands were household names in the USA without having toured there. Record companies normally want to recoup 50 per cent of the cost of videos from the artist's royalty account. For the artist, it is certainly worthwhile watching the video's budget and not spending excessively if at all possible.

Tour Support

There are often phenomenal overheads in putting a band on the road. In the early days of a band, the fees received from gigs are unlikely to cover the touring costs. It has become usual practice for record companies to advance bands some money to underwrite the costs of these first tours. This should not be necessary as soon as the band plays in larger venues. Record companies consider this support quite economic because they view a band's tours as a good way of promoting records. Tour support advances are invariably recoupable from the artist's royalty account.

All other expenses on marketing the artist's records (such as radio promotion, posters, and press advertisements) are the responsibility of the record company. The artist should not contribute financially to these. Major record companies invest vast sums of money in new artists every year. It isn't rare for a quarter of a million pounds to be spent on an act in one year. With these amounts of money involved, the relationship between band and record company can occasionally be quite strained. The record company is anxious to recover their investment quickly. The band is also in a difficult position. They are likely to be in debt to their record company for a number of years. Even though this debt isn't repayable if the band aren't successful, it is always an uncomfortable feeling to know someone else is pulling the strings.

Artists who can work with their record company effectively (often with the help of intelligent management) probably stand more of a chance than the naïve, bad-tempered or egocentric band. A potential recording artist must realize there have to be some compromises between art and business.

4. Song-writing and Music Publishing

Most bands write their own material. There is a great deal of money to be made from income generated by composers' royalties and fees as well as the earnings from performing and recording. Sometimes every member of a band writes songs, but often it is only one or two. It is a matter for the band partnership agreement to clarify each songwriter's policy on whether the non-writing band members will earn any money from his or her publishing royalties.

Songwriters and composers are eligible to join various collecting societies such as the Performing Right Society and the Mechanical Copyright Protection Society. However, many songwriters still choose to sign an exclusive publishing agreement with a music publisher, thereby giving up a portion of their royalties and fees, and assigning all rights in their songs to that music publisher for a set period of time. There are various reasons why a songwriter/artist should do this. I have listed four of the more common ones below.

Advances

Publishers often pay their songwriters fairly large, annual financial advances on account of future royalties. The size of these advances will vary, but if a writer has already several hit singles in his or her catalogue the advance may be very sizeable.

Record Deals and Promotional Assistance

Alert music publishers are sometimes quicker than the record industry at spotting songwriter/artists' commercial talent. In this situation, it is quite common for the songwriter/artist to sign an exclusive agreement with the publisher. This would include annual advances (although not as large as in the previous situation), access to a recording studio for making demos, and involvement with the publisher's various contacts in the music industry to help secure a record deal.

Administration and Collection

Later on in their career, musicians may decide to form their own publishing company and to seek only the administration services of a large corporate publisher. In return for a small share of the songs' royalty earnings, the larger company takes over the day-to-day business of administering the musicians' song catalogues while the musicians retain all copyright and control of their material (see the 'Self-Publishing' section below).

Covers

Not all songwriters are active performers. A non-artist songwriter will need a music publisher who can promote his or her writers' songs aggressively, trying to place them with major recording stars. Some music publishers certainly have a better track record in this area than others. It can be worthwhile to look through trade magazines and check on various companies' success in placing their songs with artists. Also, talk to other writers, solicitors and friends in the music business to confirm your research.

Earning Money as a Songwriter

The following areas are the most common ways of earning money from your songs.

Mechanical Royalties As well as the recording artists receiving a royalty from record sales, the songwriter is also entitled to a royalty payment from each record sold. These royalties are collected from the record company, on behalf of the songwriter, by either the songwriter's publisher or, provided she or he is a member, by the Mechanical Copyright Protection Society (MCPS). Unlike artists' record royalties, all songwriters receive the same royalty which is a rate agreed between the record industry and the MCPS.

Performing income Money is also payable to songwriters from radio and TV stations in the form of 'air play' money. All songwriters should join the Performing Right Society when they become eligible. The PRS collects this portion of money for writers.

Synchronization fees These are one-off payments made by film or television companies to the copyright holder of a song. They buy the right to incorporate a piece of music into a film or television programme's soundtrack.

Sheet music Some songs sell well in sheet music form (ballads are usually very popular). There is a royalty payable on sales from this area.

The Publishing Agreement

All of the areas mentioned below are subject to negotiation. It is very important to stress that the relative bargaining strength of each party governs the kind of a deal which is made.

Length of contract An agreement may be for one song, or for everything a musician writes over a number of years. Longer term contracts are often known as 'blanket' deals. The most common period of time for this sort of agreement is three or four years, and the advances payable should reflect this. As with recording advances, there is no such thing as a typical figure, but for a non-performing writer, enough money to live on should be sought.

Assignment of copyright Copyright exists in a musical work until fifty years after the end of the year in which the songwriter dies. At the end of this period, the musical work becomes public property. Until quite recently, most music publishing agreements assigned all rights in a song to the publisher for this full copyright term. However, the publishing business has recently become more competitive and it is now possible for songwriters to restrict the length of the assignment of copyright to what is known as a 'retention period'. This is usually for the length of the publishing agreement (normally about three to four years) plus a period which could range from five to twenty-five years, depending on the writer's bargaining position.

Royalties and advances For a songwriter/artist who the music publisher believes has a good chance of success, it is quite usual for there to be a royalty split of 70:30 in favour of the writer. This should cover all the areas mentioned above except sheet music where a royalty of between 10 and 12 per cent of the full published price is the going rate. As with record royalties, those songwriters who sign on less advantageous terms are sometimes successful in securing increases throughout each new year of the agreement. For example, a writer who signs an agreement with a 60:40 split may be able to negotiate a rise of 5 per cent in every year of the contract.

Accounting As with record companies, this tends to be twice yearly. It is important that the agreement gives a songwriter a 'right of audit', the right to inspect the publisher's books.

Reversion and determination clauses These are particularly important clauses for the songwriter. If the publisher has failed to exploit the song in any manner, within a given period of time, the songwriter is able to have all rights in the songs returned. Also, if the publisher enters into liquidation, the writer must have the right to terminate the agreement and get back all rights to his or her songs.

Self-Publishing

At a certain point in a writer's career, he or she may want to set up his or her own publishing company. This is the usual route to self-publishing.

Unless a writer is eligible to join the PRS as a publisher member (in addition to being a songwriting member) there is little point in setting up a new publishing company. On the release of a writer's first album, it is unlikely that he or she would have enough qualifying works to become a publisher member of PRS (see the 'Copyright and Performing Right' article for details on these qualifying requirements). For this reason, some writers enter into an 'administration deal' with a corporate music publisher. In this case, the songwriter should retain his or her songs' copyrights, and the publisher is responsible for administering the song catalogues (collecting the money payable to the writer's songs). The publisher will charge around 10–15 per cent of the royalties received from the writer's songs for this service. Usually, these deals can be negotiated for a short term. This allows the writer to join the PRS as a publisher member when he or she has enough qualifying works, to end the administration deal, and to sign the rights in his or her songs into a personally owned published company.

For a songwriter, the main advantages of owning a publishing company are usually regarded as keeping total control of, and earning 100 per cent of the income generated by, his or her songs. Some writers set up publishing companies for tax purposes. Others believe it looks more professional. However, there are disadvantages. The most obvious is that a larger amount of time is required from the writer. This is particularly evident when the writer has to organize the negotiations for the essential deals with foreign sub-publishers who collect royalties in non-UK territories.

5. Booking Agency Agreements

The brief of booking agents has changed radically in recent years. In the past, a band would acquire an agent fairly early in their career. The main job of the agent would be to assist the band in moving up through various grades of gig. Currently, bands seem to be facing a shrinking number of live venues coupled with the enormous expense of going on the road. This has resulted in no one making a profit from most bands' early tours. Indeed, some bands are unable to tour without their record company's financial support. Not surprisingly, established booking agents have reacted to this situation by being ever more wary of signing bands without a record deal.

Another factor which has affected the band/agent relationship has been the prominent role of strong legal advice. Lawyers always advise clients to limit the term of any music business agreement to as short a term as possible. Recently there has been a certain amount of paranoia from agents who have been tied to short-term agreements, and then have lost a band to the highest bidder just as the act is becoming successful. As a result, agents are becoming even more cagey about developing raw talent.

In the artist/booking agent agreement, the most important areas of negotiation are as follows.

Commission

Most booking agents charge a commission of 15 per cent which is payable on the gross fees for any live work. As an act's appearance fees become higher, the agent may settle for a smaller percentage.

Length of Agreement

This is variable, depending on how the two parties perceive the relationship. Most agents prefer a term of about three years, whereas bands want to work on a yearly basis. Some larger acts engage an agent for one tour at a time. If an agent is insistent on a three-year agreement, it is quite common for the artist to negotiate performance clauses. These call for a minimum level of earnings at strategic intervals throughout the relationship.

Territory

Agents invariably want to represent an artist throughout the world. This may not necessarily be useful to a band if the agent is a small or new company. Larger companies have contacts throughout the world and reciprocal arrangements with foreign agencies. Any commission paid to a foreign sub-agent should not be charged to the artist. It should be paid by the artist's UK agent, out of his or her commission.

Collection of Money

This concerns the collection of revenues arising from the artist's live appearances. The ideal situation for the artist is that all money should be paid to the artist. Then the agent either sends an invoice to the artist for the commission, or arranges for the commission to be paid by the promoters. However, some agents prefer to collect all gross revenues from promoters and, having deducted their commission, pay the balance on to the artists. For a band, this is not at all desirable because their earnings are out of their direct control.

The Need for Legal Advice

All the long-term agreements facing a potential recording artist are highly complex legally binding documents which have a great effect on an act's career. The value of good legal assistance cannot be overstressed. I always advise musicians to digest at least a certain amount of knowledge about their business affairs. There have been far too many examples of artists 'living for the moment', putting their faith in others to run their career, and waking up to find themselves penniless, out of favour with the public and feeling rather stupid. As an aspiring recording artist, I can only hope you will enjoy your music and live the lifestyle, while you remember that the music business is a career, just like any other.

23 Music Business Accountancy

. . . .

MARK BOOMLA works in the Entertainments Division of Touche Ross, one of the biggest accountancy firms in the world. He has considerable experience of advising major pop artists and companies on all aspects of their finances.

E verything about a musician's life concerns money. Whether it is hiring the local scout hut for rehearsals or the huge expenses of a worldwide tour, someone has to count the cost. However, although your accountant is your 'servant', he or she isn't clairvoyant. Your accountant relies on the information and explanations which you make available. Then he or she can help you get the best financial return from your music.

The first stage of any band's life is playing for fun. Unwittingly, the members of the band have formed an unincorporated association. They aren't trading because they don't receive income. All expenses are paid by the band's members as with any hobby, so an accountant doesn't need to be involved, although there are certain precautionary steps which should be taken at this early stage. Firstly, all equipment should be bought and owned by specific members of the band, and all purchase invoices should be kept. To avoid unnecessary disputes, draw up a list of equipment and its owners so that it can be agreed by all the members of the band. Similarly, all songs composed by the band should be credited to those members who actually wrote them. If songs are co-written, then each songwriter should be credited with the proportion of the song which they created.

Turning Professional

This is the second stage in a band's life, when they first receive income. This can happen in a number of ways. A band could sign a recording contract, or receive income from live performances or session fees (the receipt of prize money from a talent contest is tax free and does not give rise to taxable income unless this occurs on a regular basis). Now, the band has been transformed from an unincorporated association into a partnership. The existence of a partnership has significant legal consequences, and it is best practice for the members of any partnership to have a written agreement, drafted by a lawyer.

In this article, I have assumed that a band has reached this second stage by being offered a recording contract. It is now that the band requires an accountant. The band should meet their accountant before signing the recording contract to discuss the following:

1. The accountant, in conjunction with the lawyer, will advise the members of the band whether they should form a limited liability company before entering into any legally binding relationship with a record company.

2. The accountant should inform the band that, as they are about to start trading, it is necessary to notify the Inland Revenue (the tax man). The accountant will be happy to do this on the band's behalf.

3. It is likely that any 'advance' paid by a record company will be in excess of the minimum level of income for compulsory VAT registration purposes, so the band should be aware of their obligation to register for VAT immediately. Once registered there is a requirement to file a VAT return every three months with the Customs and Excise and the accountant will discuss how these will be completed and filed.

4. The band will need to open a bank account, if they haven't done so already. It is best practice for the accountant to discuss with the band who should be the cheque signatories on this account. A cash book should be maintained for each bank account to record every item of income and expenditure, analyse these into appropriate costs and back them up with supporting documentation. It may seem a chore to gather invoices to document your expenses, but without these, items of expenditure may not be allowed as a deduction from income by the Inland Revenue. Then the band would have to pay more tax than would otherwise be necessary. For instance, when the accountant produces the band's first accounts, and files them with the Inland Revenue, the invoices for the band's musical equipment may need to be produced so that the accountant may obtain tax relief for these items, although they were purchased in the first stage of a band's life.

5. As the accountant will, if required, help produce the annual accounts, he or she will want to ensure that adequate cash books are maintained. To do this, the accountant will discuss who will be responsible for them (this might be a band member, the accountant

or the band's manager). If necessary, he or she will advise on the detailed layout of the cash books, and suggest that he or she reviews them occasionally to ensure their adequacy.

Also, the accountant will wish to establish who is responsible for completing and filing the VAT return for the Customs and Excise. It may be appropriate for the person who maintains the cash books to do this, but because of their technical nature it may be necessary for the accountant to do this instead.

6. There may be an obligation for the band members to deduct income tax (Pay As You Earn) from the salaries of any employees. In this case, it is necessary to set up a PAYE scheme with the Inland Revenue, to deduct tax and National Insurance, and to pay these over on a regular monthly basis. For the band members' own 'salaries', a Certificate of Tax Deposits can be purchased from the Inland Revenue. The advantage of this scheme is that you don't need to remember to save the money which you would have paid to the Government later on! The accountant will identify whether there is a need to establish a PAYE scheme and, if the band or their manager aren't willing to take on this responsibility, the accountant will operate this scheme on their behalf.

The Record Deal

The band is likely to negotiate a large non-returnable, but 'recoupable' (out of future royalties earned) advance from the record company. The accountant will try to ensure that the band have given enough thought to how long this money is likely to last, and how best to use it until the next payment or earnings are due. The budgets of anticipated income and expenditure which are prepared at this stage are vital if the band are to appreciate the limits of their financial resources. All too often large advances can seem like a ticket to stardom. In reality they are mercilessly small when you realize for how long they have to be eked out!

As an example, consider the situation of a three-piece band who are about to receive £100,000 as a record company advance (and they have taken the decision to delay any possible publishing advances until after the release of two singles from the forthcoming album). Out of the £100,000, it is likely that the manager of the band will take 20 per cent (£20,000). Various other costs such as administration, legal accountancy fees, as well as paying off any debts of the individual band members, could all amount to a further £20,000. This leaves the band with £60,000. From that, each member of the band is likely to have a 'salary' equivalent to around £20,000 per annum before tax. Although this is a fair wage, it isn't going to sustain a rock 'n' roll superstar lifestyle for longer than a few weeks, so it is only by sensible use of budgets that the real size of the advances can be put in context.

This example might seem unrealistically pessimistic, as a new band may feel confident of being able to record and release their album in just a few months, with money from sales and royalties quickly starting to flow in. In practice this is never the case. Recording an album inevitably takes longer than expected. Songs may have to be rewritten, particular studio engineers or producers may not be available when first required, band members may fall ill and the record company may delay the release of the album 'until the market is right'. There are innumerable reasons why albums take longer than expected to get into the shops. Also, because of the type of accounting system adopted by all record companies, it is quite feasible for royalties generated from record sales in the UK to take nine months before they are paid to the artist. Record sales in foreign territories can take up to two years before they are paid. Furthermore, the three-piece band's advance was to be 'recoupable'. This means that all of the band's percentage of the royalties generated from their record sales are spent first on repaying the record company advance. When that has been paid off, the band will start to see some profit from their records. So, although the advance of £100,000 may appear a vast sum of money, it can result in a lack of spending power in the pockets of individual band members.

Recording Costs

Recording in a top flight studio is often new and exciting for any band. Suddenly, musicians can be working with engineers, producers and a whole host of technical equipment which previously had been the stuff of their dreams. Musically, this can seem like an Aladdin's cave, but financially it can be a nightmare. The band may not realize all the costs of recording and of hiring an engineer or producer. The band must remember that recording costs are treated in a similar way to advances. To start with, the record company will pay the costs of the recording studio, the producer and the engineer, but these will all be charged to the band's account at the record company. The record company recoups this expenditure by making the band liable to pay these costs from their share of the royalties generated from record sales. The band's earnings from their recording contract go towards paying this debt to the record company as well, putting off even further the stage when the band earns money from its records.

It is worthwhile for the band to keep some diary notes as to the studios they have used and on which days. Also, record which engineers, producers and backing musicians were employed. This information will be particularly useful when checking the recording costs debited to the band's royalty statement.

Touring

Once the recording has been completed, it is likely the band will go on tour to promote their album. The accountant, in conjunction with the lawyer, will consider using a separate limited company to undertake the touring activity, and advise accordingly. The main advantage of a limited company is that in general only the company and not the individual is liable for the business debts. Once the coffers have run dry, there is no recourse to the individual band members to pay any outstanding bills personally. There are important exceptions to this rule on which advice will need to be sought. The principal disadvantage is that a limited company invariably incurs some additional costs.

Touring generates two particular problems for the accountant. At the beginning of a career, any band's tours are likely to make a loss. It is likely that this loss will be funded (at least in part) by the record company and, in this case, the band are likely to receive an advance against future royalties. This is usually recoupable, so the band should realize that they are spending their own money on tour, and not the record company's.

The second problem of touring is that the volume of the band's financial transactions will increase dramatically. From the dozen or so per week when the band is in the studio, there will be up to 100 per week as they go on the road. Clearly, if a member of the band has maintained the books until this point, it wouldn't be practical for him or her to continue. For small tours, a tour manager is the most suitable person to do this book-keeping. For larger tours, bands need a tour accountant to travel with them and record all transactions as they are made. The tour manager or tour accountant must maintain adequate books to reflect these transactions so they can all be accurately included within the band's finances.

Publishing

If a band delayed signing a publishing contract until the singles from their album had obtained some success, it was because they believed, not unreasonably, that they could negotiate a better contract by demonstrating their chart success to a publisher. But how do writers' royalties arise?

There are two main sources of publishing income. The first, and usually by far the largest, is the 'mechanical' royalty. This is payable when a copy of a writer's or composer's song is made mechanically (or these days electronically). Consequently, a mechanical royalty arises each time a record company makes a copy of an album, cassette or compact disc. The second source of publishing income is public performance. This is collected by the Performing Right Society (PRS) from the licensing of TV, radio and venues for the public performance of music (See the 'Copyright and Performing Right' article).

Songwriters, both lyricists and composers, have two alternatives for publishing their work. Either they sign one contract with a world-wide publisher, or several contracts with music publishers in each individual country throughout the world. The first option is referred to as a world-wide contract, and the second is known as a territory-by-territory contract. The band's lawyer will advise as to which is appropriate, depending on the artist's circumstances. The accounting for royalties by a music publisher, for a world-wide or territory-by-territory contract, is very similar to record companies' methods. A music publisher will give writers an advance. Like advances from record companies, this will be recoupable out of future royalties. However, the main difference between the record company's and publishing company's advance is that the publisher usually has no large expenses to pay such as the recording costs of an album. As a result, publishers have few costs to charge writers and composers against their publishing royalties. This often makes songwriting more profitable than performing. Doing both is ideal. As with many of a band's activities, the accountant will consider whether a separate limited liability company is required in order to act as a vehicle for the publishing royalties.

Music publishing deals are often referred to by two figures, like 95:5 or 85:15. The first figure relates to the writer's or composer's percentage (95 or 85 per cent), and the second to the amount retained by the publisher (5 or 15 per cent). From the writer's point of view, the larger the first number and the smaller second, the better. Before signing any deal, the band's writers and composers should discuss with their accountant and lawyer the proportion of the band's publishing royalties which they will receive. It is quite feasible that band members will have contributed to the composition of songs in different amounts, so the income received from the band's songs is often split to reflect this. In order to minimize the accountant's workload (and the accountancy bill), ask the publishing company to undertake this quite laborious division of royalties. If the company are unwilling to do this, the accountant, possibly with the assistance of a computer bureau, will generally be happy to get this done.

It is important for musicians to appreciate the difference between an 'income received' deal and an 'at source' deal. It may save bands a lot of money. If a writer or composer signs an 'at source' deal, they should receive the negotiated percentages of the royalties arising in foreign territories *intact*. If they sign an 'income received' deal, they will only receive *their proportion of the royalties sent to their UK publisher*, after the foreign publisher has taken a percentage.

Royalty Examination

When the band have achieved considerable chart success (when they have sold approximately a million copies of their albums), they should consider whether a royalty examination should be done. The right to carry out a royalty examination of a record or publishing company should be set out in the recording or publishing contract. The recording artist or the writer and composer will have the right to appoint a firm of accountants to examine the accounts of the record or publishing company. This is to ascertain whether these companies have paid over the correct royalties to the band. Recording contracts can be particularly complicated due to the different royalty rates and 'packaging deductions' which can be applied to different types of record, and to where it is sold, when it is sold, and in which cover it is presented. As a result, errors can occur in the processing of the royalty payments and the contract may be open to various interpretations.

A royalty examination usually begins with an analysis of royalty statements by the band's accountant to see if there are any peculiarities which warrant further investigation. Usually there are a number of these which makes it necessary for the accountant to visit the record or publishing company. There he or she examines the record or publishing company's accounts. As a result of this visit, the accountant will prepare a royalty examination report, in conjunction with the solicitor, which will set out the claims for underpayment of the band's royalties by the recording or publishing company. The lawyer, often with the assistance of the accountant, will then negotiate the claim with the particular company and reach a settlement.

Clearly, it is only worthwhile for the band to request a royalty examination if the potential claim will exceed the professional fees incurred. As a result, this is usually only undertaken if a band has enjoyed significant record sales. However, settlement payments by the record company or publishing company are often in excess of £100,000, while the accountant's fees are measured in tens of thousands.

The Right Advice

The music business is very fickle. Careers at the top can be mercilessly short. Usually, a band or artist will have only a short working life in which to earn sufficient money to live on for the rest of their lives. While it is important to choose an accountant with whom you feel comfortable and professionally secure, you will also need the best available financial advice. By the time you realize your accountant has been second rate, your career may be over.

Choose an accountant who specializes in the music industry. When you meet your potential accountant, ask him or her about who else he or she acts for. If he or she doesn't act for a number of successful bands, he or she is unlikely to have a thorough understanding of accounting in the music business. You need to know whether your potential accountant could undertake royalty examinations, and if he or she has colleagues in other countries to assist with international tax problems at very short notice. Deciding on an accountant isn't easy. It may involve visiting several firms before you find the right one. But with a good accountant, it could make the difference between you, the pop star, being rich and famous, or just famous.

Index